Praise for Shen
More than One

'This is the voice of China's Invisible Generation – vividly written, well balanced, brilliant, humorous and very sharp – it elicits a rollercoaster of emotions that breaks through the silence shrouding the lives of excess children born during the One-Child Policy.'
—Xinran, author of *The Good Women of China*

"The One-Child-per-Family policy was a tragedy forced upon China's mothers, children and their families. Finally, in this book, Shen Yang has dared to tell the truth, speaking out bravely about the experiences she lived through."
—Ma Jian, author of *The Dark Road*

"Now that the one-child policy has been relaxed, the stories of these illegal children will soon be a part of China's national collective memory. But to those who grew up tainted with this humiliation, the scars are permanent. One is Chinese writer Shen Yang, who wrote her story in part to extinguish the nightmares that still haunt her."
—Vincent Ni, *The Guardian*

"More Than One Child would be important and interesting as an historical record regardless of its literary merits, but these are considerable. It is vividly-written and thoughtfully-structured. Though as a child Shen Yang was often weeping, her recollections of doing so never descend into self-pity. She can write about the bleakest circumstances with humor."
—Rosie Milne, *Asian Review of Books*

Balestier Press
Centurion House, London TW18 4AX
www.balestier.com

More than One Child: Memoirs of an Illegal Daughter
Copyright © Shen Yang, 2021
English translation copyright © Nicky Harman, 2021

Cover design by Sarah and Schooling

First published by Balestier Press in 2021

A CIP catalogue record for this book
is available from the British Library

ISBN 978 1 913891 09 1

Shen Yang

More Than One Child

Memoirs of an Illegal Daughter

Translated from the Chinese by
Nicky Harman

BALESTIER PRESS
LONDON · SINGAPORE

For the invisible lives;
for N. Harman, without whom the world
could never hear our voice; and for G. Tempesta, who
is always there for me

CONTENTS

Introduction   xi

New Year baby   *1*

An abandoned bumpkin   *12*

Goodbye to being illegal   *25*

Careless!   *38*

Eighteen grape vines   *47*

A pair of red boots   *59*

Bold-as-brass and happy-go-lucky   *69*

My desk buddy, Yuan Xiaohui   *80*

School uniform   *92*

What do you want?   *102*

Wei Wanjun   *111*

King of the mountain eagles   *122*

The sunshine boy   *130*

Brightly coloured days   *140*

English class monitor   *151*

The volcano erupts   *164*

Where is my home?   *176*

Spilling the beans   *188*

Breaking free   *199*

The way they were then   *212*

Sungrass   *221*

Photographs   *229*

About the author

About the translator

The Family

Mother, or Mum

Father, Shen Wenming

Nana, maternal grandmother

Grandad, maternal grandfather

Granny, paternal grandmother

Grandpa, paternal grandfather

Auntie Wenjie, Shen Wenjie, father's sister

Uncle, Li Yige, Auntie Wenjie's husband

Their two daughters, Li Ruomei and Li Mingmei

Their son, Li Mingze

Other aunts, mother's sisters, unnamed

Shen Yang's sisters:

Eldest sister, Shen Yue, Moon

Third sister, Shen Ning, Serene

Fourth sister, Shen Xing, Star

Names have been changed to protect the privacy of the individuals except for the author's, which is her real name: Shen (family name) Yang (given name, meaning Sun) or Yangyang (childhood nickname).

Introduction

Goodbye to my childhood, goodbye to an era

In 1971, the Chinese government launched a family planning campaign which, by 1982, had become a fundamental national policy. The aim of the policy was to solve the problems of poverty and limited resources by slowing the rate of population growth; couples were limited to a single child, any further babies were considered illegal, 'excess-birth' children.

However, in November 2011, the policy was relaxed: a couple where both were only-children could have two children; and in November 2013, a couple where only one of them was an only-child could also have two children. On 29th October 2015, a further change was announced: all married couples in China could henceforth have two children. Then, on 1st January 2016, the 'People's Republic of China Population and Family Planning Law' Article 18, paragraph 1, was amended to read, 'The state encourages a couple to have two children.' After more than thirty years, the one-child-per-family policy had been scrapped. Finally, on 31st May 2021, the Politburo of the Chinese Communist Party announced that every couple is henceforth allowed to have three children.

The reason for the two-child policy was that the gender ratio in China had become seriously skewed. China has a large number of elderly people, too few children, and labour shortages. An aging population and the burden of caring for the elderly are huge social problems. The skewed gender ratio has created another problem: there are thirty million more males than females in China. It is difficult for men to find a wife, and this has led to social unrest. These problems have persisted in spite of the two-child policy, and China's birth rate is now at its lowest since the 1960s, hence the new ruling allowing every family to have three children.

The slogans have changed with each new policy. In the early days, it was 'One is best, but no more than two', then 'For every couple, one child', then 'A second child for only-children couples', 'A second child where one parent is an only-child', and finally 'Everyone can have three children'. Family planning in China has always been accompanied by strident propaganda.

'For every couple, one child' was always the most controversial and the hardest policy to implement. At the end of the 1980s and the beginning of the 1990s, when family planning was strictly enforced, and social controls were tightest, the ubiquitous wall slogans were intimidating and even contained direct threats.

> If you have children illegally, we will legally demolish your house.
> Abort or miscarry it, it can never be born.
> If you refuse a coil or sterilization, we'll get you. You want to hang yourself? We'll give you a rope. You want to poison yourself, we'll give you a potion to drink.
> If you don't pay the excess-birth fine, detention will teach you the error of your ways.
> Give the snip to poverty, coil yourself in money.
> The first child gets born, with the second, we tie your tubes, with the third and fourth we abort, abort, abort.
> If you won't have your tubes tied, we'll come down on you like a ton of bricks; if you won't have an abortion, we'll pull a ton of bricks down on you.
> One excess birth and the whole village gets their tubes tied!

In that kind of an atmosphere, when only the first child was sanctioned, a second or third birth (and some women even had five or six) only happened in the utmost secrecy. These hidden babies were the lucky ones compared to those who were aborted, but they were much less lucky than the privileged only-children. They had at least managed to come into this world, but then the world turned its back on them. They were called heihaizi, 'black' children, not a reference to the colour of their skin, but to their lack of a birth permit. These 'illegals' were, and are, a community bereft of resources and support.

Couples who have a son, want a daughter to follow; those who have a daughter, want a chubby baby boy next; the bigger the family, the greater their happiness; boys are preferable to girls... all these axioms are deeply rooted in Chinese culture. And so, during the years of strict family planning, the 'Excess-Birth Guerrillas' came into being. These were parents who were determined to get what they wanted, come what may. They were constantly on the run from the authorities, trying every trick in the book to bring one baby after another into the world.

In recent years, public attention has largely been on the aborted babies and or on the legitimate only-children. As for the excess-birth babies, those who by some miracle survived, does anyone really care what happened to them?

Simply by virtue of being born, they broke the law. They were, and are, an encumbrance to their family and a burden on society, they don't count.

By contrast, only-children have enjoyed the care and concern not only of their families, but also of the state, for more than thirty years. This has given them hukou residence certificates, and only-child certificates too. They are gloriously legitimate, pampered little emperors and princesses: as children, they benefitted from the undivided attention and material benefits that were never available to their parents, who had to share with siblings. With the struggle to succeed in China growing ever fiercer, only-children have been reared to be the elite. China's family planning policy has created a generation of only-children who have lapped up all the advantages offered to them.

But what about excess-birth children, the illegals, those who escaped becoming victims of abortion and infanticide, who have been socially excluded since birth? They are the same age, but their treatment could not be more different. They have been punished for the mistakes made by their parents, and have never known what it is like to be pampered and adored, let alone honoured by society.

And yet, perhaps for this very reason, they have the vitality of weeds. They thrust into the soil, tenaciously clinging on to life. The particular environment in which they grew up, squeezed into crevices between rocks, has given them extraordinary qualities. Their misfortunes as children have made them into formidable adults.

Chen Danyan's *Only-Child Manifesto*[1] tells the true stories of a generation that became unique as soon as the two-child policy was fully implemented, and of the loneliness they suffered as they grew up. It is one of a huge number of books on the subject. There is no similar interest in the excess-birth children, yet they are a unique generation too. The truth is that they have grown up shrouded in silence and secrecy.

According to official statistics, there are thirteen million illegals, but this is hard to believe. With China's population of 1.4 billion, there must be more than that. Someone must be made responsible for the tragedy of an era, because history cannot simply be erased. China must not forget its recent past as it develops and goes forward. Otherwise, with the abolition of the one-child policy, excess-births will become no more than a folk memory.

Everyone on this earth comes with an unseen history. But we can all have our own voice, we can all write that history down and record our own insights and experiences. Writing opens our minds and enables us to discover ourselves. It offers an authentic voice for the

---

[1] 陈丹燕《独生子女宣言》 [in Chinese], Nanhai Publishing Company, 1997.

world to hear. And a reality that has been written down and described is no longer ephemeral – it is a lasting record.

As far back as I can remember, I was always an embarrassment because I was an excess-birth child growing up in an era of strict family planning policies. That single fact defines every memory – both happy and sad – that I retain from my childhood. So I have to bear witness. I have to stand up and make myself heard. I have to record the truth, on behalf of an enormous invisible community of my peers. I have to say what it was like, physically and mentally, growing to adulthood, the difficulties we faced, and how we lived. Otherwise, our entire generation really will be buried in the abyss of history.

The voices of excess-birth children must be heard. Their stories must be told.

This is not only my story, it is their story too. This book commemorates the childhoods of all of China's excess-birth generation.

This book is my way of saying goodbye to my childhood, and goodbye to an era.

1

New Year Baby

On 1st January 1986, on a bright sunny morning, I finally saw the light of day. My mother, with me in her belly, had been on the run from the authorities for nine months. Because I was a New Year baby, they gave me a warm name, Yangyang, or Sun.

However, I was hardly a little ray of sunshine to my family. I had a sister who was four years older than me, I didn't have a little willy, I broke a law simply by being born, and if the family planning authorities discovered my existence, my mother would be carted off to the clinic to have her tubes tied, and our family would be heavily fined.

So there I was, swaddled in a thick quilt. I may have chosen a lucky day to be born on, but I could not change my destiny.

Come what may, my mother had to give birth to a son in order to carry on the family line. The family could not afford the excess-birth fine and did not want my mother to be sterilized, so as soon as I was born, I was sent to my mother's parents, Nana and Grandad. They lived in Sunzha Village, Yanzhou County, in Shandong.

Nana and Grandad had lived in Sunzha for most of their lives. The area was relatively undeveloped compared to the nearest city, Jining; the air was clean and there was plenty of space to play outside. Grandad liked to get up early in the morning and stroll around the village, one hand behind his back, the other playing with two large walnuts, turning them in his palm. When he met someone he knew, he always stopped for a chat. Then he would walk to a little store at the entrance to the village to buy some baijiu liquor from a big vat, and take it home to enjoy.

My grandfather's biggest pleasure in life was to have a few cups of baijiu, a few peanuts, and some snacks every morning. It didn't matter whether the snacks included meat or not as long as there was the drink. Without it, the day was incomplete. In his words, baijiu was the best thing on earth, it made everything, even a few scraps of pickled vegetables, taste wonderful. Nana called him an old wino, but he saw himself as kin to the wine-quaffing poets of ancient times. He used to listen to Chinese opera as he sipped, and when he had finished, he would lie back on his bamboo recliner, gently turning the two large walnuts in one hand. He had had them so long that they were worn smooth. From the small radio on the table came the guttural sounds of Beijing dialect. Warm sunshine filtered through the half-open door, making dust particles dance merrily in the air. Grandad lay with his eyes half-closed, rocked, hummed, and turned his walnuts.

Nana was the polar opposite to Grandad. She was always busy with something, usually at work on her flowers, herbs and vegetables in their yard. It was more of a vegetable garden than a yard, with every inch of earth planted. A big elm tree stood in the northwest corner, and there was a small plot with greens nearby. There was a large patch of peanuts on the east side, while the south wall sheltered pots and planters. In winter time, these were piled against the wall, the withered stems and flowers in them rustling in the chill wind as they waited to be revived by the coming springtime.

One cold day before there was any sign of spring, my mother and father arrived with their new-born, me, then left. I was a burden to them, but I became Nana and Grandad's little treasure. At a little over one year old, I learned to walk by hanging onto the furniture as I followed my grandfather around the house. At two, I could walk well enough to stagger after him, pulling my toy duck along with me, as he walked to the shop. Sometimes, I messed around in the garden with my Nana; when she picked beans, I threw them to the hens; when she dug up her peanuts, I stamped around in the earth; when she put fertilizer on the flowers, I ran around the yard pulling the basket of cow dung.

The seasons passed, and soon four years had gone by. My parents visited me from time to time, bringing treats and toys, but I loved Nana and Grandad best. They took care of me every day, they loved and spoiled me, and no matter how naughty I was, they never laid a finger on me.

I liked to snuggle up to Nana and listen to her stories. I used to pull her eyelids open when she was asleep. I liked going to the market with her. She swayed along in front, with a big bamboo basket over her arm. I trotted behind with a little ragbag over my shoulder. We strolled around all morning, and Nana's basket was always full of all kinds of snacks. I spent the whole time stuffing my belly until it bulged like my little bag.

I liked to go with Grandad to get water. He went in front with the carrying pole over his shoulder, a bucket swinging from each end, and I skipped along behind, pulling and dragging on the back one. As I waited for him to draw the water, I sat and played with pebbles. When he was ready and had the heavy buckets loaded at each end of the pole, he set off home, walking on the balls of his feet, with me at his heels. As Grandad puffed and panted, I thoroughly enjoyed myself splashing in the little puddles of spilled water.

Once, we met an enormous speckled cockerel that had slipped out of someone's yard. He strutted around under a big locust tree, the picture of Mr High-and-Mighty. Grandad drew his water, I sat and played with pebbles, just as we usually did. Suddenly, the cockerel erected its large red comb, craned its thick neck, glared at me and charged. Quick as a flash, just as it was about to give my bottom a vicious peck, Grandad grabbed the carrying pole and lunged at it. The cockerel turned tail and fled. My terrified tears turned to laughter. At that moment, Grandad was my guardian angel.

In the big room of our house, in the northwest corner, there was a carved chest full of patterned ceramic jars of different sizes. They held Grandad's favourite spicy salted peanuts, some fruits and pastries that Nana loved, and the cakes and biscuits that I could never get enough of.

Although Mum and Dad were not around, they gave Nana living expenses every month. Nana, of course, spent all this money on me. In the countryside in the early 1990s, not many children got to eat thin-skinned dumplings crammed with stuffing the way I did. My Nana was a clever cook. She not only produced all sorts of stuffed dumplings, but every once in a while she made me cakes with big red jujube dates in them.

Jujube cakes are always eaten at Chinese New Year in southwestern Shandong. The dough is rolled out flat, and then pulled into long strips; the cake is formed by coiling the strips around a date in the middle. These are arranged in circles and layered up into a tower. The shapes vary from family to family, everyone does it differently. They're delicious and have a special meaning too, symbolizing people's hopes for prosperity and a better life in the coming year.

Nana's jujube cakes came in different flavours and shapes. With her nimble fingers, she used to push a few jujubes into the dough and just like that, she'd made a small animal. When the cakes had been steamed and taken out of the steamer basket, she deftly rubbed a little bit of the jujube paste between finger and thumb to form very small round bobbles which she stuck on top of each one, where they sat looking at you, like funny little eyes.

I would rush out of the door, clutching the little animals that Nana had made so carefully, and show them off to the other urchins. I was only four and a bit, I didn't know any better. Yan, who was three years older than me, once managed to get a cake off me. I didn't care, I gnawed at the stale mantou bun she'd given me in exchange, grinning and giggling.

Jujube cakes were a big treat, and the kids who didn't get any were jealous. There was one six-year-old who was tormented by the sight of Yan gobbling down the tempting morsel, and the little swine sneaked into our yard when he knew I wasn't there and told Nana about Yan persuading me to give up my cake. Nana was furious and I suffered the consequences too.

From that day on, Nana announced, she would not be making New Year jujube cakes again. 'You can go and ask the moon and the stars,' she told me. I begged and begged, and Grandad begged on my behalf, but he got short shrift. 'Don't you play Mr Nice Guy,' she told him.

Grandad couldn't say anything to that, so he just puffed and snorted through his whiskers.

And that was the end of the fragrant smell of steaming jujube cakes in our yard, for a good long while.

One day, guests arrived to see an uncle and aunt whose house was at the back of ours. My aunt produced a table full of delicious food and steamed a pot of jujube cakes. I was playing with the chicks in the yard, but the moment I smelled them steaming, I started walking, drawn by the smell.

I didn't ask for one, or help myself, I just stood staring at the freshly cooked jujube cakes with big, round eyes. Jujube cakes are not my favorite, but I had not had any for a long time and the fragrance made my tummy rumble.

My aunt looked at me and smiled. She took out a cake from the steamer basket, put it on a small saucer and gave it to me cheerfully. My eyes shone as I took it and ran away.

When the family were sitting in the back yard preparing dinner, I brought the saucer back, now empty. I stood there biting my lip, ogling the jujube cakes on the table. My aunt gave me another one without saying a word. But ten minutes later, I was standing in her yard with the saucer empty again.

'This girl must be starving!' my aunt said. 'She's had two jujube cakes, and it looks like she's going to scoff the lot!' And she ran to the front yard and called my Nana, 'How many days has Yangyang gone without food?'

Nana rushed out of the house where she was cooking flatbreads, 'What's going on?' she demanded.

'I just gave Yangyang two big jujube cakes, but twenty minutes later, she's eaten all of them! And now she's back with an empty saucer again. She can have as many as she wants, it's not that, but I don't want her to overeat,' said my aunt anxiously. 'Her uncle can only manage two at most before he's full.'

Nana said nothing. She went straight to the coop at the foot of the north wall. On the ground, the chickens were fighting over the pieces of cake I had thrown to them. My aunt came in and looked astonished.

The thing was, her jujube cakes were doughy and didn't have many jujubes. I had been spoiled by Nana. I had picked out all the jujubes and eaten them, and given all the rest of the cake to the chickens.

Nana was extremely apologetic. 'I'm so sorry,' she said. 'Don't ever give her anything again, she's a spoiled brat!'

My aunt stood looking at the cake bits, as if she did not know whether to laugh or cry.

In spite of my misdeeds, my adored grandmother never laid a finger on me.

And after that, she used to cook up a few jujubes on their own if I was peckish.

While I was being kept out of sight and having the time of my life at my grandparents' house, my two younger sisters came into the world. As soon as they were born, Third Sister was spirited away to Granny and Grandpa's house, and Fourth Sister joined me at Nana and Grandad's. The day she arrived, there was a buzz of activity in the little yard. There was my father, busy unloading the car and carrying bags into the house. There was my mother, washing baby bottles and making up formula milk. Nana was happily moving furniture around and making up a cot bed. Grandad was walking around the house, this new little baby in his arms, crooning to her.

I sat outside in the yard, bawling my eyes out.

'What's up? What's up?' Grandad was the first to come out to me, still holding the baby.

'No! No!' I went into full tantrum mode, rolling around on the ground and screaming.

'Ai-ya! Don't lie in the dirt, get up!' Nana heard me and came out too.

There was a roar from my father, 'Whatever's the matter? Get up, you little brat!'

That only made me cry harder, and the tears poured down my face.

'Now, now, Yangyang, what's upset you so much?' This was my mother.

She squatted beside me on the ground and put her arms around me. I snuggled up to her, still casting glances at Grandad and the thing he was holding. Grandad twigged immediately and brought the baby over, 'Meet your little sister.'

'Little sister?' I frowned at her puckered purplish face. I thought I'd never seen anything so hideous. 'I don't want an ugly-mug sister!'

They all roared with laughter, Nana and Grandad, Dad and Mum.

When everything had settled down, my parents slipped away. It was towards the end of 1989, the calm before the storm.

The purple-faced ugly-mug not only stole my grandparents' love away, she stole my place in the family bed too. I hated her. That evening, I had one tantrum after another. And when I finally crawled into the big bed, a pair of big strong hands plucked me out of it.

'Yangyang, you have your own little cot now,' said Nana with a smile as she put me down in it.

'No! No! I'm sleeping with Nana!' I yelled and jumped out of it.

'Be a good girl, Nana has to look after your little sister.'

'No! No! I don't want an ugly-mug sister!'

'What are we going to do with you, girl? So pig-headed!' Nana was beginning to lose patience.

I'd always been Nana's pet and now she didn't like me anymore! I sat on the floor and howled in despair.

'You pig-headed, disobedient little girl!' Nana was angry.

'Who's the pig-headed one out of the two of you?' Grandad came over with my sister in his arms. 'She's old enough to have her own ideas. Why are you putting her out of the bed without any warning?'

'You old fool, it's all very well for you to talk. I'm the one who has to look after them, so you keep out of it.' Grandma glared and took the baby from him.

'Nana, Nana! I want to sleep with Nana!' I grabbed her leg and held on tight.

Nana looked at Grandad helplessly, 'What do we do now?'

Grandad chuckled and clapped his hands, 'Make do!'

Night fell and all was quiet. In the big bed, Nana slept with the baby in her arms on the east side, while on the west side, next to the window, I slept happily cuddling Nana's pointy bound feet.

With my baby sister's arrival, I was no longer the only chick in the nest for Nana and Grandad. I couldn't get my young head around it. So I became endlessly, inventively, naughty.

If Grandad put the full washbasin down on the floor in the corner of the room, as soon as his back was turned, I put my feet in it. That made him swear crossly, while I pulled devilish faces in my delight. If Nana had a busy morning, made a good lunch, got my sister to sleep, and lay on the bed for a quick shut-eye, I crept up to her and forced her drooping eyelids apart with my little fingers, 'Open them! Open them!'

'Ai-ya! You're such a brat!' Nana rubbed her eyelids, half-amused, half-irritated.

Once, Grandad was lying in his chair listening to opera, and Grandma sat at the door in the sun sewing a baby's padded jacket, I sneaked into the bedroom when they weren't looking, picked up the little bundle that was my sister, and hugged her very tight, just like the grown-ups did. But she was too heavy. By the time I got to the door of the big room with her, my 'bundle' had slipped out of my arms and crashed to the floor.

I was constantly getting into trouble and being told off, until I felt like I didn't love Nana anymore, and Grandad wasn't as much fun as he used to be. As far as the grown-ups were concerned, I was just getting naughtier and harder to control. If only they had known that inside the devil I had become was a little girl crying out for attention.

By that time, I was almost five years old, and running wild in the village. I went out in the morning and came home filthy dirty in the evening. At first, my grandmother used to go looking for me in case something had happened to me. But as my sister grew into a toddler, she needed watching, and my Nana had a lot to do at home. She had no time to go out searching, so she just let me be. My grandfather had always been a free spirit and didn't believe in interfering with my immersion in the world of nature.

Even though with my sister's arrival, I no longer had my grandparents' undivided love, this was still the happiest time of my life. I joined a gang of other little devils and explored every corner of Sunzha. The village was our world, and there were cliffs to climb and rivers, heaps of earth and mud and sand, and other people's yards to play in. Just so long as I wasn't shut up at home, I was in seventh heaven. We played war games on the hill, fished for tiddlers and pebbles in the river, and threw mud balls into boggy ground, to see who could make the loudest splash.

But it couldn't last. Although my mother had escaped forced abortions, the family could not escape the family planning fines. In January 1991, someone reported the existence of Third Sister. My parents were fined 5,000 yuan. My father went cap in hand to anyone who would lend him the money, while my mother was 'escorted' by the head of the Women's Federation to the clinic to be sterilized. However, this was just the beginning of a guerrilla war.

News quickly got out that the Shen family had two more daughters (myself and Fourth Sister) squirreled away in Sunzha. However, there are good messengers as well as informers. By the time the Jining Family Planning Officer arrived in Sunzha, Grandad had heard rumours that they were coming, and had ferried Fourth Sister and me a dozen kilometres in his three-wheeler to the house of another aunt of mine, my mum's sister.

My aunt's house was nice. There were good things to eat and drink. But there was no Nana. And a place with no Nana held no attractions for me. It was dark when we arrived and Fourth Sister was already asleep. I dragged on Grandad's hand and whined that I wanted to go back to Sunzha, to Nana.

No, no, said Grandad, it was much too far to go back tonight, we were one old man and two kids, we might have an accident, and besides, what if we were caught by the family planning officers, all his efforts would have been for nothing, wouldn't they? He cheerfully reassured me that he'd come and fetch me and my sister first thing next morning. I wasn't giving up, I sat on the ground, hanging onto his leg and wailing.

Grandad grew increasingly frantic, 'Dammit, dammit!' But still he could not bring himself to hit me. Eventually, my aunt had had enough. She picked me up and put me into the three-wheeler. 'You sit there and I'll take you to Nana,' she commanded.

Then she made a sign to Grandad, and he scuttled away around the corner and was gone.

I clung to the side bar of the three-wheeler and sobbed, 'I want Nana!'

'Yes, yeeeees, we'll look for Nana...' drawled my aunt.

And she got in and through the twilight, she took me around the village, jolting over the ruts, until finally she succeeded in getting me to sleep and cautiously pedalled back to her house.

Early the next morning, my sister and I were woken from our bed by Grandad, and he took us back to Sunzha.

Back home, my face was wreathed in smiles as soon as I saw Nana busy at the stove.

"'I want Nana, I want Nana!" This brat made such a fuss about getting back to you…'

Grandad sat down in his recliner chair, looking exhausted.

I pulled a monkey face at him, grabbed the warm steamed bun that Nana handed to me, and ran outside.

'Hey, where are you off to?' Nana shouted after me.

'To play with Zhengzheng,' I called, without even bothering to turn around, and hopped and skipped away.

'Dammit, the girl never stops shouting that she wants her Nana, then as soon she's back, she runs off to play!' Grandad sighed.

Nana looked at him and went back into the house, hiding a smile. Grandad had always been a strict, stern father with his children. But he seemed unable to keep me under control. He was turning into a doting grandfather as he got older. Well, everyone has their weaknesses!

As for me, just so long as I knew Nana was at home, I felt secure. I could run around and play as much as I wanted, but I knew she'd always be waiting for me. Home was where Nana was.

2

An abandoned bumpkin

Family planning regulations came into force in 1979, and were fairly strict in the first few years. They had relaxed considerably by 1984 or 85; and a number of families secretly had more than one baby, though they did not dare apply for a hukou certificate for them. So when it came to the census in 1990 (the fourth since Liberation), the government offered an amnesty – a chance to register the unregistered children for free, in order to get a more accurate result. Huge numbers of children popped up all over the country, and there were some flabbergasted faces when the central government saw the figures. So in 1991, a strict excess-birth ban was re-imposed. One way or another, the birth rate had to be brought down.

The family planning officers began to make frequent raids on the village, and my little sister and I were no longer safe with Nana and Grandad. Fourth Sister was just a baby, and my grandparents sent her back to the aunt where we had spent the night, because they were afraid she would make too much noise and bring the officers to our door. And I, after five years of security and happiness, had to play cat-and-mouse with the family planning officers.

At first, the raids only occurred during the day, but later they came by night too. I clearly remember one night, I was sound asleep cuddled up to Nana, when Grandad rushed in from the big room and

12

picked me up in his arms. He held me under one arm and grabbed the bamboo ladder in the other. Nana held the ladder tight, and he scooted up to the roof space. After we had curled up safely on the big cross-beams, Nana quickly stowed the ladder downstairs.

'Open up! Open up!'

'Hurry up! Open the gate!'

'We'll break it down if you don't open it!'

It was the middle of winter, and the middle of the night, and the knocking on the door was deafening. I cringed in Grandad's arms and clutched his thick padded jacket, staring with terrified eyes at the faint chinks of light between the floorboards.

Nana tottered outside on her bound feet and opened the big wooden gate with trembling hands. The family planning officers rushed in and began to turn the house over. They even turned the big bed upside down.

I was so frightened I buried my head in Grandad's jacket and blocked my ears. I couldn't look or listen. I was afraid that if they discovered me, I would vanish into the dark night and never see my grandparents again.

After that night, if there were any rumours that the family planning officers were making night raids, Grandad took me to sleep in the roof space, leaving Nana waiting on tenterhooks downstairs.

Grandad's familiar smell of alcohol gave me a great sense of security. I nestled in his arms and listened to his powerful heartbeat, and felt very warm.

I thought this warmth would last forever, and I would grow up happily sheltered under the wings my grandparents spread over me. But one day, my so-loving Nana who, along with Grandad, never laid a hand on me no matter how naughty I was, played a monstrous joke.

It was a foggy morning, and a middle-aged woman who said she was my father's older sister turned up. I was five years old but I'd never seen her before. Her name was Shen Wenjie, and she had moved to Nanyang in Henan when she married.

My father had written to tell her that he had four daughters and was heavily in debt, so she packed her bags and got on an overnight train. Her plan was to take Fourth Sister, Star, away with her, because she was still too young to remember and miss us, and Auntie Wenjie was prepared to adopt her as her daughter.

Auntie Wenjie's own children all had factory jobs, and the family was not badly off nowadays. Besides, Nanyang was hundreds of kilometres from where we were in Jining, more than twelve hours by bus or train. If Star went there, she would be much safer than in Sunzha. However, when everyone thought that Star was about to be taken away, Nana said the words that changed my life.

'Wenjie, take Yangyang with you. She's getting too much of a handful, she spends all day running around the village. My old bones can't keep up with her anymore.'

Compared to my cute little sister, I had become a demon-child in the eyes of my grandmother. I ran wild all over the village, I was out in the morning and back home filthy dirty at night. I got into all sorts of trouble every day.

'Yangyang, you want a gun, don't you? Auntie Wenjie's going to take you to town to buy one.' Nana had told her that I envied my neighbour Zhengzheng's toy gun, and that was how she bribed me to go with her.

Just before we left, I couldn't help running over to tell Zhengzheng my news, 'I'm going to get a gun,' I boasted, 'You just wait till I get back. We can play with guns.'

That evening, Grandad stood with his hands clasped behind his back at the entrance to the village and saw us off. I waved happily at him out of the back window of the car, 'Grandad, Grandad, wait till I come back and show you my gun.'

Grandad opened his mouth as if to speak but no sounds came out. Our car drove further and further away, until he lost sight of the little girl who had dogged his footsteps ever since she could walk. Then his mouth twitched, he turned around, and took the road back home. It was almost dark as Grandad's lonely figure stumbled through the trees.

Many years later, my mother told me that after I left, my grandmother was devastated. She would cry quietly every time she thought of me. The first night, she lay awake, tossing and turning. Then the cocks crowed, and it was dawn. That was when she suddenly realized that her Yangyang really had gone. She sat up slowly, and caught sight of the strap of the little ragbag she had made me, stuck in a crack of the bed. She pulled the bag out, and finally burst into floods of tears.

She begged Grandad, 'Please, go to Dongzha as quickly as you can, see if Yangyang's left yet. If they haven't, fetch her back!' And she wept bitterly, 'I miss our Yangyang, I miss our Yangyang.'

Grandad looked at his distraught wife and his eyes welled with tears too. 'Don't be upset, I'm going right now!'

Grandad pedalled the three-wheeler as fast as he could along the tarmac road, the beads of sweat running down his face, still hopeful he could get his favourite granddaughter back. He was unaware that I was already in the train being carried far away from him.

'I want my Nana! I want my Nana!' I sobbed.

As the train in its dark-green livery sped through the forest, my heart-rending cries could be heard all through the carriage. My tears dripped onto the big steamed bun I clutched, uneaten, in my hand.

I was getting some very unfriendly looks from our fellow passengers. My aunt was greatly embarrassed. She had already had enough of me.

'If you don't stop crying, I'll throw you out of the window,' she threatened me.

The warm and friendly face she had presented to Nana and Grandad had completely gone, and there was a snarling lioness in its place.

I ignored her and carried on crying loudly. Tears and snot mingled and gathered in a big bead at the tip of my nose. Auntie was so furious that she sat glaring at me, her arms folded across her chest. A young woman passenger sitting opposite had finally had enough. She pulled some toilet paper from her bag and leaned over to wipe my nose. But before she could press the folds of tissue against my nostrils, I wiped it for myself, on the sleeve of my jacket. Just like that, my nose was clean and dry, but everyone who was watching this little scene wrinkled their noses in disgust. The kind-hearted girl clutched the toilet paper awkwardly, unsure whether to give it to me or not.

Eventually, Auntie Wenjie said, 'Don't cry, be a good girl and eat up your bun. I'm taking you to see your Nana.'

As soon as I heard the words, 'See your Nana', my tears stopped abruptly. I sniffed, and looked at her with brimming eyes, then at the tear-soaked bun in my hand. Slowly I raised it to my mouth, and stuffed it in. The warm sunshine shone through the train windows, onto my cherry-red cheeks, and my snotty, tear-sodden sleeves.

'I want Nana, I want Nana!' When we reached Auntie Wenjie's, I stood at the gate, bawling my eyes out.

Her daughters, Li Ruomei and Li Mingmei, leaned against the gate, arms folded, watching me curiously. The looks on their faces suggested I was some sort of circus monkey. It was mid-winter and I was bundled up in a patterned padded jacket that Nana had made for me. I had been wiping my nose on both sleeves for the whole journey, and the north wind that met us when we got off the train had dried the goo to a shiny crust.

My habitually rosy cheeks were horribly chapped by the cold, and my very proper, clean and tidy cousins clearly saw me as a little peasant, a country bumpkin.

'If you go on crying like that, your scabby cheeks'll crack all over!' Mingmei shouted impatiently.

This bumpkin was getting anything but a warm welcome. Back in Sunzha, I was the pet of the family. If I ever cried, my grandparents would rush to comfort me. But now, I'd been standing at the gate crying for ages, and everyone was ignoring me. My aunt had had enough of my wailing like a banshee for the whole journey, and had gone straight indoors, while my cousins, instead of consoling me, were laughing at my chapped cheeks.

So I ignored them back. But no matter how I cried that I wanted

Nana, there was still no sign of her. I looked around me at this strange place, and was terrified.

By the time I arrived in Xiaoliangzhuang village, Nanyang, Auntie Wenjie's family was prospering. They had their own land, their house, and steady incomes. Uncle Li Yige used to teach in the school, but now he had switched to working as a quantity surveyor. In fact, he was known in the district for his engineering expertise. Auntie Wenjie was a good hairdresser and had opened a salon, where her no-nonsense bluntness attracted plenty of customers. Ruomei, my eldest cousin, had an office job in a pharmaceutical factory, and Mingmei, and my boy cousin, Mingze, who was the youngest, worked in a cotton mill.

They all lived at home: Ruomei and Mingmei were unmarried and Mingze was only seventeen years old. The family lived in a large compound, with three single-story buildings, and a shelter with a tiled roof that served as a kitchen. Under the pile of firewood in the kitchen lived a skinny little tabby kitten.

To start with, I slept with Ruomei and Mingmei, but I kept wetting their bed in the night. My cousins hated this and complained to their mother every day. So for the time being, Auntie Wenjie had to squeeze me into the end of her bed, where I slept at her and my uncle's stinky feet. They obviously didn't know that Nana always used to get me up to pee in the potty every night.

They treated me like just another kitten they had taken in, a talking one. As for me, I was completely confused, everything had happened too suddenly. All I knew was that everything that had been familiar in my life was gone forever.

Xiaoliangzhuang village was on the fringes of the city, and was much larger than Sunzha. On weekdays, everyone was busy at work with no time for me. So I became more of a wild child than ever.

Every morning, my aunt prepared breakfast and opened the gate to her customers. The warm sunlight flooded in, shining on the swivel chair, the wooden table with its mirror, and the lime-washed walls from which hung a variety of scissors and other hairdressing tools.

The layout was much the same as the barbershop my Grandad used to take me in Sunzha and I had a sudden vision of Grandad putting me on the swivel chair and spinning me around. I scampered over happily, climbed on it, and spun till I was dizzy. Or rather, until Auntie Wenjie pulled me off it.

'That's enough messing around! Out, out, out! Go and play somewhere else, you damn brat!'

While she got busy cutting hair, I played with the kitten in the yard. My aunt didn't have time to cook lunch, so I scavenged a chopped onion roll or whatever else I could find in the kitchen, and hunkered down in the corner of the salon watching the stream of customers coming and going. When she could take a break, Auntie Wenjie napped in the swivel chair and I would run out to play with the children at the gate.

I used to follow them all over the village and only come back, filthy dirty, when my aunt was busy cooking in the kitchen. Then I could sneak onto the swivel chair and spin around and around, as if I had never left Sunzha, as if Grandad was watching me and laughing.

At night, when my aunt and uncle fell asleep, they snored loudly and rhythmically. I found it hard to get to sleep. I used to sit up and lie down, sit up and lie down again, making the bamboo cot bed they had bought me creak. Finally I dozed off, but sometimes in the middle of the night, I fell off the bed with a thump, still wrapped in my quilt. I simply curled up on the floor and carried on sleeping.

One day at the beginning of March, not long after New Year, while my aunt was busy with her customers, I sneaked out with a box of matches and a handful of our leftover firecrackers to join the kids at the gate. Together, we laid them out one by one in some open space.

We didn't spot that one of the firecrackers had dropped into a barley strawstack in one corner and set it alight. The flames roared and brought the stack owner to the scene. He grabbed a thick stick and chased us with it as we scattered. I ran as fast as I could but luck wasn't with me, and I was caught. The stack owner told my aunt, and my aunt grabbed me by the ears and bawled me out in front of everyone.

One day in summer, Auntie Wenjie took me to the city. On the way home, she stopped at a small store a couple of li outside our village, and bought me an ice lolly. It was the first ice lolly I'd ever eaten and I loved it.

The next day, Auntie made lunch but couldn't see me anywhere. She was so anxious that she rode her bike all around the village looking for me. Then, far in the distance, she saw me coming along the street, sucking a half-eaten lolly.

Back home, she was furious, 'Where the hell have you been, you damn brat? And who bought you that?'

'I bought it myself,' I said innocently.

The truth was I had quietly sneaked ten cents from the drawer in my aunt's salon. To my surprise, I'd managed to find my way back to the lolly stand too. That day, I went faraway alone and bought myself something for the very first time. Of course, I had also stolen my aunt's money for the first time too and so I got my first beating.

By the time I was five and a half, I knew all the kids in the village. I was used to going out to play, I'd done that in Sunzha. But here in Nanyang, the whole family were busy by day, and even when they were all at home, they ignored me. So I explored every corner of the village of Xiaoliangzhuang, and its bigger twin Daliangzhuang, on the other side of the road. After breakfast, I rushed out of the house, still with porridge all over my mouth, to find somewhere to play – a barley straw stack, piles of sand and bricks, and even graves covered with bristle grass.

Here, I was king of the children. The village boys liked to get over walls, jump off brick piles, and play cards and war games, and none of them could beat me. The girls played with skipping ropes, played catch, kicked shuttlecocks, and made dolls out of bristle grass. And I was just as good as them.

At lunch or dinner, Auntie Wenjie's loud, clear voice could be heard the length and breadth of the village, 'Yangyang! Yangyang, you damn brat! Come and eat!'

By the time six months had passed, 'damn brat' was all my uncle and aunt ever called me. Whenever I was naughty or got into trouble, that was what my aunt yelled. My uncle, when he was in a good mood, called me 'good girl!' But when he was annoyed, it would be, 'What's the good of you, you damn brat!'

Anyone in the village who heard my aunt bellowing from the house would tell me, 'Yangyang, you better go home for dinner, your aunt's about to flip.'

My aunt's voice was so loud it was called the Shen Bellow. For miles around, everyone knew what that meant. She certainly had a sharp tongue, but in one way she protected me: we were the only Shens in the family (my uncle and cousins were surnamed Li), and she used to tell them that she was the only one who had the right to hit another Shen. That didn't stop her from beating me frequently herself. I was pig-headed but I was no match for my bull of an aunt.

Once, when they were having a new wall built around the compound, a huge pile of bricks was left on an empty patch of ground at the entrance. I used to get a bunch of my mates in and we'd climb up, and then jump down with whoops and yells. But a brick pile is a dangerous thing, it looks solid on the surface but, if you're not careful, you can easily start an avalanche and get injured or crushed.

I don't know how many times Auntie Wenjie told me not to play on the bricks. But as often as I was told, I forgot. I used to sneak up there when no one was watching. Finally, one day, I didn't manage to dodge in time and a tumbling brick landed right on my toes.

It was a scorching hot day and I was wearing sandals, no protection for my poor big toe, which was pouring blood.

No more playing on the brick pile for me. But there couldn't be any harm in climbing a sturdily built wall, could there? I was wearing a new outfit my aunt had just bought me when I went with the boys to climb up to the top of a wall. But I wasn't paying attention. I fell, scraped the skin off my hand, and tore a big hole in my new trousers.

I went back home, making sure not to be seen, and tucked my trousers away as far back in the cupboard as I could get them. I thought Auntie Wenjie wouldn't find them there. No such luck. I got my ear twisted savagely for that. I burst into howls of tears, not only because it hurt, but because the whole scene reminded me all too vividly of Sunzha; of my friend Zhengzheng who was always getting his ear twisted by his father; and of my grandparents who, no matter how naughty I was, never laid a finger on me.

Although my cousins didn't hit me, they tormented me when their parents weren't looking, especially the boy, Li Mingze. Before I arrived, he was the baby of the family and everyone's pet. He was also the all-important grandson. But now, he was no longer the kingpin and his nose had been put out of joint.

One day, we had meat patties to eat as a treat. I was the youngest and got first go. I grabbed my pie and ran outside to play, stuffing it into my mouth as I went. The honeycomb briquettes didn't produce a lot of heat, and the patties took ages to cook. Meantime, I'd been running around outside like a wild thing, got hungry again, and helped myself to another one. Mingze had been watching intently, having waited a long time for that patty to be ready, and as he saw me take it, he exploded in fury. He yanked it out of my mouth, yelling, 'You just wait your turn!'

In those days, the family still had a field or two allocated by the village, and any food they grew that was not eaten straightaway was stored in an underground bunker. The bunker was by the gate against the wall, and was quite big, about two metres deep and three metres wide. Every few days, Mingze tied a thick rope around my waist and put me in. I got the job because I was small and scrawny. Once inside, my job was to fill a basket with moolis, potatoes and sweet potatoes. Once my cousin had pulled the basket up, he would take his sweet time getting me out, and would scare me with stories about mice and snakes, or pretend to put the cover on and leave me to suffocate. Even when I bawled in terror, and he finally agreed to pull me up, he would deliberately let the rope slip so I dropped back down. Of course I never gave up trying to get my own back on him, and one day my chance came: I got a potato and smashed it in his face, giving him a bloody nose. Truce. But there was a price to pay: his big flat nose bled copiously, and my aunt beat my bottom black and blue with her shoehorn.

As I got bigger, my friends and I often played on the big iron gates of the prefab concrete factory near my home. One of us would hang on to the gate while someone else pushed them, making it swing back and forth. But one day, just as I was getting up there for my turn, my right thumb got caught and, as the gate swung hard away, the whole of the nail tore off. My ear-piercing screams and the blood gushing from the nail scared my companions, and they stood rigid with shock, watching as I stumbled off home, holding my hand in the air, crying and dripping blood.

My aunt took one look at my bloody hand and erupted in fury, 'Ai-ya! You damn brat, whatever have you done now?!' She poked me hard in the head with her finger, 'Don't you ever do that again!'

'Serves her right! She's always messing around,' exclaimed Mingze, ever ready to add fuel to the flames.

No consolation from that quarter. It really was quite an achievement to be so disliked.

Time passed, my thumb grew a new nail, and the kids in the alley all started school, leaving me to wander around the village on my own. Auntie Wenjie wasn't coughing up kindergarten fees, and I had no one to play with, so I made my own amusements. I used to go clambering over gravestones, which were covered with tussocks of bristle grass as far as the eye could see, and catch crickets and grasshoppers. They were plentiful, and in an afternoon, I could get dozens.

I used to plait little cages out of bamboo, put my prizes in there, and tease them with a stalk of bristle grass. When the light started to fade and it was time to go home, I would take them out carefully, one by one, and let them go. That way, there would be plenty more to catch the next day.

But good times don't last forever.

I began to hear comments from the adults in the village, 'She's a heihaizi!'

'The heihaizi seems quite happy playing on her own, doesn't she?'

'The only heihaizi in the village, she's from Shandong, you know.'

In my wanderings around the village, I kept hearing the grown-ups gossiping, some with more malice than others. 'Heihaizi!'

I thought they were talking about my dark sun-tanned skin. What did I know? I had no idea they were pointing me out because I was an 'illegal', a kid with no official status. I'd managed to hide in my aunt's house thousands of miles away from Shandong, I'd escaped the clutches of the family planning officers, but I couldn't get away from tittle-tattle and gossip.

The existence of illegal kids made a mockery of the family planning laws. Women concealed their pregnancies, but the very act of being born was openly to flout the law. The government's reaction, when parents refused to pay the excess-birth fines, was to take it out on us innocent children. If we were not legalized, we were deprived of our citizenship.

Although I wasn't in hiding, the way other illegals were, I was still terrified by a knock at the door, and since I had no hukou, or official ID, I grew up without a sense of belonging. Inevitably, the feeling of not being accepted, or even of existing, took its toll over the years on my physical and mental health.

The villagers were not looking that far ahead. My lack of hukou didn't even arouse their pity. They just enjoyed making fun of me because I was too small to understand. Because I had no hukou, I was an illegal; because I was an illegal, I couldn't go to school; because I couldn't go to school, people laughed at me.

'Auntie, what's a "heihaizi"?'

I put my question cautiously one evening at dinner, when everyone was sitting round the table watching the TV news.

My aunt and uncle exchanged glances. Aunt Wenjie sucked her teeth and frowned impatiently, 'Eat your dinner. Don't talk while you're eating!'

'Why not? Why can't I ask a question?' I said, leaning across the table with my bum stuck out behind me, to forage in the serving dish. Just when I had picked up a piece of meat with my chopsticks and was about to pop it into my mouth, my aunt began again, 'Why are you always so greedy for meat? If you're so keen on it, why don't you just take your shoes off and jump in and fish around!'

'Good-for-nothing, such a pig!' Mingmei, who enjoyed stirring things up, chimed in.

Too many questions, too much meat, in just one minute I'd been told off on two counts. I was really upset. The tears flowed down my cheeks and into my bowl, dripping onto my rice. I bent my head and began to shovel the salty rice grains into my mouth with my chopsticks.

'You're such a cry-baby, I don't know where you get all those tears from!' Auntie Wenjie not only had no words of comfort for me, she carried on ranting.

I picked up my bowl and went out into the yard. In this family, no matter what I said or did, it was always wrong. I missed my Nana and Grandad, but I was angry with them too. I didn't understand what I had done wrong; why had they sent me away to live on someone else's charity? Why did my aunt's family hate me so much?

3

Goodbye to being illegal

The fifteenth day of the first lunar month was the Lantern Festival. The city streets were crammed with people and cars, and the trees were hung with the prettiest, cutest lanterns. My aunt always liked a good festival, and was in high spirits when she took me to see them. But the streets were too jam-packed to move, and she quickly lost patience. She looked around her, and came up with what she called a 'perfect solution'. She got onto a big stone at the side of the street and lifted me into the fork of a tree about two metres up. 'You sit here and watch the lanterns. I'll come back for you later.'

Before I could say anything, Auntie Wenjie had disappeared into the throng. In front of me was a great sea of humanity, a heaving dark mass as far the eye could see. I had never seen anything like it. Ten minutes passed, then half an hour, then an hour, then two. My bum had gone numb from sitting in the tree fork, and I was in a panic because I couldn't see my aunt anywhere. The beautiful lanterns had completely lost their attraction and I began to wail, 'Auntie! Auntie!!'

I was sobbing my heart out, 'Auntie! Auntie!!'

I was overwhelmed by that familiar feeling of helplessness and terror. I had been abandoned again.

I heard voices, 'Eh? Who does that little mite belong to? How could they have left her alone in a tree?'

'She's a clever little girl! She climbed that tree all by herself when she got lost.'

'Don't cry, little girl, your mum'll be back soon.'

By now, I'd collected quite a crowd around the tree, with everyone arguing at once.

Suddenly, I heard a strident voice, 'Ai-ya! Damn brat! You never stop crying!' My aunt grabbed me by the collar and pulled me down forcefully. 'I told you I'd be back for you, you had nothing to cry about.'

The harder I cried, the angrier she got. She kicked me hard with her foot. It was a cold day, and we were out on the street, and I was getting a terrible telling-off from my aunt, surrounded by a throng of curious spectators, as if I were a monkey. I was mortified, and terrified. I put my reddened, chilblained hands over my eyes and tried to stop crying, but the tears kept leaking through my fingers.

Many years later, I realized that crying never aroused her sympathy, only her desire to hit out. Luckily, girls were considered worthless back then. If I had been abducted by a trafficker, how could she have faced my grandparents in Shandong? She had been full of enthusiasm when she took me on, but in fact, that was all she had to offer, enthusiasm, nothing more.

Her impatience, her fiery temper, and her carelessness were evident in all aspects of her life. That was the same year that the streets were full of women with permed hair. Auntie Wenjie bought the kit, and did a home perm, which gave her a head of hair like an exploding cauliflower. Then, on a whim, she smeared lotion all over my head, put the plastic cap on me, and plugged it in. I was not at all happy. What six-year-old would want a ridiculous head of big curls? But my aunt made me sit in the salon chair. I was going to get a perm, willy-nilly. And pretty soon, I got an electric shock.

I don't know what went wrong. I just remember that when I put my hands on the metal armrests, needle-sharp pains shot up my arms. I screamed, and passed out. That scared my aunt, and she never tried to force me to have a perm again.

'I work my fingers to the bone for this family, morning, noon, and night. Where am I supposed to find the time to do things carefully?' was a frequent cry of hers.

When she was young, she and my uncle were forever at each other's throats. The years went by, and the children grew up, but their fights didn't stop. It seemed like they'd been saving up all the seething resentments they hadn't had time to get off their chests in their younger years.

One night, at dinner, we all sat around the table and watched the TV news. There were a couple of stir-fried dishes in the middle, and we each had a bowl of sweet potato and maize porridge. Suddenly, my uncle frowned, put down his bowl and stuck his hand down his throat. Out came a long thin bit of wire wool.

'What the hell is this?' he stuttered, bug-eyed and literally spitting with rage. 'Are you trying to kill me?'

Auntie Wenjie looked at him rather unwillingly, 'Eat it or not, as you like. If you're so pissed off, why don't you do the cooking?'

My uncle trembled with rage and went purple in the face. He looked like he was going to explode, and I slipped out into the yard with my bowl, and hid as far away as I could get. A few seconds later, I heard the sounds of a massive, ear-splitting row breaking out indoors.

I knew all about my aunt's carelessness from personal experience. Once, I was astonished to find a worm in my bowl of sesame leaf noodles. I put down the bowl and ran into the yard to retch, but Auntie Wenjie was quite unperturbed. 'What are you making such a fuss about? Eat it up, it's extra protein!'

Cooking aside, her washing-up left a lot to be desired too. I always insisted on washing my bowl again before serving out the food. Leaving them greasy didn't matter so much, but bits of dumpling dough from two days ago were still stuck on them, as well as yesterday's porridge, and now there was a bit of wire wool thrown in for good measure. If it weren't for my sharp eyes, heaven knows what I would have been putting in my stomach every day.

She was slovenly, unkind, ignorant and stubborn, and you could see that in every part of her life all the time. Once, she hung her trousers over the back of the chair and her money fell out. When she went to put them on in the morning, the pocket was empty – and she accused me of stealing it. For that, I got a box on the ears with a spatula, and she grabbed my mouth and twisted it hard. And guess who found the money scuffed into a corner? She did. Another time, she lost a gold earring. On no evidence at all, she decided to blame me for taking it and beat me till I howled. Soon after, I was hunkered down in the yard washing the dishes, and I found the earring glinting in the mud. Even then, she insisted that I'd stolen it and thrown it there deliberately.

The house was always full of mosquitoes in summer. She never lit the mosquito coils before they arrived. She waited until we went to bed, to close the window and light the coils. The smoke was thick in the room, and we humans almost choked to death before the mozzies did. The point was, she was incredibly stubborn, and the more you complained, the more coils she lit, until we were practically hallucinating on the fumes.

One summer, all the neighbours went on a trip to swim in the Baihe River. My aunt refused to buy me a flotation ring, and she certainly didn't have the patience to teach me to swim. When we were in deep water, without any warning, she got me under the armpits and dunked me under. I was so scared that I wailed when I came out of the water.

'Crying again! How many times have I told you, relax! Relax! And don't breathe, don't breathe!'

I was still crying, with my mouth wide open, so she ducked me again. And that time, it really shocked the neighbours. What kind of a way was that to teach a child to swim? She might drown!

'Ai-ya! Mrs Shen! Mrs Shen! Why are you trying to teach her like that? That's enough. You go off and have a nice swim and I'll take over with Yangyang,' said one of the men.

If this kindly neighbour hadn't intervened, she really might have been the death of me.

In the early 1990s, every household used honeycomb briquettes for cooking. Every day, the cooker had to have the cinders at the bottom removed with a pair of long tongs, then two smouldering briquettes were put back in, and finally a fresh briquette was added on top. The same operation, every single day.

Auntie could not even manage this simple everyday task. Either the briquettes she picked up were soft or they were crumbly. Even when luck was on her side and she got them to light, for one reason or another the briquettes always went out.

'Yangyang! Put a new briquette in!'

'Yangyang! Come and use the bellows!'

'Yangyang! Take this briquette and go over the road, and get them to give you a lighted one!'

Auntie Wenjie and briquettes just did not get on, but I was at her beck and call to help. In those dark days before the gas became popular, I became known as the village 'briquette girl'. Every other day, I could be seen carrying a fresh one in a pair of tongs to a neighbour's, and then running back home carefully carrying a flaming briquette.

My aunt didn't give a button for these trivial domestic things, or for her family, but she was different when it came to outsiders. She was full of enthusiasm, and endlessly patient. Sometimes too enthusiastic, but she never got tired. One summer night, after dinner, she went out alone, and about half an hour later, she came back in a great hurry.

'I just met X and Y having a fight with kitchen knives when I went out! What a coincidence that I happened to bump into them! I went up to the man and grabbed the knife off him.' She stood in front of the TV, gesticulating as she described the alarming scene proudly to the family.

My uncle was not impressed, 'Are you dopy or something?' He glared at her angrily.

'Mum, that's dangerous, and you're an old woman! Why are you getting involved in a ruckus like that? You might have got slashed yourself, then what?' Mingze muttered, frowning.

'That's right, steer clear of that stuff,' my girl cousins chimed in.

'Why should it matter to you all if I die in the street?' was my aunt's riposte. She imagined herself as a swashbuckling hero from *The Water Margin*, Lu Zhishen for instance, but in her family's eyes she was more of a simple-minded hunk like Zhang Fei, from *The Romance of the Three Kingdoms*. She was so annoyed with them that she didn't speak to them for days. In the meantime, she was on a very short fuse, and took out her resentments on me.

When I was living openly at my aunt's house and suffering all this abuse, three-year-old Fourth Sister, Star, was carefully being kept out of sight of the officials. My grandparents were popular with the villagers, and every time the family planning squad were planning a raid, someone would warn them. The officials got so frustrated that they rented a place to stay in Sunzha and settled in.

In desperation, Grandad stayed in Sunzha to hold the fort on his own, and Dad took the risk of fetching Star and Nana and taking them to live in Jining. It was hiding in plain sight. No one would suspect him of hiding his child in his own home.

But a kid is not a hamster. Star was fed up with being shut in, and naturally wanted to get out of the house. Although the grown-ups had told her over and over that she was never to go out, she took her chance one day when Nana was napping. She got onto the stool, quietly opened the gate and sneaked out.

She certainly caused a stir. Anyone in the village only had to look at her to know she was Shen Wenming's little girl. If it hadn't been for my Granny who spotted her as she stood gossiping in the street, the village officials would have had Star in custody in no time at all.

When Nana woke up and couldn't find Star, she was frantic. She was rushing out to look for her just as Granny arrived at the door, 'This little one scared the living daylights out of me! She ran into the street alone. You better pack up straightaway and go. Otherwise, they'll be here looking for both of you!'

My father and mother were due to do their factory shift early next morning, so they got their eldest nephew to pedal Nana and Star to another aunt's house in the north of the city on the bicycle. The nephew was a sturdy young man in his early twenties. Dad told him to be very, very careful – he should leave out of the back gate and take the lanes. He patted his chest confidently, 'Uncle, you can depend on me, I'll get them there safely.'

He cycled steadily away, with Nana clutching Star in her arms on the back. But in no time at all, he was back again, with the bicycle but without his passengers, and looking panic-stricken. Mum and Dad had been about to leave for work. They looked at his bleeding hand and got a terrible fright. 'What happened with you? What's up?'

'Uncle, Auntie, hurry! They're down that lane there. I– I was pedalling alone fine, when– when suddenly we hit a big rock that some idiot had left in the middle of the street. I didn't have time to brake, and Nana fell off, with Star in her arms.'

'What?!' Mum and Dad pushed the boy out of the way, and headed off on the bike.

They found Nana sitting on the ground, still holding Star. She was groaning, and her head was bleeding heavily. The blood had flowed down her face and neck, and soaked into the front of her jacket. Star was frightened but uninjured.

Dad put Nana on the bicycle and very carefully pedalled off to the hospital. Mum picked her daughter up, 'Star, Nana's had a nasty fall, so you've got to be a good girl in future.'

Star's little mouth turned down. She was only just three, and the tears welled in her eyes as she nodded obediently. Many years later, talking about the hair-raising events of that day, my mother was still traumatized, 'If Nana had suffered serious injury, I would never have forgiven myself for the rest of my life.'

Nana had stitches in her head, and Star and she returned to Sunzha.

Back in Jining, the family planning officers, who had amassed a good deal of evidence, didn't let the grass grow under their feet. It wasn't long before they found out that my parents were out for the day, and arrived at our house with a posse of men armed with a stout wooden stake.

The thuds on the gate were deafening.

'Who is it? What do you want?' my big sister, Moon, hands on hips, yelled from inside.

'Open up! Open the gate! Otherwise we'll break it down!'

'Wah!!!' There was a wail of terror from Third Sister, Serene, who was only four and a half.

'Don't cry, Mum'll be back soon!' Big Sister put her hand over her mouth to stifle the wails.

There was a crash, and our big iron gate suddenly fell in.

The whole posse rushed through the yard and straight into the house. They yanked the cable out of the TV where a cartoon film was on.

'Mummy, Mummy!' Third Sister's cries rose to a shriek.

'Stop crying! We've got to stop them!' Big Sister rushed forward and grabbed the leader's arm. The man tried to shake her off, but she got her arms right around him and wouldn't let go. Third Sister went to her defence, throwing her small arms around his calf and sinking her teeth in hard.

The man yelled, snarled, and flung both of the girls away with all the strength he could muster. There was mayhem. Big Sister and Third Sister sat on the ground bawling their eyes out. The man sat down too, rubbed his bitten leg, and ordered his companions to take all the furniture out of the house.

My two sisters watched wide-eyed as the bastards carried everything out and took it away: TV, washing machine, sideboard, sewing machine, pots and pans, even a torch and a cigarette lighter. When we were all grown up, whenever Big Sister described the events of that day, the four of us couldn't help laughing. Amazing that the dramatic events of twenty years ago could still make us laugh!

That evening, Dad arrived at the Family Planning Office with Third Sister in his arms.

'Fuck it, we have laws in this country, right? Look what you've done to my kid!'

'Your kid?! That fucking brat almost chewed my leg off!' The officer yanked up his trouser leg angrily.

'It serves you right, you fucker! You're just a thug!'

And Dad handed my sister to Mum, who was standing behind him, and squared up to the family planning officer.

'Who fucking gave you the right to break into our house? I want every single one of those things you stole back right now! Otherwise, you'll see what I'll do to you!'

Dad's spittle sprayed the man's face. He wiped it off with his sleeve. His lip twitched, and he narrowed his eyes as he spat out scornfully, 'Do you really think we don't know what's going on in your family? Let me tell you, I know just what you're hiding in Sunzha village!'

My parents were taken aback. It had never occurred to them that these thugs at the Family Planning Office already knew about Fourth Sister, Star.

'Eight thousand yuan, that's what you owe us. Go and sort it out. When you bring it to us, you can have this trash back again, every single bit of it!' The officer dropped into his chair and looked at Mum and Dad in disdain.

'Eight thousand yuan? Where are we going to get eight thousand yuan from?'

'Borrow it! You can pay it back in dribs and drabs.'

'I don't know how they found out. However will we pay so much money back?' Mum said frowning as they returned home. Dad walked in silence, carrying Third Sister in his arms.

'It means Yangyang may not be able to come back for a while.'

'Well, if she can't, she can't.'

The road back seemed endless to my mother. She was overwhelmed with despair. Many years later, she told me that, at that moment, she could hardly see the way home, let alone how all this was going to end.

At the height of the family planning campaign, the officials in charge of it were universally loathed. In China, raising children, caring for the elderly, and keeping the family line going, were deeply-rooted cultural traditions. As far as sons went, it was the more the merrier. But nowadays the government enforcers had their eyes glued to every woman's belly, carried out inspections and raids on a regular basis, confiscated cattle and pulled down houses, and carted pregnant women off to have forced abortions. The implementation of the law left a lot to be desired, as did the calibre of some cadres, and excessive brutality was common, especially in the countryside. At that time, everyone was poor, and few people could afford the fines that were the only way to keep your children with you. Violence between cadres and the villagers frequently flared up, and the latter gave as good as they got.

It was tit for tat: if the cadres confiscated a family's food grain, they'd find their own crops destroyed; the cadres pulled a family's house down, and their livestock would be poisoned; if the cadres used violence against a pregnant woman, her family would attack the cadres' old folk or kids – 'If you kill my child, I'll do the same to yours,' was a threat that was carried out. An eye for an eye, a tooth for a tooth. Cadres and villagers fought running battles, the one openly, the other by subterfuge.

Of course, rules were sometimes bent. Even among the cadres whose job it was to enforce the law strictly, quite a few were supportive of the villagers and were as lenient as they could be. They would let it be known that pregnant women should hide themselves; someone who had been arrested might find themselves surreptitiously released; some cadres preferred persuasion and went to visit excess birth families over and over again to try and change their thinking; when a family's house was demolished, they would make sure the roof tiles were carefully stacked in the yard, and they'd leave one room undamaged for the family to take shelter in; when they confiscated grain, they quietly left half behind, enough to keep the family alive.

Theoretically, family planning work should have been done by women, but most were men. Why? Because as soon as the officers arrived in a village to enforce the law, the villagers set the dogs on them. When the women heard the dogs barking, they didn't dare go into the village, let alone bang on someone's door.

There were considerable risks in having excess births, yet families did it, putting up stubborn resistance, and never giving up. Some women bought forged 'tubal ligation certificates' or made a small wound in their bellies and stuck a dressing over it to look like they had been sterilized; women would hide away anywhere they could, or the family would pay for a sterilized woman to have her fallopian tubes reconnected, or they would try to pull strings. There was no limit to what people could actually do, only a limit to what they could dream up.

Family planning was supposed to benefit the nation and the people. 'Have one, have the best.' 'With only-child families, the government will look after the old folk.' Everyone knew the slogans, they rang out loud and clear. What effect family planning would have in the end was anyone's guess, however.

In any case, China used to be an agricultural country, and feudal attitudes linger: a big family is a thriving family; more children means more workers and a stronger family; a single, solitary child has no one to help if things go wrong, and no one to stand up for them if other villagers cheat them. In the countryside, only a son is considered to belong to the family, able to set up a household and keep the family line going. Daughters will marry out, so they don't count. A family with only daughters will be mocked because the line will soon die out. In any argument with the neighbours, you'll hear someone shouting, 'When you die, there'll be no sons to lead the mourning ceremony!'

As far as country folk are concerned, the only thing they can control is their bellies. The one thing they long for is children, and children are also their support in old age.

Compared with the family planning battles in rural areas, enforcing the policy in cities and towns was a simple matter. Government organizations, public institutions, state-owned enterprises, and the military were ideal for implementing the policies, because employees had no land to live off and had to rely on their jobs to support their families. If a couple dared to have a second child, then both husband and wife would be kicked out. What else could they do except obediently toe the line? Of course, some did manage it. They were either people with the right connections and power and courage and money, or those like my parents with no money, or power, or connections, but the determination to do whatever it took to have one child after another, and hide the evidence.

At the beginning of 1993, when my parents had paid off the fine, Fourth Sister, Star, finally got her wish and was able to go home to Mum and Dad. She had spent three years in hiding, being shuttled from pillar to post. I was not so lucky. I had spent five years hidden away in Sunzha with Nana and Grandad but 'home' for me was further away than ever.

Meanwhile, in Nanyang, my uncle and aunt grovelled and pulled strings, and scurried from one office to another for several months, and spent 3,000 yuan, and finally managed to get me a hukou residence card.

A girl cousin called Wu Shanying had had a hukou in another city bought for her at great expense so that she could apply for college there, and of course the hukou was registered in a different name. As a result, she did not need her own hukou and my uncle managed to wangle it for me for the exorbitant price of 3,000 yuan. Of course, it was my aunt and uncle who paid up. After that, my cousins used to make fun of me by calling me Three Thousand Shen when the grown-ups weren't listening.

But things were rather more complicated than just buying a hukou.

My aunt and her family lived, and were registered, out of town. If I registered myself as living with them, I would have a rural hukou just like they did. Back then, the document that everyone wanted was a city hukou. So my uncle went and talked to his older brother and sister-in-law in the city again. After some discussion, I was finally added to their urban hukou under the name Wu Shanying.

In law, I had taken someone else's name (not that I minded that) and become someone else's niece. However, on the hukou, I was registered as, 'Wu Shanying, female, date of birth 24th December 1984,' instead of 'date of birth 1st January 1986', my real date of birth. In other words, two years had been added to my age, which made me a very late starter at school. My uncle thought he had been very clever and done me a favour because I'd be able to retire early, though actually it meant that I was teased mercilessly by my classmates.

'Auntie, why do people call me "illegal"? What does it mean?'

'It means you don't have a hukou.'

'What's a hukou?'

'It's a document that proves who you are, it means you can go to school.'

'Ah...'

'Your aunt and uncle scraped together the money to buy you a city hukou, they paid 3,000 yuan for it. Don't forget, your name's Wu Shanying from now on. When you get to school, you make sure you do what the teacher says and work hard. And don't let us down – we spent a lot of money on you.'

On 1st September 1993, I, Shen Yang, was seven years old. Except that in the eyes of the law, my name was Wu Shanying and I was nearly nine years old. At least I was no longer an illegal, a girl who didn't exist. I really did start school, at the newly built Changzhuang Primary School.

In the meantime, Star, my fourth sister's name was finally entered onto the Shen family's hukou, and in the position where I should have been, Third Sister's name appeared as, 'Second Daughter, Serene'.

4

Careless!

At the age of seven, I walked into school, my schoolbag on my back, and took my place in the bright, spacious classroom. I liked the teachers straightaway. There was Ms Feng who taught Chinese, Ms Yang who taught maths, and Ms Yao who taught music. They had just graduated from Teachers' Training College, and were young and pretty, funny and energetic. The most important thing was that they all genuinely liked children. I had come from a family where all I got was harsh words, and I loved every aspect of school life. I looked forward to it every day.

In class, I paid attention and worked hard. After class, I was equally happy with the boys playing with their cards or marbles, or joining the girls with their skipping or Slam-the-Sandbag games. If I saw a boy bullying a younger girl, I would always stand up for her. I was a knight in shining armour. I was a tomboy with pigtails.

Ms Feng was the class head and was observant enough to have spotted my willingness to take the lead. At a meeting for selecting class 'cadres', she picked me to be head monitor. Happy days! That year, I was a good student, a good monitor in the eyes of my classmates, and a good kid at home. I couldn't wait to get to school every day. I even dreamed of rushing to school in the mornings. If only I'd been allowed to eat and sleep there too.

Every morning before school, I went through the same ritual. Most times, it went like this: I went to scrounge for food in the kitchen, I took the lid off the pot, then looked in the bamboo baskets hanging on the wall. Frowning, I picked over yesterday's steamed mantou buns, which by now were cold, hard and curled at the edges, pinching this one and that. Finally, I acknowledged defeat and chucked them back into the basket.

Having rooted through everything in the kitchen without success, I pushed my aunt's bedroom door open gently and poked my head in. 'Auntie,' I whispered.

My aunt lay unmoving, her big bum making a hump inside the quilt. I tried again, and finally she opened one eye unwillingly, 'What?'

'Breakfast money.' I whispered as I squeezed in through the crack in the door, tugging on my dangling satchel straps.

'Take a mantou with you, damn brat! Why d'you always want to waste good money on buying street food? Can't you be happy with what we've got?' my aunt spluttered.

I said nothing. I just stood there, head bowed, biting my lip.

'Huh.' She reached reluctantly for the trousers that lay next to the bed and fumbled in the pockets. She took out a handful of notes – there were bills of ten yuan, five yuan, two yuan, fifty cents and twenty cents, but there was no one-yuan note.

She held onto the two-yuan note and hesitated. Then she threw the fifty and the twenty onto the chair by the bed.

'Seventy cents isn't enough!' I muttered with a rebellious pout.

'Of course it is! Take it or you won't get anything!' my aunt snarled.

I snatched it up and fled from the room. 'Door!!' she bellowed after me.

She'd only given me seventy cents, so why should I stop and shut her door? I pulled a face at her bedroom window as I ran outside and through our gate.

'Damn brat!' Behind me, my aunt cursed. She crawled out of bed in her baggy patterned undershorts and shut the door herself. There was a freezing draught and she shivered and hugged her chest as she dived back under the covers again.

Asking for money, getting sworn at, talking back, getting sworn at, being given money, getting sworn at again. It was compulsory, every day.

'Pepper soup and a fried laomo bun!'

'A bowl of soft tofu and a fried youtiao stick!'

'Give us two bowls of babao congee and two egg pancakes please!'

In front of the stall that sold breakfasts, my schoolmates brandished notes of one, two or even five yuan and shouted. I kept a tight grip on the seventy cents that was all I had and kept watching. When everyone else had made their orders and gone away with their takeaway trays, I jumped in, 'A fifty-cent laomo to take away.' The stall-holder took the note and chucked it into his cash box on the side. Then he deftly picked out a steaming-hot laomo with his tongs and popped it into a white plastic bag.

I took the bag and stuffed my remaining twenty cents into my jacket pocket. Just when I was about to sink my teeth into the laomo, I caught a glimpse of Yuan Xiaohui, one of my schoolmates, who was sitting at one of the tables gulping down a bowl of soup and munching on a fried youtiao. His mother, Wang Jixia, who was sitting beside him, watched him fondly. Every once in a while, she took out a handkerchief and wiped the grease from his mouth for him. I was dead jealous, but I acted like I couldn't care less. I took a large bite of my laomo then wiped my mouth on my sleeve, stuck my nose in the air, and marched off to school, munching as I went.

Yuan Xiaohui had thick eyebrows and big eyes. He was the only child of the Yuan family of Xiaoliangzhuang village, so he was one of those pampered little emperors. His mother, Wang Jixia, took him to school and collected him every day, come rain or shine, regular as clockwork. Sitting in the classroom looking out at Wang Jixia, who stood under an umbrella waiting for her son, I used to daydream of having a mother who loved me like that, one who would come and fetch her darling girl from school in all weathers. But my daydreams never came true, and every time it rained, I'd run madly home on my own, hugging my schoolbag in my arms.

In the autumn of 1994, when I was eight and in year two, I lost my first front tooth. I did what my aunt told me to do and threw the tooth up on the roof. Everyone said that was the way to get big, strong, regular, white teeth. The neighbour's kid saw I was missing a tooth and sang out, 'Eight years gone, tooth gone too, throw it on the roof, grow like new.'

It was a sad autumn. I had not only lost my front tooth, I had lost my two favourite teachers as well – they were now teaching the new year one children. I hid away in the corner of the sports ground, and cried and cried, my toothless mouth gaping. Those teachers had been like mothers to me.

The new Chinese teacher was kind and friendly, and everyone liked her. But Ms Hua, the maths teacher, was a plump older woman, one of the senior teachers, stern and unbending. To start with, a group of boys, the class mischief-makers, acted up. But a few things happened and before long, she had an unusually quiet classroom.

We used to have double maths classes. Ms Hua began by writing the names of any children who made trouble in the first session in pink chalk at the top right corner of the blackboard. In the second class, punishment was meted out.

The first time, it went like this. Ms Hua called out, 'Zhai Jingchi, Liang Bo, Li Maozhi. Come and stand on the podium, the three of you!'

The boys smirked and obeyed. Ms Hua took a fountain pen from the teacher's desk and unscrewed the cap. Then she bent down and wrote couplets on their faces: a line of characters down each cheek.

'You can all stand there and listen for the rest of the class so everyone can see how naughty you've been!' she hissed furiously.

The rest of the class burst out laughing, and the three wretches on the podium bowed their heads and looked subdued. I was so shocked by how suddenly this had happened that the rest of the lesson passed me by. For the whole of the second class, the boys stood heads bowed, without moving. They were just naughty little eight-year-olds, they could never have anticipated such humiliating punishment.

I was a kid who normally obeyed all the rules in class, but from that day on, I was extra careful in the maths class. I didn't dare make any mistakes. I was afraid that if I slipped up, it would be my turn next.

'Have you come to class to use your brains, or have you not? Huh?' Ms Hua raged at us in one lesson. She flung our homework books down on the desk, and bits of chalk bounced up as if they were going to bite us.

'This is all stuff you've already been taught. Why are you still making mistakes?'

She stalked up and down the podium, her hands clasped behind her back.

'If I read your names out, come and line up here on the podium.' She paused at her desk and picked up a workbook. At that moment, the classroom was so quiet you could only hear breathing.

'Zhou Lu, Zhou Gang, Wei Xu, Guo Jianwei, Wu Shanying!'

When I heard her say 'Wu Shanying', I felt faint. I don't remember how I got to the podium. I only remember that the moment I got to my feet, I started trembling all over.

'I've told you and told you, and you're still making mistakes like this! Now you can all tell me what you're thinking about in my class!'

Zhou Lu and I kept our heads down, but the other three, all boys, acted like they couldn't care less. The rest of the class were whispering to each other. Ms Hua glanced at us. She picked up her pen, unscrewed the cap, and walked calmly over to Guo Jianwei.

Then she bent down and wrote 'Brainless' in big red characters on his forehead. That wiped the devil-may-care grins off the faces of the other two, especially when she followed it up by writing on their foreheads too.

The rest of us hardly dared breathe as we watched what was happening to our luckless classmates.

'I don't know how you have the nerve to cry!' said Ms Hua as her pen landed on Zhou Lu's forehead. Zhou Lu's mouth was agape in a wail.

'And you're not allowed to wash it off until I say so, do you hear?' Ms Hua instructed us sternly.

Zhou Lu bowed her head, still weeping. I stood next to her, my head held high, eyes lowered, fists clenched.

Ms Hua yanked my burning face towards her. Mercilessly, she wrote, 'Careless.'

I bent my head and the tears poured down my cheeks. I forced myself not to sob, but I couldn't stop a shiny rope of snot from running from my nose.

I heard muffled laughter from the children below us, and forced my head down even more. Through my tears, I looked at my plastic shoes, which were filthy and falling to pieces. Then I looked at the torn leggings I was wearing under my trousers. I felt desperate.

At that moment, all I wanted to do was to pull my head right inside my shell like a tortoise and never come out again. Only two questions wrong, and Ms Hua had humiliated me like this. She was a government-funded teacher and she was supposed to serve the people, but instead of patient, systematic teaching, all we children got from her was abuse.

The school bell rang and all the kids swarmed out into the school yard, shouting and yelling. Then the yard was empty too.

Zhou Lu and I poked our heads out of the classroom and watched for ages before making a run for it. We made straight for the washbasins in the sportsground and put our faces under the tap. We rubbed and rubbed, but the marks of red pen were still faintly visible.

Just then, Yuan Xiaohui came out of the boys' toilet, which was not far away, with his schoolbag on his back. He pointed at us and laughed, 'Careless! Careless!' Zhou Lu bent her head and ignored him, then picked up her own schoolbag and broke into a run. But I was so angry that I picked up a stone and threw it hard at Yuan Xiaohui. It hit him bang in the middle of his forehead, and he burst into tears. Before he could get his own back, I grabbed my bag and fled with an evil smile on my face.

Ms Hua had a daughter who was grown up and working. One day, she turned up at the school looking very smart. Ms Hua took her outside where they sat and chatted and laughed in the sunshine. When the daughter's hair was mussed by the wind, her mother smoothed it down. When the daughter was thirsty, her mother took a thermos from her bag and gave it to her.

I was perched on the parallel bars watching goggle-eyed. It was hard to believe that this was Ms Hua, the stern, unbending teacher, now full of laughter and affection. If it was her own daughter standing in front of her on the podium, could she bring herself to write on her face?

At some point around then, I stopped dreaming that I was rushing to school in the morning. Whenever I opened my pencil case and looked at the unending maths classes on my timetable, my hair would stand on end. By the time the school bell rang and Ms Hua stepped into the classroom, I was a bag of nerves.

I never dared tell my family about that humiliating ordeal at school. I knew that they would not only not challenge the teacher, they'd instantly side with her and tell me off too, 'Why are you so stupid? If you're making mistakes in your homework, you can't have been listening to the teacher!'

In those days, the teacher was God, her words imperial edicts, and her farts fragrant.

Ms Hua had decreed that mistakes in homework were not permitted, so we just had to find a workaround. Those children who were good at maths lent out their homework books to kids who wanted to copy them. My maths was getting worse and worse, and I had to take desperate measures to save myself. The first time, I rushed home in great excitement and asked my uncle for help. He had been a teacher, a government-funded one too.

He peered at the questions in my workbook, then frowned and asked me, 'How do *you* think you should do it?'

I'd been asking him for help, I didn't expect him to throw the question back at me. I stood there with my head lowered, mute. My uncle looked stern and bellowed at me, 'Read me the question again!' I shook with fright, and even my aunt quivered. I repeated the question in a trembling whisper as my uncle frowned even more severely at me. I felt dazed.

'Damn brat! Why are you so stupid? Can't you even do a simple question like this?' Uncle bellowed again.

There was a stunned silence. The pitter-patter of my tears on the workbook were the only sounds to be heard.

'Such a crybaby! Is that all you can do, stupid girl?' Uncle was working himself up into an even greater rage.

My nose began to run and I stood there as if I'd been turned to stone, my mind a blank.

My aunt had had enough. 'Why are you shouting at her like this? If she's come to ask you, it's because she can't do it herself! Otherwise, she wouldn't ask you, would she? You think you're so clever, but you never went to college. You spend all the time looking down on other people but you're not so bright yourself!'

My aunt had touched a sore spot here. When my uncle was young, he hadn't been allowed to go to college because of his 'family background', and he never got over the injustice of it. My aunt's words just added fuel to the fire and he flared up at her. A blazing row between husband and wife erupted.

In school, I didn't dare to ask Ms Hua if I couldn't do the maths problems. At home, I couldn't go to my uncle and invite more humiliation. Over time, I developed a violent dislike of mathematics which has never left me.

When he wasn't losing his temper, my uncle was affectionate towards me. He taught me to read classical Chinese poems, told me stories, took me on days out to town, and played badminton with me.

He even taught me to ride a bicycle, patiently holding the seat and jogging along behind me as I pedalled along.

I was only small, and couldn't reach the seat of the big heavy machine with its 28-inch wheels, so I stood over the crossbar and pushed the pedals down as hard as I could, first on one side, then the other. Once I could balance on my own, my uncle stood at the gate watching his young pupil, roaring with laughter.

'When your cousins were young, your uncle never played with them. He certainly didn't teach them to ride a bicycle,' my aunt commented.

By now, I knew enough about my uncle's temper not to ask him for help with my maths again. In turn, he never bothered to ask about my schoolwork. He often said to me, 'It doesn't matter what marks you get in school, so long as you're healthy!' This axiom stemmed from bitter experience: he had wanted to become an intellectual – he was clever enough – but never got the chance to make his dreams come true.

5

Eighteen grape vines

In the spring of 1993, my eldest cousin Li Ruomei got married. The family were given another bit of land, built a new house and we moved. My uncle, to his delight, was given eighteen grape seedlings by an old friend. They reminded him of the time when, as a young lad – more than fifty turbulent years ago now – he had hunted through a certain vine trellis for grapes. For the rest of his life, he never forgot the taste of the beautiful, succulent grapes he had found. This was the story he told us:

Uncle's mother died young, his father was away working, and his brothers and sisters were busy on the farm. They were very poor. He was a scrawny kid, always hungry and shy as well, so he was bullied by the boys in the village.

There was an abandoned yard in the village where two lone vines bore bunches of red and purple grapes every summer. Everything was in short supply back then, and folk counted themselves lucky if they had enough food and clothes. So fruit was an unattainable luxury for almost everyone.

One afternoon when the sun was blazing down and the cicadas were chirring loudly, the bigger village boys descended on the grape vines. Uncle hid at a safe distance and watched as these monkeys stripped the trellis clean of grapes. If only they had given him just

47

one grape, he would have been satisfied. But they picked the vines clean, and stuffed their mouths and pockets, and once there were only leaves left, they swarmed away, shouting and yelling.

He sneaked into the yard and, standing under the trellis, he peered upwards and carefully scanned the foliage. A gust of hot wind hit him in the eyes, and the sun's rays dazzled him painfully through the gaps in the leaves. Suddenly, in the corner, some leaves moved in the wind and, magically, a bunch of dark purple grapes came into view. Elated, he scrambled ever so carefully up the mud-brick wall, leaned across and reached out for the grapes.

Sitting astride the wall, his face burned red from the sun, he began to savour his hard-won prize. The juice filled his mouth, and he closed his eyes and relished their sweet nectar on his taste buds.

'I normally never had grapes, the older kids never gave the younger ones any. Finally, I had a whole bunch to myself and they were so sweet!' Decades had passed, and my uncle could still clearly remember that brilliant midsummer sweetness. Every time he told the story, his face would light up.

Life had been difficult for Uncle, and as a young man he had had to work hard to support his family; but at least he could enjoy a bit of leisure now that he was old. Those eighteen vines embodied his childhood dreams and his wordless love for his family.

One warm spring day, under his guidance, I dug holes and planted eighteen grape seedlings, backfilling them with soil, around the new house. They filled the whole yard. In the days that followed, my uncle studied every manual he could get his hands on, and in his spare time, he squatted by his precious seedlings and checked on their progress.

We put up bamboo trellises, applied fertilizer and insecticide, and pruned. Spring turned into summer, and summer into autumn, and the vines grew tall, to the delight of my uncle. Every morning in winter, we heard him striding through the main room of the house in his big boots. In his cheerful footsteps, we heard his high hopes for the eighteen vines, which by now lay under a thick blanket of snow.

One morning in the spring of 1995, the vines in the yard seemed to have sprouted tender young leaves overnight. We had had some spring rain, and our small yard was bursting with green foliage. But although the plants were flourishing, I was not. I had caught mumps at school, and the whole of the right side of my face was swollen like a giant bun.

'Damn brat! How many times have I told you not to play with the kids with medicine patches on their faces. You never listen and now look what's happened! You're so disobedient!' My aunt scolded me as she rode me to the hospital on the bicycle.

She acted like it was my fault for catching the mumps! But with sixty children, half of them infected, all breathing the same germ-filled air in a stuffy classroom, I would have needed the Monkey King's superpowers to escape the infection.

In the hospital, the elderly doctor prescribed topical Chinese herbal medicine and a large black sticky plaster was applied to my face. That night, under my aunt's eagle eye, I held my nose and forced myself to drink a large bowl of bitter-tasting Chinese medicine. The next day, my aunt again boiled up the medicine for me but I sneakily poured it away under a vine in the corner of the wall. I thought I'd got away with it, but my uncle found me out: he saw the dregs on the ground when he was checking his precious vines.

He gave me a furious telling-off as soon as I got home that lunchtime from school. 'Damn brat! Don't you want your face to get better? We spent time and money on you, taking you to a doctor, buying medicine and boiling it up, and you pour it all over my vines!'

I knew I was in the wrong, and stood with my head bent, not saying a word. Auntie came out of the kitchen, a dish in her hand, 'Damn brat! Why do you always cause us so much trouble?' She called to the tabby cat lying in a plant container, 'Puss, puss! Here!' She lifted a large piece of streaky pork out of the dish and threw it down.

Uncle was tending his vines, carefully snip-snipping the branches with his secateurs.

I looked from one to the other then, with my schoolbag in my arms, went miserably into the house. I wished I was a cat or a vine. I would have been better looked after in this family.

'I like going to school and playing with my classmates because it's the only place I don't feel lonely, and no one shouts at me,' I wrote in my diary in my careful handwriting.

Come June, bunches of green grapes covered the vines, and I surreptitiously picked a bunch and took them to school. In the classroom, the teacher was in full cry on the podium but all of my classmates in the rows in front and behind mine had their eyes on me.

'Zhou Gang, stand up and read Li Bai's poem "Gazing at a Waterfall on Mount Lu", please.' The teacher had spotted something was going on, and the unlucky kid she picked on was Zhou Gang. Zhou Gang stood up slowly. He picked up the textbook and tried his best to look serious, 'The sun shines on Incense Burner Peak, purpling the smoke. A distant waterfall hangs over the river.' He had just started on the third line, 'Water flies straight down three thousand feet', when a trickle of saliva fell from his mouth just like in the poem.

The class erupted in laughter. I laughed so hard I nearly wet myself. Poor Zhou Gang panicked, grabbed his workbook and tried to stem the cascade before it dripped onto his jacket.

'Zhou Gang!' The teacher was really furious now. She hauled the poor boy out of the classroom by his collar and made him stand outside, 'Are you really that hungry? You just stand here and think about how to behave in class!'

The teacher found some grapes Zhou Gang had grabbed off me inside his desk, and hung them over his ear. Zhou Gang stood looking at me reproachfully, but I callously hid my face behind my workbook. All that laughing threatened to give me cramps.

The longed-for summer holidays finally arrived. The news that my aunt and uncle had grapes soon got around, and every few days, one of my classmates would come knocking on the door. For the first two days, my aunt greeted them with a smile, but then it was almost every day that some grubby boy or girl would turn up on the pretext of wanting to play, but really because they fancied our grapes. Auntie roared like a lioness at them and sent them away. This was too bad. The upshot was that no one dared come and play with me. So if I wanted to play, I had to sneak out while the lioness was taking her siesta and take a bunch of stolen grapes to a classmate's house.

A girl in my class, Zhang Sen, lived in a nearby village called Lixianggongzhuang. There was a big pond in front of her house. On hot summer days, adults and children alike used to go and splash around in the water. One afternoon, I stood on the bank with a bag full of grapes and shouted at my classmates who were having a swimming competition. They swam over and got out straightaway. They had had enough of playing and my grapes were tempting. They took them and went in to watch TV.

Looking at the sparkling water, I felt a sudden urge to jump in and swim, just like fishes did, but the problem was that I couldn't swim a stroke. Then, my eye was caught by a glinting metal basin at the water's edge. I had a brainwave, threw off my jacket and sandals, grabbed the empty basin and walked slowly into the water. It gradually got deeper, but I gripped the rim with both hands and doggy paddled with my legs. Hah! So swimming wasn't such a big deal after all.

I swam splashed happily back and forth, and shouted to my friends. They came out with the few remaining grapes in their hands and stared open-mouthed. I let go of the basin with my left hand and waved and shouted again, but just as everyone was about to shout back, I lost my balance and, in my panic, I nearly upturned my life-saver basin.

'Get out! Get out now! You're scaring us!' Zhang Sen yelled at me.

'Hey, I'm fine! I'm still having fun!'

I'd never had such fun, in fact, and there was no way I was going to stop. I turned and headed to the opposite bank.

'Whose kid is that? She's got a nerve!'

Zhang Sen's grandad was standing behind her, puffing on his pipe and laughing.

'She lives with her aunt and uncle. Her mum and dad are away,' said Zheng Sen, stuffing her mouth with grapes. 'They've got eighteen vines at their house.'

'Eighteen!' he laughed. 'No wonder you've covered my floor with grape skins!'

His granddaughter took the hint and hurriedly got the dustpan and brush to sweep up.

If Uncle had known that his precious grapes were causing such a lot of trouble, I don't know what he would have thought.

That summer holiday, I used to get a gourd scoop and stand on a stool, crane my neck and pick out the best of the grapes. When I had a scoop full of the darkest purple fruit, I washed them in well water, then strung them one by one on pared-down chopsticks and popped them in the freezer.

The first thing I did when I woke up after my afternoon nap was to get the frozen grapes out. In the sitting room, I lay under the fan in the rocking chair my aunt had just bought, watching cartoons on TV and eating my frozen grapes. Bliss.

But my days of leisure didn't last long. I woke up after my nap one day with a raging fever. 'Serves you right for pigging out on grapes,' Auntie said. 'Damn brat.' And she ignored me. I begged a bit of money from my uncle and staggered off to the village clinic.

'There you go,' said the plump doctor wiping the puncture mark on my bottom with cotton wool soaked in alcohol and deftly pulled my trousers up for me.

'Go home, drink warm water and have a good rest. Come back tomorrow for another injection and you'll be fine,' she instructed me, giving her hands a wash. I nodded obediently, thanked her, and set off for home.

I hadn't gone far when I met an old man who took one look at me and yelled, 'Hey, girl, hey!'

At first, I didn't realise he was shouting at me. I was feeling a bit dizzy and carried on walking slowly.

'Hey, girl, you're bleeding from your bum!'

'Bum? Bleeding?' I came to a halt and twisted round to look at my bum.

There was a big patch of blood on the right side of my trousers, and I let out a wail. Back to the clinic.

'Doctor, doctor, my bum's bleeding!'

I had been feeling queasy, but I shot back to the clinic like I'd been given a chicken blood tonic. Everyone hanging around on the street, gossiping and laughing, laughed until they had a bellyache.

Back in the clinic, they gave me some alcohol-soaked cotton wool to press down on my bum where the doctor had inserted the needle. I pressed for a very long time. Ever since then, I've had a horror of bleeding after an injection, and I always make sure to press down for a long, long time.

'Damn brat, you do nothing but stuff your face and watch TV all day long. And you keep the fan on from morning till night. No wonder the electricity bill's shot up this month! You never do any homework or open a book. You're good for nothing!'

My aunt went on and on at me every day, once I'd recovered from being ill. One day, she really flipped, and to get me out of the house, my uncle sent me to the market to sell his grapes. I put on a white sleeveless T-shirt, blue knee-length shorts, and a straw hat, and pedalled the family three-wheeler loaded with a basket of purple grapes to the market near our home.

The vegetable sellers were mainly elderly men and women. I was shy and found a space in the corner of the market where I stood in silence. That whole afternoon, just one man came up and asked how much the grapes were.

It was too bad that the scales I'd brought did not work. 'Two yuan a bunch. Help yourself,' I said, flustered and sweating.

'That's great. You certainly know how to make a sale, girl!' said my customer, a middle-aged man.

He chose five big bunches, gave me ten yuan, and went off very happy.

'Ai-ya! Your mum'll kill you when you get home!' exclaimed one of the women. 'Grapes are so expensive this year, and you're practically giving them away!' She came over and looked at the grapes left over in the basket, sounding genuinely distressed.

I laughed. 'My mum never beats me; she couldn't even if she tried. Here, have two bunches, Missus, I won't charge you.' I handed them to her with a smile.

'What a sweet girl! But I can't take your grapes for nothing. You give me grapes, I'll give you green onions.' She turned around, picked two bunches of green onions from her three-wheeler and stuffed them into my arms.

When it got dark, I pedalled home with half a basket full of grapes and two bunches of onions, and the ten yuan in my pocket, feeling like I had done a good day's work.

Uncle will be pleased with me, I did good! I said triumphantly to myself.

According to my aunt, I'd made big losses. She was so angry, she couldn't eat her dinner. But at least I got praise from Uncle. I was so happy! For the first time ever, I was quids in: ten yuan and two bunches of onions!

After that first time, it wasn't long before my uncle sent me out again to sell grapes. My aunt did not want me to go, but my uncle insisted. He said it didn't matter how much I sold, what mattered was getting experience of life. I was too young to understand what he meant, but I did know that it was fun to go out and sell grapes.

This time, instead of skulking in a corner, I spread a piece of cloth on the ground next to the butcher's stall and laid the grapes on it. The butcher was very enthusiastic. He actually recommended my grapes to his customers, and they were too embarrassed to bargain with a small girl. So they all bought some and, before long, I had sold more than half my grapes.

I liked the butcher. He had a big round face and crinkly eyes when he smiled, which was often. He not only helped me sell the grapes, he also did conjuring tricks to entertain me when he had no customers. He got a coin in his hand and touched behind his ear, and the coin disappeared. I couldn't figure it out. I pulled his big fat ears down and looked behind them, then picked up his fat, greasy hands and peered at them, but I couldn't find the coin.

'Ai-ya! It's no good. I didn't see properly. Do it again for me!' I would implore him, pulling at his arm.

'OK, watch carefully then.'

He waved the coin right in front of my eyes then suddenly, popped it in his mouth. It had disappeared!

I burst out laughing, 'It's in your mouth! I know it is!'

I poked his puffed-up cheeks.

'Aaaah...' he opened his mouth wide.

But there was no coin inside, and his hands were empty too.

'You swallowed it!'

I kept trying to pull his lips open again.

'Hah!'

The butcher suddenly made a grab in the air, opened his hand and – hey presto – there was the coin in his palm. How did it get there?

'How did you make that happen?' I asked, taking the coin and turning it over and over. The butcher squinted at me, and wouldn't tell.

About halfway through the summer holidays, the butcher suddenly left and went back to his home village. I never saw him again, but I have never forgotten him. He remains a magical childhood memory.

In the early nineties, candles were a necessity in every household. We often had power cuts on summer evenings. I used to get very excited when the lights went off. Somehow, dinner in candlelight always tasted better, and I loved listening to night-time stories sitting under the poplar tree. We would spread a small mat under the tree by the front door, put out a bowl of freshly picked grapes, and set out some stools. When my aunt and uncle had finished their dinner, they would come out into the yard bringing a palm-leaf fan. Usually, old friends of my uncle would turn up, strolling down the alley, hands clasped behind their backs, and then there would be a lot of gossip about goings-on past and present. I used to take off my sandals and chuck them on one side, and settle down on the mat to listen.

There was nothing I liked more than sitting cross-legged on the mat, eating grapes, listening to good stories, looking at the starry night sky, enjoying the blessed evening breeze. I liked to snuggle up next to the adults and listen to them talking about the past and telling stories from books. Many times, I couldn't bear to leave even to have a pee, for fear of missing the most exciting bit.

'Hey, during the Cultural Revolution, didn't Jin Zhou's dad live in our village? He said he'd rather spend his money on two ounces of pig's brawn than Chairman Mao's Quotations. So the next day, the Red Guards got hold of him and tied two big pig's heads on him, one on each shoulder, and paraded him through the village!' Our old neighbor Jia Jizhang said one evening.

I thought that story was hilarious. I was too young to understand the bizarre and terrible things that people were forced to endure back then. All I knew was that someone with a pig's head on each shoulder was very funny.

The adults' stories got taller and taller as they gossiped about anything and everything. One very hot summer night, an old neighbour called Pang suddenly came up with a ghost story. I sprawled on the mat, picking at the grapes as usual, and had soon demolished several bunches. At first, I was caught up in the story, but then I had to admit I really needed to pee. I held it in for dear life for as long as I could, because I was scared to go to the toilet alone. It was in a pitch-dark corner of the yard.

'Auntie, will you come with me?' I crept over and whispered to her. I was really desperate by this time.

'Just go to the toilet if you want to, damn brat!' my aunt yelled at me. 'Why d'you need someone to show you where it is?' Everyone stared at me.

'Ai-ya! I...' I clenched my legs together and jammed my hands between them.

Pang was carrying on with his story, 'It was the middle of the night, and the driver was so tired he couldn't keep his eyes open. When he saw the lights on in the hotel, he parked then and there under the tree. He peered through the darkness and walked up to the door. It creaked, and opened by itself.'

I stood there frantically jigging on the spot. Old Pang was a good storyteller and though it was a very hot night, I had goosebumps. 'The door opened, and an eerie draught blew out.' His voice grew quieter.

I couldn't hold it in any longer and with a despairing wail, I raced off to the toilet.

There was a roar of laughter from the grown-ups.

In the toilet, I muttered as I squatted, my eyes tight shut, 'There's no such thing as ghosts. There's no such thing as ghosts.'

Suddenly, I heard a creak from the grape trellis right above me.

'Ai-ya! Ghosts, ghosts! Auntie, there's a ghost in the toilet!' I stumbled out, holding up my trousers and wailing loudly. It wasn't until I heard a familiar meow that I realized that the 'ghost' was in fact our tabby cat.

Our yard, burgeoning with foliage and fruit, was my holiday retreat, my earthly paradise, and my secret hideaway, where I could invite my friends and satisfy my cravings to play teacher. It was also the place where we played practical jokes on each other.

On these scorching summer days loud with the chirring of cicadas, the grown-ups simply slept through the long hot afternoons, and Auntie and Uncle's snores reverberated in the back room. I used to go to the gate and call the children waiting there into the yard. In the shade of the grape trellis, I had arranged some stools and a big chair. There was a small blackboard, and a twig from one of the trees. My rudimentary classroom was fully equipped. My time had come to shine. I taught them how to write their characters and how to do arithmetic, and I rewarded those who did best with bunches of ripe grapes. Had there ever been such highly motivated and cooperative pupils in the history of education?

As for pranks, in the winter when the snow was heavy on the branches, I used to get hold of the grape trellis and give it a shake while my cousin was in the roofless toilet in the corner of the yard having a crap. It was an unmissable opportunity and he never saw it coming. Freezing cold lumps of snow hit him slap-bang on his lily-white bum, and he howled like a stuck pig every time. Most times, I managed to get away, with an evil smile on my face, before my cousin could rush out, catch me and beat me up.

If those eighteen vines fulfilled my uncle's dreams and made up for the frustrations of his youth, then for me, who grew up alongside them, they provided me with my happiest childhood dreams.

6

A pair of red boots

'It's New Year, it's New Year!' On the morning of New Year's Day in 1996, firecrackers exploded and popped all over the village. Children in brightly coloured clothes and new shoes yelled and shouted as they followed their parents around, wishing relatives and friends a Happy New Year. The streets and alleys were bursting with noise and excitement.

My aunt, uncle and cousins were busy in the kitchen making jiaozi dumplings, but I was fast asleep in bed with my head under the quilt. This was the only day in the year that I was not going to get shouted at for sleeping in. The family was superstitious: they believed that if you lost your temper on New Year's Day, there'd be no peace for the rest of the year.

They also believed that if you slept in on New Year's Day, you'd be lazy for the rest of the year. But I didn't care two hoots about New Year. No one gave me new clothes or new shoes, and there were no relatives dropping in with cash-filled red envelopes for me. In my end-of-year exams I was near the top of the class, and I had won a certificate of merit too, but still my aunt wouldn't buy me the red leather boots that I pined for.

'You should count yourself lucky to have enough to eat and drink!' That was what Auntie and Uncle used to say. They had been through hard times. They did not give themselves new clothes, so of course they were not going to make my wishes come true. Although my three cousins were earning by now, they detested me and were hardly going to buy a present for someone as annoying as me.

I imagined my sisters at home in faraway Shandong, racing up and down the alleys of our village in the new clothes and shoes our mother had bought them, enjoying the celebrations. They didn't know of my existence, and my own memories of everyone had started to fade over the past five years. The Nana and Grandad I adored as a small child, I could now scarcely even remember. Time and distance not only erased pain, they could also wipe out a child's best memories.

After a brief, boring winter holiday, the term began again and it was back to the grindstone. Spring was a prime time for getting sick, and soon after school started, white-coated doctors turned up in the classroom, sat themselves down on the teacher's podium and set to work.

'Hurry up now, you're going to be vaccinated, take off your jackets and push up your sleeves so you're good and ready,' our teacher instructed us.

My classmates did as they were told, chattering and laughing. I looked at what they were wearing: almost all of them had new sweaters and new padded jackets. I bit my lip and looked down at the thin, threadbare padded jacket that I had on under my outer jacket. I really did not want to pull down the zip.

'Don't forget to roll your sleeves up!' Our teacher reminded us again. Taking advantage of the noise and confusion, I hurriedly stripped off both my jackets, bundled them both into a ball and stuffed them inside my desk.

When it came to my turn, I stood on the podium, wearing just a pink long-sleeved vest, one arm bared.

'Haven't you got a sweater? Aren't you cold?' asked the middle-aged woman doctor, sounding worried.

'I'm fine!' I stood up straight and acted unconcerned.

She smiled as she pulled the needle out and gently pressed an alcohol-soaked cotton wool ball against my arm. 'Good.....Next!'

I pulled my sleeve down and strolled slowly back to my place. I reached into my desk, glancing oh-so-casually around the room, and hurriedly put my jackets back on. As soon as I had zipped up, I heaved a sigh of relief. Thank goodness no one had discovered my little secret.

I couldn't help being envious of the nice clothes other kids had. I often begged my aunt to knit me a jumper or sew me a padded jacket, but I always got a sarcastic response, 'What a little madam! Damn brat, you're a bit young to be dressing up, aren't you?' The words were spoken carelessly, but they stung. And with every jibe, I developed more of an inferiority complex. I was only young and I could not understand why things that came easily to other kids were always out of reach for me.

We had a cold snap that spring and a few days after our vaccinations, there was heavy snowfall. The grape trellises in our yard were blanketed with a thick layer of snow, and our naughty little cat left trails of paw prints along the top. That day, I got up early as usual and was just about to leave for school with my schoolbag on my back, when my cousin Mingmei, dressed in a thick coat, stopped me as I was passing through the sitting room. She looked suspiciously at me. 'Come back! It's freezing cold, why aren't you wearing your jacket?' She was holding my grubby old padded jacket in her hand.

'I'm not cold,' I said stolidly.

'You're not cold? Don't say that when you've frozen to death!' She glared at me.

'Really I'm not!' I insisted with determination.

'Come here and put it on! Otherwise, you're not going to school today.'

I went over reluctantly, dragging my feet. As soon as I was within reach, she yanked the collar of my outer jacket down and peered inside, 'Who said you could wear my jumper?' she demanded. Then she slapped me across the face and yelled, 'Take it off this minute!'

I rubbed my flaming cheek as my tears poured down my cheeks.

I stood there, shivering and sobbing as I took the jumper off. She flung my threadbare jacket at me, and kicked a pair of battered rubber boots over. I put the jacket on and swopped the thin worn-out shoes I had been wearing for the boots. My feet swam in them. I stood there feeling wretched.

'Disgusting brat! You've made it filthy!' She gave the mauve jumper she had just knitted for herself a vigorous shake. 'I knew you were up to no good, getting up so early for school! Think you look pretty, do you, wearing other people's clothes? Don't you dare to wear my clothes again or I'll beat the living daylights out of you!'

I cried all the way to school that day. My tear-streaked face froze in the biting cold wind, and I seethed with hatred for Mingmei. All that morning I sat in our unheated classroom, freezing in boots that had let the snow in, my heart as ice-cold as my feet.

'We should have kept the old jacket and trousers you had on when you arrived from Shandong. The sleeves were so shiny and hard with snot, you could have struck a match on them!' Mingmei used to taunt me.

I didn't like her, and sometimes I was afraid of her. She was a difficult young woman who had inherited her father's unpredictable temper and her mother's harshness. She was always having a go at me: she made fun of me, she slapped me round the face, she made me kneel on the corrugated washboard. Her cruelty is engraved in my memory.

I reached such a pitch of loathing for her that one sunny afternoon, when I was ten years old, I sprayed air freshener in her cup. Then I hid in a corner of the yard, and watched with bated breath as she picked up the cup and drank it. If I could poison her and she died, I would never have to suffer her bullying again. But she stayed perfectly healthy and unaffected all day long.

All these years later, I still feel apprehensive when I remember what I did. If she had really died, I would have been marked down as a criminal my whole life. But at the time, all I felt was hatred. I had no idea that the reason why she was like this was connected with her own miserable childhood.

My aunt rejected Mingmei from the moment she was born, because she was a girl. When she had to go to work in the fields, she would feed the baby, tie her tightly to the bed and leave her there all morning. Morning after morning, for a whole year. As a result, Mingmei didn't learn to walk until she was almost two years old.

She was not a pretty child and my aunt used to call her 'ugly brat'. When she learnt to speak and could answer back, mother and daughter were always at loggerheads, and the rows usually ended with the latter getting slapped. She quickly learnt not to cry, because that only drove my irascible aunt into a fury. Her patience had worn thin with all the work she had to do: tilling the fields then coming home to wash, cook, and feed the family. Apparently, she used to grab the salt pot in the kitchen and pour the salt into Mingmei's mouth whenever she opened it to start crying.

When the boy, Mingze, was born, it was all very different: my traditionalist uncle and aunt adored their son and heir. He always got first go when there was anything nice to eat, or drink, or play with. The rest of the family doted on him too. They were always dropping in with goodies – all of which went to little Mingze. Mingmei never got a look in. If Mingze did something wrong, he never got scolded or beaten, they took it out on Mingmei instead. He was their precious boy: his dad took him wherever he went, and he was the apple of his mother's eye.

Growing up unloved and rejected cast a shadow over Mingmei's childhood. At the age of five, I suddenly burst into their lives, a wilful little girl, spoilt by my doting Nana. I was a thorn in the flesh of dire, joyless Mingmei, and she vented her rage on me at every opportunity. If I cried, she never took pity on me, and there were a few times when she looked like she was going to pour the contents of the salt pot into my gaping mouth. She was completely unaware that she was just reenacting her own wretched childhood all over again. Every time she hit me, she was repeating the pain that my aunt had inflicted on her. She had been miserable as a kid, so why shouldn't she make someone else's life miserable?

Whose fault was this? Mingmei's? Auntie's? Or Uncle's? He didn't love his wife, so the mother didn't love her daughter, was that it? And what about Uncle who had never experienced his mother's love either? How could he give if he had never received it? It was a vicious circle of lovelessness, in which I came off worst. They were all victims as well as perpetrators. Only I was one hundred percent victim.

I was beaten and scolded so often that from being a carefree happy child, I turned into an oversensitive girl with an inferiority complex. A pain in the neck, who was always in tears. The trauma of my childhood has never left me. I never learnt from the Li-Shen family how people who love each other communicate.

My cupboard was full of cast-offs from my two cousins, clothes that no one else wanted. I really wanted to have pretty clothes, nice shoes, and schoolbags with cartoon prints like other kids. I wanted to be dressed up by my aunt so I could look nice instead of looking like a grubby urchin all the time. So, when I saw that newly knitted mauve jumper hanging in Mingmei's room, I couldn't help myself. Even if it was never going to fit my scrawny body properly, I could wear it to school for half a day, and I'd feel so good.

Not long after that incident, I finally got a mulberry pink jumper, very ordinary without any patterns. Mingmei had knitted that for herself too, but my aunt washed it and it shrank. I was the only one skinny enough to wear it.

I did not like the hand-me-down pink jumper. I dreamed of having a pretty jumper with a cartoon design on it that was all mine one day. But that day never came. I was stuck with that dull pink thing every spring and autumn while I was young.

After five years of living with my aunt's family in Nanyang – from the beginning of 1991 till early spring 1996 – I had forgotten my Nana and Grandad, and my parents only lived in my dreams.

Then on an ordinary evening in March 1996, everything changed. I walked into the yard, and Auntie Wenjie came over, her face wreathed in smiles. That gave me goosebumps. I was so used to her fierce glare, I did not like that smile.

'Yangyang!' A middle-aged man and woman whom I did not recognise burst out of the house.

I stood rooted to the spot, and my schoolbag slipped off my shoulders to the ground.

'Don't just stand there, silly, say hello to your mum and dad!' Auntie gave me a shove.

Just then, a chubby little girl came running out of the house and grabbed the strange woman by the hand, 'Mum! Mum!'

For the last five years, when my friends were mollycoddled by their parents; when it rained and they were picked up from school, and I went home alone; when I was abused and got sick and there was no one to look after me, I had dreamed time and again that one day, my parents would suddenly turn up and take me by the hand, and tell me, 'Yangyang, we've come to take you home!'

Now here was this nicely dressed little girl, my Fourth Sister, Star, standing with my mum and dad. But I felt like a country bumpkin, like I had nothing to do with them. I stuck my hands in my trouser pockets and looked this doll-like creature up and down. On her feet, she was wearing the red boots that I had longed for.

'Our Yangyang's grown so tall!' Mum exclaimed and came towards me with a smile. The moment that I had dreamt of so often had come. But just as she got to me, I turned tail and fled through the gate.

'Hey, damn brat, where are you off to?' I heard Auntie yelling after me. I didn't look back, I ran to the cemetery that I used to go to when I was little, and curled up with my schoolbag in my arms, my heart racing and tears pattering onto the grass. I don't know why I reacted like this. I longed to feel my mother's arms holding me close, I longed to be her baby. But when I saw those red leather boots on Star's feet, tears of disappointment flooded my eyes.

How many times had I begged my aunt to buy me a pair? How many times had I almost tripped over in those oversized patched rubber boots? How many times had I longed for the kind of red boots that all my girl classmates had as I walked out in freezing weather in my tatty slip-ons. But my aunt wouldn't buy them for me, and all I could do was dream.

I clutched my bag in my arms, as a crow flew over my head, cawing.

'Yangyang! Yangyang!' I heard my aunt coming nearer.

'Damn brat, where are you?' Auntie's voice came closer.

I picked fiercely at the patches on my rubber boots, and as my aunt's shouts got farther away again, I hurriedly opened my schoolbag, tore a page out of my workbook and blew my nose hard. These days, I was still a crybaby, but I didn't wipe my snot on my sleeve anymore. I was learning to take care of myself, growing up day by day, and gradually become independent.

At dinnertime, the whole family sat around the table, eating, talking and laughing. Mingmei kept putting titbits into Star's bowl, teasing her and making her giggle. I sat between Mum and Dad, bent over my bowl, silently raking the rice into my mouth. To my amazement, my aunt put a large piece of meat into my bowl. I could hardly believe my luck. Up until then, if I even held my chopsticks in the air above a dish of pork for a second, my aunt or Mingmei would taunt me, 'Why don't you just take off your shoes and wade right in?' I just wanted a piece of pork, but all I got was ridicule.

According to the Seven Principles of Child-Raising, Chinese children are supposed to be loved and cared for, but apparently none of the seven principles applied to me. I was constantly belittled. Everything I said and did was wrong. I wanted to be praised. Fat chance. I was humiliated and beaten in front of everyone as a matter of course. Even if I knew I was in the wrong and admitted it, I wasn't spared. Even in the middle of the night, they made me kneel in the yard. When we were eating, they needled and abused me, until the tears fell into my bowl, and I scooped them up with my rice, and still they showed no sympathy. They just got angrier and shouted even louder, 'Cry cry cry, cry yourself to death and be done with it! Where on earth do you get all those tears from?' When I got good marks in my school tests, I was thrilled but they sneered, 'You must have been cheating. You must have copied from someone else!' Even if I ran a temperature and was aching all over, there was no one to comfort me or to take me to the clinic. All I got was, 'You deserve it, damn brat!'

This is the environment in which I grew up: a family where everyone put me down, and destroyed my self-esteem and confidence. I did not know then that I was being abused. I got so used to being ill-treated that when I was treated with kindness, I had no idea how to react.

Mum shared my bed that night, and as I lay next to her, she whispered, 'Yangyang, do you like school?'

After a long pause, I grunted, 'Uh-huh.'

'Is there anything you want?' she asked again.

My nose prickled, and I wanted to yell at the top of my voice, 'There are so many things I want! I want a new jumper, a new schoolbag, red boots, I want to go home…' But I didn't say anything. I just pulled the quilt over my head, and wept silently into it.

I kept completely still for a long while and my mother probably thought I was asleep, so she turned on her side and did not say anything more. Outside the window, the vines swayed in the moonlight. Each of us busy with our own thoughts, Mum and I fell asleep in the darkness.

At the weekend, my parents took Star and me to the children's playground. We had a fantastic time playing together, and finally I had a smile on my face. A child of only ten rarely holds grudges for long. Even if I were worlds apart from them, and they left me there my whole life, just a few words and a hug, and I would instantly forget my unhappiness.

On the way home that evening, my mother took my hand and I took my sister's hand. At that moment, I was very happy.

'Mum, shall I sing you a song?' I said.

'Okay, what song are you going to sing?'

'The children in the village don't believe that I have a mother, they call me a stalk of grass. Now I've finally got a Mum, and my Mum's prettier than theirs! I'm going to sing you, "I love my Mum"!'

'Okay!'

'Mother's the best,

A child with a mother is her darling.

With your mum's arms around you,

You'll be perfectly happy.

Mother's the best,

A child without a mother is like a stalk of grass.

Without your mum's arms around you,

You'll never be happy,' I sang.

Mum's eyes reddened and she choked up. For years after, she could not remember that moment without a flood of emotion.

Three days later, one overcast morning, my parents took my little sister on the train back to Shandong. I was still fast asleep, and unaware of their departure. I was dreaming of snuggling in my mother's warm arms. They must have thought it was best to leave without saying goodbye. Maybe when I woke up and opened my eyes, I would think it had all been a wonderful dream.

Mum had gone, but there on my bedside table were the red boots I had dreamed of.

7

Bold-as-brass and Happy-go-lucky

My aunt called 'Damn brat!' so often and so loudly that the villagers always knew it was me she was shouting for. In Xiaoliangzhuang, Damn Brat was the girl from Shandong, the niece of Shen Wenjie, the woman with the Shen Bellow.

Ever since my aunt brought me to Nanyang to live with them, I had never lacked for a nickname. It was the family's way of showing me how unwelcome I was. Money-Grows-on-Trees, Guzzle-Guts, Piss-Taker, Pig-Brain, Touchy, Pain-in-the-Neck, Bold-as-Brass.

My aunt never got up early to make breakfast for me, and I always had to beg her for my breakfast money. Every morning, as I stood by her bed with my schoolbag on my back, she would mutter, 'Damn brat, you're always asking for money! You think money grows on trees?'

At Nana's house, I always had something to nibble on. The Li-Shen family was not poor and there was no shortage of good things to eat here, but my aunt liked to squirrel things away. Sometimes it was a case of fizzy drinks, or a box of red apples, or a packet of biscuits. As soon as I found out about this foible of hers, I got into the habit of searching the house. When I found some goodies, I would quietly remove some. I hid them in my tummy and in my schoolbag.

Whenever Auntie found me out, she launched into a tirade, 'You damn brat, you're such a guzzle-guts, I've never met a kid so fixated on food!'

This hurt my feelings but I wasn't going to change. Food was bought to be eaten, wasn't it? Why did she insist on hiding things? If she'd put them on the table, I might not want them, but the more she hid, the more I ate.

One winter, my aunt bought a large bag of candied jujubes to make jujube cakes for the New Year. She was determined to keep them out of my reach and, after a lot of thought, she finally hid them in our semi-automatic washing machine that had not been used for a long time. She was sure that was a safe hiding place. Whoever would think of looking for food in the washing machine?

God may have given her the knack of hiding things, but her niece had a god-given nose for sniffing them out. Not three days had passed before I caught the delicious whiff of jujubes. I opened the washing machine and was ecstatic when I saw so many candied jujubes. As a small kid, I used to dig out the jujubes and throw the pastry away. How could I let such a huge bag of goodies lie there all alone and lonesome, shrivelling away?

The days passed and one by one the jujubes made their way from the washing machine into my tummy. Just before New Year, Auntie had made the dough and was about to steam the dumplings when she suddenly remembered the jujubes hidden in the washing machine. She lifted the washing machine lid and stared dumbstruck. The drum was completely empty. There was not a single one left!

At first, she thought she must have mis-remembered. Maybe she had not bought any jujubes. But something wasn't right. She knew she had wrapped the jujubes in a plastic bag, tied it tight, and hidden it in the washing machine, just a month ago. Surely we didn't have mice? Even if we did, how could a mouse get in and eat all the jujubes? And without leaving any traces. The drum was completely empty, there was no sign of a jujube ever having been there.

'Can't you guess? I reckon our big mouse has had 'em all!'

Once Uncle had let the cat out of the bag, it was all suddenly plain as daylight to my aunt.

'That damn brat, she really takes the piss! You can't hide anything from her! It wouldn't matter if she just ate a few, but she's had every single one of them! It makes me livid!' Auntie was hopping mad. If I had been at home then, she would have whacked me till kingdom come.

My uncle did not shout and swear and torment me like my aunt, and he never laid a hand on me. In fact, when he was happy with me, he was sweet. But he had an unpredictable temper. He didn't get angry often but when he did, he would let out a roar that always made me burst into tears. He was a Li through and through and the Li way of showing anger was to glare at you out of the corner of his eye. He had a way of glaring that was scarier than the poster of Zhong Kui the guardian god stuck on our wall.

Once, the family was sitting around eating lunch, and I was watching cartoons on TV, when he suddenly slammed his chopsticks down. 'Bring me the remote!' he roared. I shook in terror and almost dropped my bowl. Even Auntie and Mingze looked frightened.

His eyebrows drew together in a deep frown and he glared at me with deep hostility. I picked up the remote and handed it over with trembling hands, my eyes swimming with tears. My aunt scowled at Uncle, picked up her bowl and got up and walked outside. It was obvious they must have had a fight.

I didn't understand why he couldn't have said in a normal voice, 'Yangyang, pass me the remote, I want to watch the news.' I had done nothing wrong, but I was everyone's punch bag.

Living under someone else's roof, I learned how to tread carefully from a young age. Auntie, Uncle, my cousins, they all took it out on me whenever they were unhappy. I was both sensitive and vulnerable. I longed for someone to confide in, for someone to care. But in this loveless family, where no one understood love or could express it, that really was asking for the moon.

I had always enjoyed playing outside and was happy to be out all day long. I loved messing around with the kids in the alley and my classmates from school. Even if we did not do anything much together, we were free as birds and I never wanted to go home.

One summer holiday, conjunctivitis (pinkeye, we called it) was going around our neighbour's family. My aunt banned me from playing with their kid. If I got pinkeye, we would all get it and that would be awful.

Auntie was actually being quite reasonable, but back then, I was not allowed to watch TV much, I had no toys to play with, and the neighbour's child was my best friend, the playmate who shared those long summer days with me. How could I not see her for a whole summer?

A few days later, my eyes started to become inflamed. We shared the same towel and after a few more days, my aunt and uncle had pinkeye too. We all lay on the bed, wiping the boogers from our eyes and applying eye drops. My aunt heaved a despairing sigh, so loud that it echoed around the yard, 'What am I going to do with this niece of mine! You damn brat, you really take the piss! Tell me, why do you do it? Why can't you listen to grown-ups? Ever since you were little, you've been like this. The more I tell you not to, the more you do it! Now look what's happened, all because of you!'

Although Auntie often hit me, it had not taken me long to discover that she was not as tough as she made herself out to be. Sometimes, she only hit me after I really had driven her to distraction with my stubbornness.

'You've got no one to blame but yourself. If you hadn't played up Nana the way you did, I wouldn't have had to bring you here,' she told me often. The subtext was that there was nothing wrong with her hitting me and only I was in the wrong because I was such a nuisance.

'I didn't ask you to bring me here. Why did you take me on when you had your own children to look after?' I shot back.

'Ai-ya! You damn brat!' Auntie would take off her slipper and slam it at me.

I just laughed.

I was a dab hand at Slam-the-Beanbag in school and I caught the slipper easily. I turned around and threw it into the grape trellises. Before she had time to react, I was gone too, quick as a flash, out into the yard.

My aunt abused me day in, day out, so of course I fought back, how could I not? One time, she bought some sweet potatoes from an old man who used to sell vegetables from his handcart, and that night she made her favourite meal of sweet potato and maize porridge. I sneaked into the kitchen behind her back, grabbed a handful of sugar from the sugar jar and sprinkled it into the mixture. When it was ready, and she took a slurp of the sweetened porridge, she hardly dared believe her luck at finding such sweet yams. She carried her bowl out into the alley and told all and sundry how good it was. Then she made them taste it too, 'You taste it, see? Isn't it sweet?' And she pushed a big bit of sweet potato into their mouths.

The next day, she rushed off to find the old man, bought half a cartload and stored them in her cellar. As I was helping her carry the sweet potatoes into our cellar, I had a hard time not laughing.

Living through the frustrations of the Cultural Revolution had made Uncle withdrawn and uncommunicative. That, together with his unpredictable temper, meant that he hardly ever talked to his son and daughters. The family all lived under one roof but unless something major happened, he might go a whole day without speaking except for yelling 'Dinner!'

I was the only person in this family who had no blood relationship with him but from time to time I could get a few words out of him. I was a strange little kid, but I was quick off the mark.

When I was little, I used to get cracked lips and hands from the cold in winter. My uncle used to point to his big nose and say earnestly, 'You take a look, this nose produces its own face cream, I'll squeeze some out and rub it on, and all those cracks will go nice and smooth!'

'You make your own face cream?' I teased him. 'Keep it for your wife, then she won't need to spend money on makeup.'

Before I went to bed at night, my uncle would get me to bring him a basin of hot water to wash his feet in. Sometimes they ponged terribly because he did a lot of walking and they sweated, so I held my nose until I could run away.

Every time I did that, he used to give his feet a good scrub in the basin and say earnestly, 'You don't know anything. So-and-so on CCTV, she's only got such a gorgeous voice because she drank my foot-washing water!'

I couldn't let him get away with that. He'd hardly finished speaking before I butted in with, 'If your foot-washing water is so magical, then as soon as you've finished, I'll ladle you out a big bowlful and you can drink some! One day, you can sing for CCTV!'

Uncle always burst out laughing at my cheekiness.

People used to tell me that Uncle said, 'Honestly, that niece of mine, she's all skin and bones but she's not stupid. She's a bright kid.'

I had to grow up more quickly than other kids of my age because of my turbulent home life. I was sensitive, so I was quick to pick up on people's emotions. I was always laughing and joking – at myself too – and I loved doing whacky things. I was often seething with anger: if my aunt beat me, or my uncle yelled at me or my cousins told me off. But the next minute, if they flashed a smile at me and were kind, I used to forget the pain, just like that. Sometimes, I even smiled grimly in the mirror, and said to myself, *You're a bold-as-brass girl who shines in the sun and doesn't know what to do with a bit of warmth!*

At home, I was a greedy wild child whom no one loved, but I was happy-go-lucky by nature. On the way to school, a bowl of steaming hot spicy soup and a fried laomo charred on the outside and soft inside was a great way to start the day. Coming home after school, though, was a different matter. My belly rumbled with hunger, and the fragrant smells from the food stalls by the school gate and in every street and alley were hard to resist. Spicy jerky, sweeties, sour plum powder, candied peel, bubble gum and chewing gum, crispy rice, crab sticks, biscuits, instant noodles, chocolate... When the school bell rang, shouting, laughing children hurtled out of the school gate, and swarmed around the brightly coloured snack stalls. The kind-hearted woman behind the counter could hardly keep up with demand, and her buckteeth were always bared in a cheerful grin.

When we kids had chosen what we wanted, we strolled away in groups, chatting and eating, and swopping bits of our snacks with our friends so everyone got a taste. And of course, in no time at all, we would have nibbled our way through almost all of it.

I used to stand at the candy stall and take a look at the candyfloss cart, and another look at the popcorn. My coins were burning a hole in my pocket, but eventually I made my choice and was parted from them.

Children are greedy pigs. I was no different from the others, I wanted to stuff myself with snacks like everyone else. But all I could ever get out of my aunt was my breakfast money.

Breakfast cost one yuan. I didn't need to buy soup, but I did need to eat something. A bun for fifty cents did not fill me up, but having fifty cents left over allowed me to spend the long morning in class dreaming about how I was going to spend it at noon.

At some point, I developed the bad habit of eating while I was walking home. It felt good to walk along chewing on something. Ten strips of chewing gum for ten cents would last all the way home. If I spent twenty cents, I could get a big lump of candyfloss and pull it out into longer strands than any of my classmates; fifty cents and I could buy two bags of jerky so spicy that it made me pour with sweat – not that I would admit it, of course.

That was only the start of fun after school. Not many of the kids had money to buy snacks, in any case, but we could all play in the countryside on either side of the road that led back to the village. In warm spring weather, we looked for cogon grass under the budding willow trees on the riverbank. We used to peel off the outer leaves and eat the pith, which was soft and white as candyfloss and filled our mouths with honey-sweet nectar.

On sunny days, the golden wheat fields by the school became a paradise for children. I loved playing hide and seek there. We chose one person and he or she had to turn their back and count to ten. The rest of us ran away and hid. 'Ten!' they yelled and spun around, but by then everyone had disappeared into a billowing sea of wheat.

Lying in the field, squinting up at the blue sky dotted with white clouds, I used to hold my breath so I could listen to the wind soughing through the wheat. I loved those times. I waited till I could hear yelling and shrieking as all the kids were found, one after another, then as the footsteps got closer, I leapt out of the wheat, teeth bared, hands outstretched like claws.

We never got tired of our games. Sometimes, the farmer might pass by and get furious at seeing the crop being trampled by a bunch of irresponsible little rascals. Then we usually got a hail of pebbles hurled at us, along with shouts of, 'You're ruining my crop, you little bastards, I'll kill you!'

Then we were in trouble. We grabbed our schoolbags and scattered in all directions. When we reached safety, we jabbed our fingers at each others' noses and laughed our heads off. If the farmers had found out we had been stealing ears of grain too, and making bonfires and roasting them, they would have skinned our hides!

When summer was here, the wheat was ripe, and the corn stooks appeared like giant mushrooms, the party really began for us. We raced from one end of the wheat field to the other in mad excitement, like the Monkey King's crazy monkey followers. As children, we never seemed to run out of energy. We ran until we were gasping for breath and pouring with sweat, but still we managed to chase each other around the field. Then we flung ourselves down on top of the piles of straw and laughed up at the sky and clouds like maniacs. Eventually, worn out from laughing and shouting, we fell asleep up there.

The wheat field brought us not just simple pleasures and wild excitement, it also left us with wonderful childhood memories, full of the heady aroma of ripened wheat.

As we got older, the days when we walked home in gangs of classmates were fewer. Most of the time, I was on my own, and I enjoyed meandering along. I would stop off at the stall selling hens and ducks by the roadside, and squat down and play with them and stroke them. I picked them up and put them back down, and really wanted to buy one, but I finally gave up the idea because I was embarrassingly skint.

Or if it was breezy, I pulled off the red scarf that tied my hair back, held it up by two corners and ran into the wind. Once, I accidentally let go of it and the wind snatched it and rolled it up and carried it over the high wall of the cotton mill. My red scarf disappeared into the great grey yonder, like a flame being extinguished.

Along the road home, there were always stalls selling second-hand children's picture books. That was a temptation I could not resist. I squatted down and flipped through them until I found one I liked. Then I sat on the ground and read it. The old man who was selling them never stopped me. He just sat on his stool and puffed away at the roll-ups that he made himself. I read until it got dark, and he closed up and went home for dinner, when I finally had to relinquish the book I was clutching.

From there, I still had halfway to go. I turned off the road and took a shortcut over a wall. The climbing skills I had acquired as a small child came in handy now. Not only had I not lost them, I was getting strong and better at it. The pleasures of walking home after school did not last long, but I have never forgotten them.

One day, a small sesame oil mill opened in Xiaoliangzhuang. From morning to night, the whole village was filled with the smell of sesame oil. Drawn by the smell, people turned up at the mill carrying bags of homegrown sesame seeds. This was a new attraction: as soon as I had finished my homework, I went there and dogged the miller's footsteps, watching every part of the process of producing the oil.

The sesame seeds were dry-fried and then crushed between huge grindstones. The mash was then slowly poured into a large iron pot set on a revolving frame where paddles mixed it with soy paste and water. I was fascinated and could happily squat there watching all afternoon until the miller funnelled the precipitated sesame oil into large glass bottles. Finally, I patted the dust off my clothes and ran back home, clutching a small bottle of fresh sesame oil the miller gave me.

A freshly steamed mantou bun, a few green chilli peppers from the vegetable patch cut into fine strips, sprinkled with a teaspoon of salt and a few drops of pure sesame oil, mixed together in a large bowl with a pair of chopsticks, and you had a delicious meal.

One night, I must have eaten too much mantou, or maybe the sesame oil was too rich, but in the middle of the night, I woke up clutching my belly with an urgent need for the toilet. I jumped out of bed and rushed to the outhouse in the corner of the yard. In my panic, I pulled the light cord at the front door too hard and it broke.

I did not know what to do. It was the middle of the night, so there was no one to fix it for me. But if I didn't wake them up, I would have to leave the light on. At ten, I was too small to reach it and fix it myself. And if Auntie woke up in the morning and found that I had been wasting electricity all night, she would kill me. What on earth was I going to do? As I squatted in the toilet, my mind was racing. I had to avoid being shouted at and beaten the next morning at all cost, so I heaved a table and chair from the sitting room to the front door, where the bright light lit up the courtyard. Under the dark night sky, barefoot and clad only in my vest and shorts, I climbed onto the table and then got onto the chair on top. I gently unscrewed the light cord cover and found the switch that the cord was supposed to be threaded through. Holding the cord between finger and thumb as if I was threading a needle, I passed it through the switch, knotted it and screwed the cover back on, and then carefully pulled the switch cord so that the yard went dark.

The stars that night were very bright, and I slept like a dream. All that practice in climbing and scrambling certainly came in handy. When push came to shove, I was able to put it to good use and it saved my bacon.

You have to practise your skills, for you never know when you might need them.

8

My desk buddy, Yuan Xiaohui

One afternoon, I was on my way back to school. I stopped at the gate of Yuan's house with my schoolbag on my back and shouted, 'Yuan Xiaohui! Yuan Xiaohui!' But no one answered.

Strange noises came from inside. Curious to know what was going on, I gently pushed the big iron gate that stood ajar and crept in.

I heard loud sobbing coming from the front room of the house.

I bent down, pressed my face against the crack in the door and peered inside. I could see a burly man with a stout hemp rope in his hand, busy tying something up. The sounds of a woman's agonized struggling became more desperate, and I leaned harder against the door as I pressed forward.

Suddenly, the door banged open, hitting the wall and making the glass door panel shake. I fell forward and landed heavily on the concrete floor. Yuan Xiaohui's father turned to look at me in alarm, still clutching the rope. I sprawled on the ground not daring to move, terrified by what I saw in front of me.

Yuan Xiaohui's mum Wang Jixia, a woman who was always nicely dressed and soft-spoken, whom I had often imagined as my own mother, was lying trussed up in a bamboo sleeping mat. All I could see of her under her dishevelled hair was a face covered in bruises, and eyes that were full of fear. She was struggling to speak, but there was a rag stuffed into her mouth.

'Come in, girl, come and see what this is!' Yuan Xiaohui's father leered at me.

Then he grabbed me in both arms.

I gave a shriek.

'Stop wriggling, otherwise I'll tie you up too!'

He was carrying me towards the back bedroom. In desperation, I sank my teeth into his arm and he let go with a yell. I staggered out of the house and fled.

It was a scorching hot day and dust swirled along the street in the wind. My small figure vanished into the distance, ponytail flying, as I clutched my schoolbag and churned up dust with my sandals. When I showed up at the school gate out of breath and sweating, I saw Yuan Xiaohui messing around with a group of boys.

Why did he get to school so early today? Does he know what's happening at home? I asked myself.

I had a sudden vision of the helpless agony in his mother's eyes.

'Yuan Xiaohui!' I blurted out, and all of them turned towards me.

I really wanted to tell him everything but when he looked guilelessly at me, I found I could not get the words out.

I stood rooted to the spot, scarlet in the face and mute.

There were jeers from the boys. 'She really likes our Xiaohui, doesn't she!'

Yuan Xiaohui looked taken aback but I was livid. I chased down our loud-mouthed classmates and beat them up, one after another. Finally he reacted – after all, they were making fun of both of us.

Although our families lived almost opposite each other on the same street, Xiaohui and I had completely different personalities and at first we never played together. He was the mollycoddled baby of the Yuan family and he was never going to spend his days running wild with me, a despised excess-birth girl. He was their precious hot-house plant, while I was a wild child, a weed in the fields.

It was not until I started school that he and I had anything to do with one another. We were in the same class for the first three years of primary school. Once he had escaped his family's clutches, a mischievous side to his nature emerged. The troublemaker at school and the little lamb at home could have been two different people. For three years, I was always getting into fights with him. Then finally in our fourth year, I thought we would be in different classes, but to my surprise, he and I were not only in the same class but also sharing a desk. The proximity meant that even though we disliked each other, we still exchanged a few words every now and then. Eventually, when I was in a good mood, I used to stop by his house and we went to school together.

In self-study class that day, I was staring abstractedly out of the classroom window when I felt him jab me with his compass points.

'Ow!' I yelled, and cradled my stuck arm. 'What are you stabbing me for? You off your head or something?'

'You're the one who's off your head,' he shot back. 'You've crossed the 38th Parallel!' (That was the line he had drawn to divide his side of the desk from mine.)

'I never have! And I never jabbed you when you drew it either!'

I had been in two minds about whether to tell him what had happened that noon at his house, but the way he jabbed me and was smirking at me was so unfair that I got furious. I clenched my fist and punched him hard on the back. In return, Yuan Xiaohui gave me a hefty shove that landed me on the ground. The girl on the other side of me came to pull me up, but I did not need a helping hand. I jumped to my feet and kicked Yuan Xiaohui in the belly.

'Yay! A domestic! A domestic!' The boys in the row behind us started yelling and cheering.

He and I came to blows properly then. The class erupted. There were shouts of, 'Yay! Left hook, right hook, yay! Go on! Keep going! Hit her hard!'

Suddenly, Ms Hua appeared at the door of the classroom. Silence fell. Yuan Xiaohui and I pulled apart and glared at each other angrily.

'Just look at the two of you scrapping like a pair of dogs! For shame!'

Ms Hua was almost spitting with rage. 'Come out outside right now! You can stand in the corridor!'

The kids who had been jeering shrank back into their seats and kept their heads down, hardly daring to breathe.

I glared at Yuan Xiaohui, then turned and marched out of the classroom, my head held high. He had started it by pricking me with the compass, I was in the right, there was no way I was going to bend my head.

'Stand up properly, keep still!' Ms Hua berated Yuan Xiaohui as she wrote on his face. A strong smell of garlic wafted over us.

With the couplet clearly written on his cheeks, Yuan Xiaohui stood with his head lowered, rubbing his school trousers with his hands.

'A girl scrapping with a boy?! You should be ashamed of yourself!'

Ms Hua started to write on my face, and the stink of garlic coming out of her mouth almost made me faint.

'You can both stay right here when class finishes so that everyone going down the corridor can see you've been fighting!' Ms Hua finished writing and was done with us.

I was mortified at the turn of events. I could not stand the class teacher and she was making me share a desk with a boy I could not stand either.

Ms Hua had not even given me a chance to explain. The more I thought about it, the more I felt aggrieved. Tears of frustration ran down my cheeks, over the two lines of red writing.

The bell rang after class, and I hurriedly wiped my tears away with my sleeve. The corridor filled up with kids, and the pair of us were soon engulfed.

The writing on our faces was in traditional couplet form: a vertical line of characters down each cheek, and a horizontal line across our foreheads. 'Yuan Xiaohui's in Fourth Year Class 1. He's a brawler. He gets into fights with girls!' The kids read out the writing on Xiaohui's face, laughing and chattering and interrupting each other. Xiaohui shrank away from them, looking hunted. There was not a trace of his former arrogance left.

I held my head high, as if to say, *Come on then, look all you want, I did nothing wrong and I'm not bending my head to anyone.* I stared hard at the poplar trees far away outside the window.

'She fights boys,' someone read the writing across my forehead.

I pricked my ears. I had no idea what the writing on my face said. All I heard was whispering.

What had happened was that my tears had smudged the ink, and after I wiped my cheeks dry, all I had left was what looked like splodges of rouge.

After our fight, the 38th Parallel Yuan Xiaohui had drawn down the middle of our shared desk disappeared. But in its place, there was a rift between us that could never be healed.

One afternoon when the cicadas were chirring, Ms Feng was declaiming from the podium, and I sat daydreaming, my chin resting on my hand. Class had begun twenty minutes since, but Yuan Xiaohui had still not arrived and his seat stood empty. On his part of our desk, he had drawn himself as a grinning cartoon face, with a ballpoint pen.

The door of the classroom burst open, and Ms Hua came in looking very serious. In the doorway, I could see Yuan Xiaohui's father and aunt, both grim-faced. The moment I saw Yuan Xiaohui's father, I immediately picked up my workbook and held it in front of my face. Ms Hua went to the podium and whispered to Ms Feng, who frowned and nodded repeatedly.

She put down the bit of chalk in her hand, picked up her book and left the room.

'Zhou Yu, Guo Jianwei and Cheng Fei, I want the three of you up here,' Ms Hua said gravely from the podium. The three boys emerged from the back row and shuffled forwards, their heads bent.

They left the room followed by Ms Hua, and the door closed behind her. The classroom erupted in noise and chatter. The kids in the front row turned around to talk to the ones behind them. A few of the bolder boys even left their seats and went to the front row where they started talking loudly.

'You know what? They went for a swim in the pond in Lixianggongzhuang this lunchtime. Yuan Xiaohui jumped in and never came out again,' said one of the boys up at the front, looking around mysteriously.

The girl next to him clapped her hand to her mouth in horror. 'Really? That's scary!'

'You weren't there, how do you know? Don't talk rubbish!' I hit him on the head with my rolled-up workbook.

'You don't believe me? Don't then! But I'll tell you something… I know he killed a snake before he went swimming. I bet you it was the snake taking its revenge.' The boy in the front row turned back again with a know-it-all look on his face.

I looked at the cartoon self-portrait Yuan Xiaohui had drawn on the desk and shuddered. I moved my chair further back. Outside the window, the Yuans and Ms Feng were grilling the three boys. They looked very guilty, heads bowed and their hands behind their backs.

I started to feel agitated. For some reason, I suddenly felt very upset. I had had a fight with Yuan Xiaohui and some things about him really annoyed me, but we had grown up together in the same village after all. What if something had really happened to him?

His father and aunt had come to the school to find out who had organized the swimming trip and why it was their poor boy who drowned. They even suspected that some of the boys might have deliberately pushed him in. However, the three of them were interrogated separately and their accounts were consistent: Yuan Xiaohui had been the organizer. First he killed a snake in the grass by throwing a stone at it, then he picked it up and threw it away from him, then he jumped into the pond. They were just about to follow him, when they saw him floundering and struggling in the water, and after a bit he went under.

Wild rumours flew around the class. One theory was, it must have been a big snake in the water who was avenging the little snake he killed. Otherwise, why would he have gone under when he got into the water?

The Yuan family turned up at the school for several days after the accident, making a big fuss. These were anxious times for all of us.

So, in the summer of 1996, towards the end of the summer term, our classmate and my desk buddy Yuan Xiaohui, drowned. He was just ten when he died.

On the day of the funeral, his small coffin sat in the Yuan family's yard. His grandmother and aunt bent over it, weeping inconsolably. Other family members stood by, wiping their eyes. Yuan Xiaohui's father was there, supporting his own father whose face ran with tears. The cries of grief echoed through Xiaoliang Village.

All the neighbours turned up in small groups to pay their respects. I heard them talking.

'You should never have to bury your own children. Poor them! That poor, poor family!'

'But where was his mother all this time?'

'I heard she fainted as soon as she heard the news. She was taken to hospital. She's probably still there.'

'Fate is so cruel.'

I squeezed through the jostling crowd. Once inside, I saw Yuan Xiaohui in his coffin. He was neatly dressed, rosy-cheeked, and lying quite still as if he was asleep.

When the funeral cortege was about to leave, family members came forward to comfort the two older women and pull them away from the coffin so that the lid could be shut. I was pushed aside, and a middle-aged man with a beard pulled the cart bearing the coffin around and pushed it into the street.

'My baby, my baby!' The grandmother struggled frantically.

Yuan Xiaohui's father and grandfather followed behind the coffin. The latter looked utterly desolate. Behind them came aunt and grandmother, tottering along supported by the other mourners.

As the sun went down, its afterglow lit up our faces. I followed the weeping mourners all the way to the end of the village. As the coffin receded into the distance, I stood there and watched him disappear into the setting sun.

That night I had a dream about Doraemon the robot cat. He opened his Anywhere Door, and in the bright light I saw my mother smiling at me with open arms. 'Mum!' I yelled and ran towards her. But as soon as I stepped inside, everything disappeared. 'Mum! Mum!' I shouted frantically into the pitch darkness.

Morning came and I woke up. My mother had not been there in my dream, and she wasn't there in real life either.

During our reading-aloud class one morning, Yuan Xiaohui's mother, Wang Jixia, burst into the classroom. She was dressed in a hospital gown, and looked disheveled. Silence fell and everyone stared at her. Wang Jixia's eyes fell on the empty desk that had been her son's and she headed towards me, walking slowly and unsteadily. I froze, my textbook gripped in both hands, and watched her nervously.

When she got to our desk, she stroked it with a trembling hand, and I saw a faint smile as she caressed the face Yuan Xiaohui had drawn. She looked so desperate that my eyes welled with tears and my hands began to shake. I had daydreamed so often that she was my mother. How could she have changed so much overnight?

'My son! My son!' Wang Jixia suddenly dropped to the floor, clutching Yuan Xiaohui's stool in her arms, and burst into heartbreaking sobs. Her despair had some more of the girls secretly wiping away tears.

I found myself reaching out and laying my left hand gently on her right shoulder. Still sobbing, she raised her head to look at me. Suddenly, she grabbed my arm and burst into a loud wail. For a moment, everyone's eyes were on me. I sat there awkwardly, unsure what to do.

Just then, the old gatekeeper and the director of studies hurried in. They pulled Wang Jixia to her feet and took her outside. In the school yard, she broke free and made a desperate bid to come back again. As I watched them, my tears really began to flow. By now reinforcements had arrived in the form of more teachers, and without further ado they bundled her roughly out of the gate. I will never forget her despairing expression. I could not understand why they would not let her weep on her son's desk and give vent to her grief.

In the last class before the summer holiday, one sunny afternoon, I was gazing dreamily at the classroom door when I saw Yuan Xiaohui standing there carrying his schoolbag. He was smiling and waving at me, and I could see his trademark dimple. I jumped to my feet. The sun was in my eyes and I rubbed them hard, and when I opened them again, there was no one there. Ms Hua pinged a piece of chalk at me and it hit me on the head. I sat back down, holding my head in my hands. The whole class burst out laughing.

When Yuan Xiaohui left us that summer, he took the soul of his mother with him. When her son was alive, she had everything to look forward to, and when he drowned, it broke her spirit. She had put up with her abusive husband for more than ten years. Now, her own family was useless and her in-laws bullied her even worse than before. Without a son whose glory she could bask in, she was unprotected, and her mother-in-law and sister-in-law spent the whole time finding fault with her.

She lost her mind; her in-laws drove her out and her birth family refused to take her back, so no one in the village could do anything for her either. She slept in the street or at the rubbish dump until she finally took up residence in one of the two-metre-tall wheat straw stooks. The villagers had a lot of sympathy for her and the owner of the stook declared that no one was to drive her away without his say-so.

That autumn, the stook was just a stook like all the others, open to the elements but, with winter approaching, it took on a new look. Plastic sheeting appeared, draped over the top to keep the rain and snow out. An old wooden board became a makeshift door, and there were tree branches in front of it, hung with all sorts of little knick-knacks.

On sunny days, Wang Jixia liked to sit at her stook door in the sunshine. She always had a handful of dried orange peel in her hand.

When I saw her there for the first time, I had an odd feeling. I was just on my way to school like normal. The village was bathed in early morning sunshine. I had my schoolbag on my back and was humming and kicking pebbles as I walked along. Then, I passed the wheat stook. Wang Jixia suddenly pushed away the wooden plank and emerged. I stopped singing abruptly, and the pebble I had been kicking landed in the ditch by the side of the road.

'Are you going to school, girl?' she asked with a soft smile.

I was so frightened I started to quiver. There was this woman, her face sunburnt and dusty, her black hair a mass of tangles, staring at me.

'Hey, why are you standing there? Get out of my way!' A shout from behind me broke the silence, and a straw-hatted old man pedalled past on a three-wheeler.

I turned to look at him, then broke into a run. Behind me, Wang Jixia stood in the sun looking dazed.

I ran all the way to school, but I could not concentrate all morning. All I could see in front of me was Wang Jixia's smile and her expression. I thought she was mad. That was what they said. But if she was mad, how could she remember me? Was she just fooling them all?

The next time I saw her, I was walking home from school in a laughing, chattering bunch of children. We looked at each other, and I saw a glint of recognition in her eyes. I smiled and waved to her. She jumped up in excitement and trotted towards me. The other kids took fright and ran off. I froze, rooted to the spot. Wang Jixia was very close now and I felt my heart thumping and my palms sweating.

'How's our lad getting along in school, girl?' she asked. 'If he doesn't do his lessons properly, you can smack him for me,' she said, completely earnest. Her breath smelled strongly of orange peel.

My forehead was beading with sweat by this time. I opened my mouth but no words came out.

'You go on home. I'm going to get dinner ready, our lad will be home soon,' she went on.

She got a bit of dried orange peel out of her jacket pocket and pushed it into my hand, then turned and went back to her stook. I felt weak at the knees and they almost gave way under me.

From the branch, she took a large bag of orange peel, squatted down and began to turn the pieces over carefully. Walking away, I looked back at her lonely figure and felt a sharp stab of distress. If Yuan Xiaohui could look down from heaven and see his mother in such dire straits, how would he feel?

The bit of orange peel in my hand made me remember one day when he and I were sharing a desk. When oranges were in season in October, he used to take one to school every day. Once, we were doing self-study. The teacher left us to it and had just stepped out of the door, when I suddenly got a strong whiff of freshly peeled orange. I knew without looking that Yuan Xiaohui must be eating his orange on the quiet.

'D'you want some?' he whispered to me as he ate it.

'I don't want anything you peeled with your filthy hands,' I said, looking at his grubby fingers and frowning.

'Fine, one's not enough for me anyway,' he said, and pushed half of it into his mouth all in one go.

'You can give me the peel. If you squeeze it, it makes the whole classroom smell nice.'

'You can't have the peel. I need it.'

And he grabbed the peel and shoved it into his schoolbag.

I pulled a face at him, 'Whatever…'

I didn't understand why Yuan Xiaohui thought orange peel was more important than the fruit itself. But now, squeezing the peel in my sweaty hand, it suddenly dawned on me that he was keeping the peel for his mother. He never told anyone but apparently his mother used to make tea with orange peel and use it when she was cooking too. His mother was a woman who loved her orange peel.

9

School Uniform

When I was in year five, my cousin Mingmei finally got married. The room that she had vacated on the west side of the yard became mine. I was eleven years old and this was my very own private space. I was almost too excited to sleep that first night.

In the middle of the first night, I turned over, to see a black shadow with bared fangs and outstretched claws flickering outside the window. I froze, not daring to move, one leg suspended in the air, staring intently at it from under the sheet. My heart was thudding madly. I don't know how long I stayed in that position, but my leg got heavier and heavier. Finally, I jumped out of bed and screamed, 'Auntie, Auntie!'

I raced to her room on the other side of the house and hammered on the wooden door.

'All right, all right! I heard you! Stop trying to knock the door down, you damn brat!' My aunt yelled back and opened the door, 'What's wrong? Why are you getting hysterical? It's the middle of the night!'

'There's someone outside the window!' I pointed with a trembling hand.

'Where? There's no one there! Take a look for yourself, there's not a soul in the yard!'

My aunt stood in the yard in her baggy bloomers, shouting at me. Suddenly, there was a fierce gust of wind, and the branches of the grape vine outside my window swayed and fluttered. It dawned on me that the terrifying be-fanged and be-clawed figure must be the vines that had grown up with me.

'Damn brat! Can't you even go to sleep without keeping other people awake? You drive me mad!'

My aunt glowered, and waddled back into the house, her big ass sticking out behind her. I was relieved. I didn't care about getting told off. I just happened to have an overly fertile imagination, and could scare myself over nothing. After that, whenever I got ready for bed at night, I imagined the vines in the yard as eighteen soldiers guarding me. Gradually, I overcame my fear of sleeping alone.

When I was eleven, I was chosen to be the school flag-raiser. I used to be envious when we stood in line watching someone else raise the flag as the national anthem played. If they raised it too slowly, as often happened, the national anthem would finish with the flag only half-way up the pole. I used to think to myself, *They're so clumsy. I could manage it properly if I was the flag-raiser.*

When my chance finally came, I had a problem – I did not have a school uniform. Every time the school put in orders for new uniforms, I went home and asked my aunt for the money. She always said, 'No way! They charge sixty yuan for a lousy old uniform!'

If she would not give me money, what was I to do? I had finally achieved my dream of being the flag-raiser, but I was worried stiff about not having a school uniform. I went to Ms Liu, the brigade instructor, and blurted out my problem.

'Come with me, I'll find one you can borrow.'

We tried several classes and finally a student in class two, year six, lent me a jacket and trousers. I put it on and rushed off to the sportsground where a group of flag-bearers were drilling. The morning reading session was over, and the students were pouring out of their classrooms and coming over to form up in their allotted squares. I had done my practice with the flag-bearers a few times over but now, all I wanted to do was escape.

The problem was, my borrowed uniform was too big. As soon as I took a few steps, the trousers began to slide down and droop around my ankles. I had already rolled up my jacket sleeves. If I rolled the trouser cuffs up as well, everyone would laugh at me.

I could hear their jeering voices in my head, 'Are you off to fish in the river or raise our flag? Ha-ha-ha!'

'Get yourselves ready,' Ms Liu was instructing us in a low voice. 'As soon as the head teacher finishes speaking, you go up on stage.'

Looking at all the teachers and students standing in the sportsground, I suddenly felt like a clown. I really wanted to run away but it was too late. As the music rang out, all eyes were on us.

I walked gingerly towards the flagpole. The flag bearers deftly hung the Five-Starred Red Flag from the flagpole, then spun around and stood on either side. I could feel that one of my trouser legs was trapped under my heel and I hurriedly yanked the waistband up as I walked to the centre of the stage.

'Everyone salute, play the National Anthem,' the director of studies commanded through the megaphone.

The music struck up, the flag fluttered in the breeze, and I pulled gently on the rope to raise it. But all I could think of was what I was wearing. I was convinced that everyone's eyes were on my too-big uniform.

My few minutes on stage felt like an age. Finally, when the music ended, I turned around and was about to step off the stage, when my right foot landed right on top of my trailing left trouser cuff and I tripped and went sprawling.

The sports ground erupted in loud laughter.

The flag bearers came rushing over to help me to my feet.

'Quiet! Quiet!' the director was bellowing through the megaphone, but there was still a lot of whispering and smirking going on.

I went red to my ears and wished the earth would swallow me up. At that moment, I hated my aunt, hated her for not buying me a school uniform, hated her for always yelling at me, hated her for making me lose face in front of everyone. I vowed to myself, 'I *will* get a school uniform this year, however much she shouts at me and beats me, I *will* make her give me sixty yuan!'

Not long after the flag-raising incident, on a Monday morning, the tailors came to the school to receive the orders for uniforms. We were measured one by one in our classroom. We walked up to the podium in the order of our seat numbers. One of the tailors took a tape measure to us, and the other noted down our sizes.

'I'm telling you one last time. Tomorrow morning everyone has to bring eighty yuan for their school uniform. Remember to tell your parents when you go home tonight,' our newly appointed class teacher Wang Zhongrui reminded us.

What? Eighty yuan?! Auntie thinks sixty is too expensive, she wouldn't even give me that. Now it's gone up to eighty. I sat with my head bowed, sunk in gloom, as my classmates chattered around me. My aunt's reaction was predictable. 'Spend, spend, spend all day long! That's all you know how to do! Even your teacher's farts smell sweet! The school isn't bothered about teaching you, all they do is think of ways to get money out of the students!' she yelled indignantly.

I stood without moving, biting my lip, as my aunt worked herself up into a fury. 'Damn brat! Why are you standing here? Haven't you got school to go to?' She hurled the broom she was holding at me.

I gave a loud wail, threw my arms over my head and rushed out of the hair salon.

That day, as the school uniforms were issued, I sat in the class in agonised apprehension as everyone else went up and collected their uniform.

The memory of last year was still fresh in my mind, and now this year the price of uniforms had gone up. I felt like the rug had been pulled out from under me.

When I came home from school, the door was locked and a note was stuck in the crack, 'Yangyang, get the bus to the People's Hospital after school, your uncle's broken his leg.' I borrowed one yuan from the neighbour and rushed to get the bus. At the Inpatients Reception desk, I found out where my uncle was and went straight to the ward.

'My dad was riding his bicycle, and a motorbike came up behind him. It was speeding and it hit him and knocked him off and he's broken his right leg,' my eldest cousin Ruomei was saying.

'A hit-and-run, the bastard! And he thinks he can get away with it! Death is too good for that man!'

My aunt stood by the hospital bed, cursing wrathfully. On the bed, my uncle lay with his eyes closed, a drip in the back of his hand, his right leg in plaster. The rest of the family were trying to comfort my aunt. Tears were running down her cheeks and she kept wiping them away.

I looked through the half-open door at my uncle, who was lying motionless, my tears falling too. The corridor was quite empty, and I curled up in the corner, my schoolbag still on my back. My uncle had a broken leg and the biker had made his escape. The family was going to need a lot of money to pay the hospital fees. There was no way I could ask my aunt for money for a school uniform.

'Have any students not paid for their uniforms yet?' our class teacher Wang Zhongrui asked the next morning. She was holding a bag of money in her hand. My classmates all looked at each other, but no one raised a hand or stood up.

'That's strange, I'm eighty yuan short,' Ms Wang Zhongrui said, and walked out. I ran after her, my classmates' eyes all following me curiously. I caught up with her at the end of the corridor and said, 'Ms Wang, I haven't paid for my uniform yet.' My face was burning with embarrassment.

'Well, you have to bring it this afternoon without fail,' she said impatiently, smoothing the bag in her hand.

I summoned up my courage and forced myself to speak, 'Ms Wang, can I not buy the uniform? My uncle's just broken his leg. It was a hit-and-run accident and the man ran away. We're really short of money at home.'

'You only need eighty yuan for a school uniform. Everyone else is buying one! When we have school inspections, our class will get marks deducted if you don't have a school uniform.' Ms Wang folded her arms across her chest and looked very annoyed.

I had never seen Ms Wang like this. She was normally such a smiley person, why had she turned so unfriendly when I explained why I couldn't afford the uniform? I felt deeply wounded.

When the bell rang after class, Ms Wang glanced at me and went into the office. My classmates flooded out of the classroom, my skinny figure among them. More than anything else in the world, I wanted a school uniform of my own. I had not forgotten making a fool of myself in front of the whole school at the flag-raising ceremony. But now my uncle was hospitalized and the family was having to foot quite a big bill. It would be really crass of me to nag my aunt for money for the uniform at this, of all times.

In class, Ms Wang lobbed questions at us as usual and a forest of hands shot up, eager to answer. But every time I raised my hand, she did not even look at me. All the children around me got their turn, but it was as if she was completely ignoring my existence. Finally, I stopped putting my hand up.

During the morning reading session, the school monitors in their red armbands came into the classroom to make their usual hygiene and uniform checks. One of the monitors spotted me in the corner not wearing a school uniform, my head bent as low as I could, and made an ominous note in her notebook. Ms Wang followed the monitors out of the classroom, and exchanged a few words with them, pointing at me as she did so. All eyes were on me. I sat there red-faced and head bent, my eyes swimming with tears.

At the school assembly, all the students sat in the schoolyard in orderly rows, dressed in their uniforms, listening to the principal's speech. Except for me. I was banished to the classroom, so that there was no danger of me besmirching the class reputation because I had no uniform.

I never did ask my aunt for money to buy a school uniform. Ms

Wang Zhongrui, a government-funded teacher, always ignored me after that. Even when I came top of the class in exams, my name never appeared on the merit list at the end of term. I knew that Ms Wang looked down on me. But she never knew that, ever since that day, I despised her for her hypocrisy and snobbery.

At the age of eleven, I suddenly understood something very important. I was a charity case. I was lucky to have enough food to eat and clothes to wear, and to be able to go to school. I was in no position to pick and choose.

By the second half of year five, most of the girls had started their periods. During PE, they all huddled together to share their secrets. I felt like a fool, left out because it hadn't happened to me.

On the way home from school one day, I broached the subject with my friend Hai Jing as we walked along, scuffing pebbles.

'Hai Jing, I'm a year older than them. Why have they got theirs? You…you don't think there's something wrong with me, do you?'

'My mother's told me the facts of life. She said everyone develops physically at different times,' she reassured me. 'Some girls develop early and some develop later. You've got nothing to worry about, with a strong body like yours!'

She went on, 'Yangyang, my mum says we have to be careful when we get to a certain age.'

'Be careful? About what?'

Hai Jing took a packet out of her schoolbag and pulled a pink vest out of it.

'What's that?' I exclaimed, going as pink as the vest.

'Ai-ya, don't be embarrassed, we're all developing. All the girls in the class are wearing these now.' Hai Jing straightened up and stuck her chest out, making out she was very grown up. I looked down at my white T-shirt, under which my breasts were budding ever so slightly, and hunched over in embarrassment.

'Thank you, Hai Jing,' I said.

That very day, on the way home, my first period sneaked up on me. At the age of eleven, I had changed from being a kid into being a growing girl. That night, my aunt was in the front room, watching a soap on TV and knitting a sweater. I stood in front of her, covered in embarrassment. 'What's wrong?' she snapped.

'Could...could you give me five yuan?' I stammered.

'All you do is to ask for money all day, money, money, money!' she exclaimed.

She bent over her knitting. It looked like the matter was closed.

I stood where I was and stared at her.

Eventually, she felt compelled to ask, 'What do you want the money for?'

'I've come on,' I said, even more embarrassed. 'I want to buy sanitary napkins.'

'So you've come on. Just stick a wad of toilet paper in your knickers. Why do I have to spend money on buying sanitary napkins?'

I turned around and went to my bedroom, feeling utterly dejected.

Behind me, my aunt was saying, 'In my day, we got a bit of cloth and stuffed it with plant ash. You're lucky, at least you can use toilet paper!'

That was all she ever said, 'In my day...in my day!' She never stopped going on about how things used to be! As far as I was concerned, her day was hundreds of years ago.

I shut the bedroom door and threw myself on the bed, muffling my ears with a pillow. Money, money, money, every time I asked her for money, it was an ordeal. She seemed compelled to make me feel bad. I always tried very hard not to bother her about money, what more could I do?

Before going to school the next morning, I folded some toilet paper and put it in my knickers. Then I pulled up my trousers and looked in the mirror very, very carefully. Only after I was satisfied that nothing was showing could I relax and set off for school. In the ten-minute break between classes, I bent over the counter in the school shop, staring at the packs of sanitary napkins in one corner. I had been worried there was something wrong because I wasn't menstruating. Now I was, and I was worried about how to deal with it.

I was uncomfortable all that day in school. When I got home, I dropped my bike and ran to the toilet. I was appalled when I pulled my trousers down. There was a large dark red blood stain on my knickers, and the wad of toilet paper was gone. I had been very careful, where had it disappeared to? The very thought of the blood-soaked paper slipping out of my trousers and onto the ground, and someone spotting it, gave me goosebumps.

In for a penny, in for a pound. I had to find a way myself since my aunt was refusing to give me money for sanitary napkins. That evening, I sneaked into the salon when she was cooking in the kitchen, carefully opened the cash drawer, grabbed some, and ran. As far as I was concerned, my plan was flawless and there was no way Auntie Wenjie would find out. However, by the next afternoon, she had rumbled me. When I got home from school, she greeted me with an outburst of suppressed fury, 'You needn't think you can pull the wool over my eyes! You'd rather die than admit it, wouldn't you? But I know what you've been up to!'

I knelt in the yard holding my head in my hands as she took off her trousers belt and whipped my back with it.

'You've been a thief all your life! And I've had enough!' she spluttered in rage.

My uncle sat at the front door and silently watched her beat me.

'You start with a needle, you'll end up stealing gold! If I don't beat it out of you now, you'll go to prison for it!'

She reached out and gave my ear a vicious twist. 'Own up, you stole money from the salon, didn't you?'

I protected my poor ear with my hand, and refused to utter a word.

'I'll break you if it's the last thing I do!'

She hauled me upright with both hands and pulled her belt tight around my neck. She was exerting all her strength, and I struggled and coughed, trying to get a grip on this thing that was choking me. For a moment, I really felt that she was going to strangle me. Suddenly, I felt a stream of something warm running down my legs, and realized I was still alive. Alive, and soaked in my own urine.

My survival instinct finally kicked in. 'I took it!' I cried.

'If you hadn't admitted it, I would have strangled you! You'll grow up vicious if you go on like this!' She let go, and I could see the marks from the belt on her hand.

I squatted down and cried and coughed, feeling the red marks on my neck.

'Tell me straight up,' she demanded sternly, still clutching her belt. 'What did you spend all that money on?'

I got to my feet, still sobbing, and went into my room. I came out again with a plastic bag and tipped the contents onto the ground. My aunt and uncle were dumbfounded.

Three bags of sanitary towels, and a vest, and two pairs of knickers with a cartoon design on them, lay spilled out in front of them. My uncle got up slowly. My aunt let her belt drop.

That was the most humiliating day in my life. Even after twenty years, the scene is still etched vividly in my memory. If I reach up to my neck, I can feel that belt tightening around it.

That night, I locked myself in the room and licked my wounds. Auntie would never apologize to me, because no matter what I bought with the money, there was no denying that I had stolen it. If you stole, you were a thief.

Curled up in the corner of the bed with my hands around my knees, I thought of my sisters at home in Shandong. They were with our mother, and I was sure they did not need to worry about vests, knickers and sanitary towels. Girls with mothers got school uniforms every year, for sure. In the darkness of the night, the tears scalded my already battered ego. What made me cry was not being beaten, or being poor or feeling inferior. It was because at eleven years old, I felt utterly helpless, terrified and despairing of life.

10

What do you want?

'You're going up to year six soon. You'll have a lot more homework. You all need to come to classes this summer holiday. And don't forget to bring two hundred yuan for the extra tuition next week,' Ms Wang said, and walked out of the classroom carrying her course books and her tea mug.

The class erupted, 'Oh no! Just when we had summer holidays to look forward to, we have to come to class!'

I quietly tidied away my workbook and was first out of the classroom, carrying my schoolbag. As soon as I heard her say, 'two hundred yuan', I knew I was in trouble.

Sure enough, my aunt and uncle refused to pay for me to go to summer school. 'What's all this about summer school? If you haven't been paying attention, what difference is an extra month of classes going to make?'

'Your teachers spend their time thinking of ways to make money from the students instead of doing an honest day's work.'

'Everyone's going to go, I'll be the only one not going,' I protested. 'What am I supposed to say to the teacher?'

'What's the problem? Just tell her! What have you got a mouth for? You think it's just for stuffing food in?' my aunt raged, practically spitting her food all over the table as she yelled at me.

I looked down, picking at the stale mantou in my hand, then dropping the crumbs on the floor.

A week later, on a broiling hot summer's day, Changzhuang Primary School rang with the shouts of my classmates as they recited their lessons aloud. In the classroom, my seat was glaringly, conspicuously empty. The others were all beginning on the year six curriculum, while I was at the Nanyang Bus Station with my aunt.

'Ai-ya! Damn brat! You're such a fool! You make me so angry!' Auntie yelled at me and gave my ear a vicious twist. It was so painful that I shrank away and tucked my neck into my collar. In order to get me a half-price bus ticket, she had insisted that I put on a baggy long skirt.

'Next time when I tell you to squat down when I buy your ticket, you do as I say! Now look what's happened. I've had to fork out full-price on your ticket! You make me so angry!'

I cradled my poor, red ear with one hand and silently got into the crowded bus queue, tears of frustration running down my cheeks. It was easy for her to talk, but how could I pretend to be a child with countless pairs of eyes on me? If only the floor could swallow me up.

The coach hurtled and bounced along the country roads. I was sitting in the front row with the window open, my eyes screwed up against the hot wind that blew in. Endless expanses of glossy green crops and rows of poplars flashed past. Beside me, my aunt fell asleep, her head lolling to one side. Every time we went over a bump, it shook like a rattle drum. I poked her head with my finger. Only a little while before, she had been behaving like a mad witch, but now she just looked pathetic. My ear still felt bruised. If only I could grow up quickly.

It was 1st July 1997, the very day when Hong Kong was handed back to the motherland. I was eleven years old and going back to my birthplace, Jining, in Shandong province. My paternal grandfather had died at the age of sixty-six. I had imagined I would be spending my time arguing with my aunt for the money to attend the summer classes. But then, out of the blue, came the phone call from Shandong.

My aunt packed a bag and we went to the bus station. After a bumpy day's ride, we finally made it to the door in time for my grandfather's funeral. Granny's yard was crowded with people who had come to pay their respects.

'Dad! My poor dad!' cried Auntie Wenjie. As the eldest daughter, it was expected that she would fall to her knees and wail as soon as she arrived at the house. This was my home, but it was completely unfamiliar. It was a huge shock. I looked at my aunt, sprawled over the coffin and wailing, and found myself beginning to cry as well. 'What a good girl you are, Yangyang. Such a good girl, you never even met your grandfather and you're crying as if your heart would break,' said a middle-aged woman wearing a white mourning hat, coming over and putting her arms around me. 'There, there, little one, don't cry.' She patted me on the back.

'Yangyang!' I heard someone else calling me.

My mother, also in a mourning hat, came out of the house. When I raised my head, there she was, the mother of my dreams, right in front of me, but I stood rooted to the spot like an idiot.

'Are you tired after your long bus trip?' she asked, taking my hand, and wiping the tears from my face. I wasn't used to such kindness. It embarrassed me, and I backed away, shaking my head. Although she was my mother, she didn't really feel like it. Meeting her felt stranger than meeting a stranger.

'Yangyang's crying even though she never knew her grandfather. What a dutiful child.' A dutiful child? Suddenly I had to smother my laughter. I was only crying because my aunt was crying and it was infectious, and they thought my tears were for a grandfather I had never met.

My mind went blank. I simply did not know how to handle this complicated situation.

'This is your aunt,' said my mother, indicating the middle-aged woman.

'Hello, aunt,' I whispered reluctantly.

'Hey, what a good girl! Such a good girl!' My aunt stroked my hair approvingly.

On the round straw mat in the middle of the front room, I knelt before the grandfather I had never met before and knocked my head three times on the floor. It was the first and last time I met him. Our relationship started and ended here. That night, Auntie Wenjie and my father and their brothers would watch over his coffin. I went with my mother to the home I had never been in since I was born. And yet it was as if my sisters and I had known each other all our lives, even though I lived so far away. They crowded around me and we chatted all night. Finally, we all squeezed into the big bed and fell sound asleep. This must be what people mean when they say that blood is thicker than water.

'Yangyang!'

The next morning, a grey-haired old woman appeared in the doorway and called my name.

Star rushed over and threw her arms around her, shouting, 'Nana!'

I stared bewildered at this small figure with the beaming smile and bound feet.

'Yangyang's back! Yangyang's back!' she exclaimed in excitement. She hurried forward and reached for my hand.

I was scared, and dodged out of her way. Moon and Serene laughed behind their hands, while Star hid behind Nana and made faces at me. Nana looked awkward. Sweat beaded on her forehead and dripped into her eyes, and with a trembling hand, she took out a handkerchief and dabbed at them.

My mother walked out of the kitchen with a spatula in her hand, 'Yangyang, you were your Nana's pet when you were tiny! You must remember Nana!'

I bit my lip silently and looked down at the ground. Nana was quick to make excuses for me, and for herself, 'Our Yangyang's a big girl now. I didn't mean to embarrass her.'

I looked up at her, turned and ran out into the street. It was a cruel rejection of the grandmother who had adored me, who had hurried over from Sunzha village as soon as she heard I was back. She sat on a stool in the yard, lost and alone. She probably had no idea that after all these years, she was a complete stranger to me. I was no longer the little Yangyang who clung to her in bed every night and went to sleep cuddling her feet. I didn't even remember having done that.

That night, when I was sleeping, my father carried me to the guest room, where Nana slept in the sofa bed. She took me gently in her arms, and fanned me like she used to. It had been six years, but for her, the girl she was holding was still that tiny tot.

When I woke up in the morning and opened my eyes, there was a grey-haired old woman lying next to me. I grabbed my pillow and ran into the yard, screaming. No way did I want to sleep with her. Nana awoke with a start. She sat up, her hair straggling around her shoulders, and quietly wiped away the tears.

At dinner, Nana made a big deal out of picking the nicest morsels to put in my bowl, but I put them back in the dish again. She forced a laugh, but her chopsticks trembled in her hand. On the sofa in the front room, I sat close to Auntie Wenjie, and Nana looked envious. In the alley outside, I played with my sisters, and Nana watched me unobserved.

Then she bustled around the kitchen, making dough and stoking the cooker, sweating profusely. And when she saw me eating a large piece of jujube cake and playing with my sisters in the yard, she looked gratified. At least, I still loved her steamed jujube cake.

During my time at home in Dongzha, Nana did all she could to please me. She told me stories about when I was little, in the hopes that the memories of my life with her in Sunzha might trickle back. But I shouted impatiently, 'You're so annoying! I didn't sleep with your stinky feet! Please stop going on at me!' Finally, I got in such a paddy that she gave up trying to talk to me.

Six years before, she had sealed my fate with just a few words. At five years old, I was taken away from everything I knew. Six years later, she wanted to make it up to me and be as close as we were before. No way.

While Nana was doing all she could to suck up to me, my father flew into a temper and beat me up. It happened like this. After the funeral, he was finally able to come home and rest. When he woke up, Star and Serene were playing in the yard. Something seemed to put him in a rage. He went to stand at the gate, smoking a cigarette and looking down the alley.

'Dad!' I sang out and skipped up to him, with two packets of chocolates I had just bought from the kiosk.

He frowned and looked at the chocolates. Then he spat out the cigarette butt in his mouth and ground it under his shoe.

'Why are you so greedy?' he demanded.

'Star and Serene asked me to buy them.'

'So you just do what they tell you, do you?' Before I had time to defend myself, he gave me a hard kick and shouted, 'You're the greedy one, don't blame it on them!'

I stumbled and sat down heavily on the ground. The chocolates rolled away from me.

'I've told you that you can't go out running around outside, but you just don't listen! Are you just trying to make trouble?' I got to my feet, and he jabbed me hard in the forehead with his finger. 'Are you stupid or what?'

I rubbed the mud off my hands and glared at him.

Between the bars of our big blue gate, I caught a glimpse of two pairs of curious eyes. It had to be my younger sisters, Star and Serene, who else? Their father, Shen Wenming, normally king of his castle, had met his match. It was pretty exciting for them. He beat everyone in the family, and cowed them all into silence. Slaps were a normal part of their lives. Our father was a man who believed in corporal punishment.

'This'll teach you to be so pig-headed!' He raised his arm ready to strike.

This was bad. I legged it. I had longed for a dad who was an improvement on my aunt, but he was just an upgraded version of her. I certainly did not want a dad like this! Although he later explained to me that he was worried that they would be severely punished by the people from the family planning office if they spotted me, and wanted me to remember to do what I was told, I refused to have anything to do with him.

For many days, I avoided him, not because I was afraid that he would hit me again, but because in kicking me, he had hurt my self-esteem and ruined my relationship with him. I had entered that house for the first time in eleven years, and instead of getting a hug or a present, I got a telling-off and a beating. I did not like my father one little bit. And then something happened that made me reject him for good and all.

One sunny day, he took Star and me on the motorbike to see my mother's eldest sister. My aunt remembered me as the little girl who had wailed for her Nana. Now I was quite grown up, which made her both happy and sad. She bought me lots of snacks, and secretly gave me and Star ten yuan each. It was the first time anyone had given me so much pocket money. I was overwhelmed. Having lived all those years in a family where you had to fight for every yuan and then you would not necessarily get it, I was touched by my aunt's generosity. It was not so much the money, it was the feeling of being loved.

I heard my father Shen Wenming's voice, 'You keep an eye on Yangyang. Mind she doesn't steal your money.'

His words stabbed me in the heart. That cosy feeling of being loved vanished, and my self-esteem was trampled underfoot. If I hadn't been sitting on a chair outside the front door taking a breather, I would never have known that my own father had announced to all and sundry that his daughter was a thief!

'Keep an eye on Yangyang.' What for? 'Mind she doesn't steal your money.' Whose money?

This had all come about because Auntie Wenjie had told him

that I had taken money for an ice lolly when I was little, and then I took money for sanitary napkins. So he concluded that I would steal wherever I was. This aunt was so kind to me, and I was so grateful, why would I steal her money? As a father, it never occurred to him to judge himself for his failure to love and care for his own daughter. Instead, he hurt me over and over again. He was not worthy to be my father and never would be!

That summer, when I was eleven, my father ceased to exist for me.

The short summer reunion was soon over. Auntie opened the window of the bus and poked her head out, smiling and waving goodbye to the family. I sat in the row behind with my head down.

'Yangyang, do as your Auntie Wenjie says, and work hard at school,' I heard him say, but I immediately turned away so I didn't have to see his horrible face.

Auntie turned around to try and persuade me to answer him, but I simply pulled the curtain across.

'You all go on home, it's a really hot day, the bus is about to leave,' she pulled the curtain back again and poked her head out.

'Thank you for looking after Yangyang. I hope she'll be good,' Nana choked on her words, took out a handkerchief and pressed it to her face.

My mother went to comfort her, and Star went to her too and hung onto her arm, looking like she was going to cry. I took a quick look out of the window, then bent my head again.

'Goodbye Auntie, goodbye Yangyang!'

My sisters waved at the window. The bus slowly pulled away, and Nana wiped away her tears and looked up. She took Star's hand and tottered along the road after us.

The bus picked up speed. Watching Nana and Star following behind us, I couldn't hold my tears back any longer. They ran down my face and onto my neck. Why wouldn't they let me stay? Why did it have to be me who was sent away? Why did everything land on me?

I don't know whether it was because I was crying, or because she missed her mother and her old home, but Auntie's eyes suddenly reddened, and she put her hand over her nose and looked out of the back window. The sadness of parting filled the bus and clung to us for a long time.

As the bus bowled along, the wind coming through the open window blew my hair into a tangle. I was lost in my thoughts as the rows of houses flashed by.

The evening before, in the front room of our house in Dongzha, I had silently packed my bag while my mother sat folding my clothes for me, 'You're leaving tomorrow, is there anything you want?'

I looked up at her, and shook my head with a faint smile.

I had been with them for more than a month, and my family had never once asked me how I was getting on with Auntie and Uncle. They didn't ask, and I only let slip the odd grumble. And if they had asked? What could they have done if I had told them the truth? Even though I was desperate to come home, no one even mentioned this possibility. I just had to stick it out in my foster home. A child without a mother is like a stalk of grass, no one loves her. I knew quite well that I was that abandoned, unloved stalk of grass.

As the bus drove along tree-lined country roads, I looked out and squinted up at the sun flickering through the foliage.

I want a loving family, that's what I want, I said to myself.

The sunlight cast mottled shadows over the ground, and the bus wheels sped over the tears that I flicked out of my window.

11

Wei Wanjun

'Everyone's attended summer school. You're the only one who has to be different! You don't buy your school uniform, you don't pay your tuition fees! We're halfway through the workbook, and you come swanning into class dangling your schoolbag. You're so disorganized and undisciplined! Don't you know how important year six is?'

At Changzhuang Primary School, Ms Wang marched me into the office and was ranting at me. The other teachers cast contemptuous or sympathetic glances my way as I stood awkwardly clutching my bag.

'Go home, you're wasting my time, go and tell your parents you'll either have to repeat your year or move to another school.'

Tears of disappointment ran down my cheeks as I shuffled out of the office. I could hear the sound of the other children reading aloud from the corridor. It was a very long corridor and the road home seemed even longer. I was miserable about having missed summer school. I was still struggling with having to leave my family in Jining and now here I was back in Nanyang wrestling with this problem alone. I didn't know how long I could hold on.

In the yard, my uncle was standing under the trellis busy tending his grapes. I crept up to him.

'What's happened? Why are you back? Not going to class today?' Uncle looked puzzled.

'My teacher says that I didn't go to summer school, so she won't let me go up to year six.' I choked up.

'What? That's a disgrace! Not letting children who miss summer school go up a year?'

My uncle was shaking with rage.

'Why didn't you tell your teacher that your grandfather died and you had to go back to Shandong for the funeral? Why are you crying? What's the use of crying? Your mouth's for speaking, not just for eating, you damn brat!' my aunt joined in. She had overheard the shouting and come out of the kitchen. She didn't bother to ask me what had happened.

That was the last straw. My pent-up feelings finally exploded, 'You expect me to do everything! Absolutely everything! You didn't want to spend money on sending me to summer school, and now my teacher won't let me back in school, you still want me to sort it! What's it got to do with me that my grandfather's dead? I never knew him and he never cared about me either!'

I flung my schoolbag on the ground, and shrieked and cried. My aunt and uncle were taken aback. Not that they were going to admit that they were at fault. They were my elders, so in their minds, they were always right.

That night, I heard my uncle tossing and turning. The more he thought about it, the angrier he got and the more he was convinced that the teacher had behaved disgracefully. Whoever heard of keeping a child down to repeat a year because she didn't attend summer classes?

'Yangyang, get your schoolbag ready,' he announced the next morning. 'I'm coming to school with you.' He limped along behind me with his walking stick. His right leg had never properly healed after the motorbike had knocked him down.

In the school office, he sternly interrogated Ms Wang, 'Where are your school rules? Show me where it says a child can't go up to the next year after the summer holiday!' His hand shook as he gripped the walking stick.

'Please calm down, sir, I'm only the teacher, I don't make the rules. If you don't believe me, go and talk to the head. We covered a lot of ground in this summer school. There's a lot of pressure on all the students in year six before they take the exams for junior high school. It was you who allowed her to skip these classes!' Ms Wang sounded shrill.

Uncle was seriously annoyed, 'If your grandfather had died, would you come to summer school? Huh?' He played his trump card, 'Let me tell you, young woman, you were still in split-crotch trousers when I was a teacher!'

'All right, all right, I'm not going to argue with you anymore. You go to the office and talk to the head. I've got children to teach!' And Ms Wang swept out of the room, glaring at me.

I glared back just as fiercely. We'd burnt our boats now, I had nothing to lose. I was not putting up with Ms Wang's snobbish attitude anymore, even if it meant changing schools.

I could see that my uncle was still angry at her rudeness, and I tugged at his arm, 'Uncle, I don't want to stay in this school. Don't you know the head of Zaolin Primary School, Mrs Luo? I didn't get very good marks in maths but if I have to repeat the year, I can do it there.' I had suffered too much humiliation at Changzhuang School. I wanted out.

My uncle tried to dissuade me, 'Are you sure you want to go to Zaolin Primary School? It's no fun to repeat a year. You've only missed a month's classes, I can tutor you at home.'

Him? Tutor me? Forget it, if I didn't understand a maths problem, I could just imagine how he'd rub my nose in it.

'I'm quite sure!' I declared. 'If I go to Zaolin, no one knows me there, it's no big deal to do the year again.'

'Fine, let's do that then. But I have to speak to the head before we leave here,' said my uncle with a sigh. I helped him to his feet and we made our way slowly towards the head's office.

That morning, my uncle spent two full hours closeted with her. I stood outside the door waiting for him to come out. I had no idea what they were talking about. But one day shortly afterwards, I bumped into Hai Jing and she told me that Ms Wang, the arch-snob, had not only lost her Excellent Teacher badge, but she had also been publicly reprimanded by the head at an all-school meeting.

I was humbled and grateful that my uncle had stood up for me and was perfectly happy for me to transfer. My aunt told me that it was because Wang Zhongrui's behaviour had touched a raw nerve, and my uncle firmly believed that no one had the right to deprive a child of going to school.

In the Wancheng District of Nanyang, the Yangtze River Road marked the dividing line between Changzhuang and Zaolin villages. Our little village Xiaoliangzhuang came under Changzhuang village, to the south of the Yangtze River Road. The school was close to home, so I used to walk. The Zaolin Primary School that I transferred to was in the village of the same name, north of the trunk road. It was too far for me to walk, so I was quite justified in taking the bike.

I had had my eye on Auntie's ladies bicycle, a Three-Gun model, for a long time. I was in a new school, with new teachers and new classmates. Everything was new except for the curriculum, which I had already covered as I was repeating year five. I had always done well in Chinese, and the class teacher Ms Liu picked up on that straightaway. Less than two weeks after school started, she chose me as class monitor for Chinese and I became Ms Liu's trusted helper. That year, I felt like I was back in my first year of primary school. I came first in all my subjects, no trouble at all. I made a bunch of good friends too – my outspoken and happy-go-lucky personality won them over.

I noticed this girl sitting in the corner of the first row on my very first day. She looked different. She was dark-skinned and scrawny, and very quiet. She hardly talked to the rest of us. The reason why I noticed her was because she was so skinny and thin and she had an outsize head.

When I became Chinese monitor, I used to sneak glances at her when I was handing out the homework. In spite of her big head and protruding forehead, she had a pretty face, and very cute, long eyelashes.

She was always first into school, and first out again at the end of class. Several times, when I was right behind her on our way out, I would see a middle-aged woman waiting for her, always with a calm smile on her face. But the girl used to bat the woman's hand away impatiently and walk along on her own.

In class, whenever she was called on by the teacher to stand up to answer a question, some of the more mischievous boys would deliberately make strange noises at her to get the rest of the class laughing. The teachers could not be bothered to tell the wretches off. The girl ignored them too, as if she was used to it. But this kind of flagrant bullying of someone who was unable to defend herself, happening right there in the classroom, I found hard to bear. After all, I had a fiery temper, and I had always seen myself as a protector of the weak.

One rainy afternoon, I could see a multi-coloured forest of umbrellas outside the school yard gate. I sat at my desk and watched as my classmates were picked up one after another by their parents. This was nothing new. I was always jealous of the kids who had someone to meet them, but no one ever came to hold an umbrella over me and take me home.

'Hey, you!' A ruckus at the classroom door disturbed my thoughts. I looked up to see what was going on. Some boys were clustered around the girl, pointing at her as she was about to go outside.

'Hey, you! Big Head! What d'you want an umbrella for? Your head's big enough!'

The boys were jeering and shouting, egged on by the class bully Lü Meng.

She walked out of the classroom without saying a word then when she got into the rainy yard, she broke into a run, hugging her schoolbag to her chest.

I couldn't help myself yelling at the boys, 'Hey, haven't you yobs had enough yet? You're horrible!' I grabbed my schoolbag and rushed at them.

The boys turned their attention to me and burst out laughing. I stamped hard on Lü Meng's foot, then turned tail and disappeared among the forest of umbrellas. Behind me, I heard Lü Meng's cry of pain from the classroom.

A few days later, on cleaning day, all of us competed to see who could work hardest. Some of the boys even climbed onto the window sills and wiped down the window panes. I got a watering can and sprinkled the floor with water starting from the back row. Lü Meng and the other two boys wandered around the room with long-handled brooms slung over their shoulders, doing nothing in particular.

'Hey, Big Head, you're working hard! But it's not gonna make your head any smaller!' Lü Meng jeered, spotting her standing on a bench and carefully wiping the blackboard down. He sauntered over to her, still hefting his broom. He thought he was so funny, but he was just pathetic. She rinsed her rag in the basin, completely ignoring them.

'Hey, I'm talking to you, Big Head! Are you deaf as well? Have you all got big heads in your family?' With Lü Meng egging them on, his three mates fell about laughing.

Some of the kids were indignant but dared not say anything, some clamped their hands over their mouths to cover their smirks, and some simply grinned along with them.

I was at bursting point by that time. I got behind Lü Meng, holding a plastic watering can full of water, and said, 'This classroom, the more we clean it, the more it stinks. And here's a big heap of rubbish that needs cleaning up!' Before Lü Meng realized what was going on, I had lifted the can above my head and sluiced him from head to toe with water.

Everyone stared at both of us wide-eyed and open-mouthed. She had been wiping the blackboard and now she stood rooted to the spot, even more astonished than they were.

'You cunt, I'll kill you for that!' yelled Lü Meng. He was furious, and shivering, and took off his coat.

'So young and so foul-mouthed! Didn't your mother teach you any manners?'

'Manners? You're a fine one to talk!' And Lü Meng rolled up his sleeves and got ready to fight.

'You little git, clean your mouth out!' I threw the can on the ground, rushed up and grabbed him by the collar. 'If you ever bully Wei Wanjun again, if you ever bad-mouth her again, see if I won't tear your stinking mouth off your face!'

Wei Wanjun suddenly realized I had become her protector against Lü Meng, and she jumped down from the bench.

'Wanna fight, do you?' Lü Meng reached out to grab my collar, but I used all my strength to shove him away and he fell over.

'Ai-ya!' he squealed as he sat on the concrete floor, rubbing his sore bottom.

There were shouts of laughter from the rest of the classroom, as soon as they realized that the class bully had been pushed to the ground by a girl. Suddenly, Lü Meng jumped back up again, and shook his head vigorously, so that water sprayed in every direction. I was not afraid of him, I just stood there with my arms folded, calmly watching the little monster. I think the rest of the class thought another world war was about to break out. But Lü Meng caved in completely. He walked over to me, his hands raised in surrender, and said, 'Sister, you're amazing. You win!'

I turned around to pick up the watering can but Lü Meng got there before me and took it from me, 'I'll do it! It's hard work carrying a full can. You're the boss, you can leave it to me!' And he sauntered outside to refill it, humming a little tune.

He was a pathetic sight, dripping wet, slopping along leaving wet footprints, and I did not know whether to laugh or cry. After school, I walked home with Wei Wanjun, pushing the bike. 'Thank you for helping me out today,' she said.

'Hah! I could see straightaway that Lü Meng was a nasty piece of work. He's such a bully. I don't know how you put up with it. I would have been furious with him.'

'I just don't want any worse trouble to come out of this.'

I had my self-respect but I was sensitive too. When she said that, I was suddenly worried that me teaching Lü Meng a lesson was going to get her into trouble.

'Oh, don't worry, it's nothing. I've been laughed at in class since the first year of primary school. I've been given all sorts of nicknames. I've had five years of it and I'm used to it,' she smiled, when I didn't say anything.

'Wanjun, can I ask you a personal question?'

'You want to know why my head is so big?'

I grinned awkwardly.

'Do you know about family planning?' she asked, suddenly serious, and turned to look at me.

There wasn't a soul in the world who knew more about family planning than me. I looked at her and nodded quietly.

'I have two older brothers who were in kindergarten at the time Mum was pregnant with me. Family planning was super strict back then. The family planning officers were always raiding our house trying to catch my mother and take her away for an abortion. Every time they came, Mum ran away through the backyard when they smashed the front door in. There was a big stook of barley straw on the other end of the wall, and my mother used to climb over and land on it, then go and hide at my granny's.

It got so that every time there was a wind and the bushes knocked against the door, my mother ran outside and got ready to escape over the back wall. But this wasn't a long-term solution, so my father smuggled my mother away to a relative in the country. But my mother could hardly eat and sleep from stress. She was scared they would catch up with her even there.'

As the sun went down, the afterglow lit up Wei Wanjun's face. She was telling her story as calmly as if it was about someone else.

'I was born prematurely because my mother was so stressed. At six months, I was still a scrawny little thing but I had an outsized head. At first, my dad teased my mum that his little princess was brighter than other kids because of her big head. But then my forehead began to stick out and there was something strange about my eyes, so they rushed me to a big hospital for an examination. At eight months, I was diagnosed with hydrocephalus. We're not well-off, but my parents borrowed money for my medical fees from family and friends. My mother always told me that they would get me better even if they had to sell everything they had. So I had the treatment and I'm cured. But every time I look in the mirror, and see this big head I've still got, and think about everyone making fun of me since I was a baby, I wish I'd never been born.'

'You know, Wanjun? We're the lucky ones.'

'We? What d'you mean?'

'I'm like you, I'm a family planning survivor too. I have an older sister and two younger sisters, and I'm the piggy in the middle that no one loves. The reason why we're lucky is because at least we're determined to survive.'

Wanjun's astonished expression said it all.

She had no idea that a lively, happy-go-lucky girl like me was an excess-birth child too.

'My aunt was going to bring up my littlest sister, but my Nana, who was looking after me, said I was too much for her to handle, and so my aunt took me instead. So here I am in Nanyang. I've been here six years, since I was five. My only visit back home to Shandong in six years was this summer.'

'Is your auntie's family nice to you?'

'My aunt's got a terrible temper. Sometimes, I don't even know what triggers her outbursts. As for my uncle, he's an old fossil, very traditional and unpredictable too. He doesn't often fly off the handle but when he does, he scares me to death. My cousins don't like me either, they're always trying to get me into trouble. Last winter, I borrowed my cousin's sweater without asking her and she whacked me across the face,' I burst out laughing.

'Eh? How can you laugh at that? How can you get by in such a depressing family? I'd go crazy if I were you. Our two families are really funny. Our family wanted a girl, and yours wanted a boy. I'm the pet of the family, but I look weird. You have no one to love you but you're healthy and lovely and lively.'

'I heal quickly. They beat me and swear at me, I hate them for a second but the next second, as long as they smile at me, I've forgotten it all. I've got a thick skin!' I laughed. 'Nothing bothers me.'

'Do you hate your mum and dad?' she asked.

'Of course I do. But it doesn't change anything. They're not here to hear me or see me or touch me, or even feel what I'm feeling. So I don't think about them at all. Even if I did, it wouldn't change anything. What about you? Have you always been with your parents?'

'No way! Because I'm an excess-birth kid, they demolished the house my dad built. I spent years going from one aunt or uncle to another, hiding in pitch-black wardrobes, stuffy smelly wooden chests, damp, dark cellars, dirty, prickly straw stacks…there's nowhere I haven't hidden!'

I was stunned. The only place I'd hidden was in the attic with my Grandad.

'Even when I went back home, if there was any talk of raids by the family planning officers, day or night, my mum used to grab me and look for a place to hide. As I grew up, it became a reflex for me too. If I heard someone come to the yard, I used to run to my parents' bedroom and bury myself under a pile of clothes, just leaving a tiny gap to breathe through. I was so terrified of being discovered as an illegal. I can't remember how old I was when I developed this knack for getting away and hiding but I've never lost it. Still nowadays, I can run faster than anyone else when it's an emergency.'

'You ran so fast back then just because you were so afraid. The darkness makes you anxious and afraid, but it gives you a sense of security too. Hiding in dark places means safety, no one's going to find you and you won't be caught, right?'

'Yes, I like to be alone in the dark, no one can see me, no one can find me.'

'Wanjun, you don't need to hide in trembling fear anymore. From today on, we can walk hand in hand in bright sunlight!'

'Shanying, you know what? That's how I see you, a girl who's bathed in sunshine.'

'Haha, me, a sunshine girl! You know what? I've actually got the character 阳 for sun in my name. Wu Shanying is the name on the hukou my aunt bought me. My real name is Shen Yang.'

'They bought you a hukou? What a complicated life you've had! How did that happen?'

'You want to know? That's the next installment.'

I jumped on the bike, and pedalled off, then turned back and shouted, 'I'll tell you next time. If I don't get home soon, you'll hear the Shen Bellow all the way from Xiaoliangzhuang!'

Many years later, Wanjun told me that that day, watching me pedal away into the sunset, she had mixed feelings. She had always felt she was the saddest, unluckiest person in the world. She certainly never imagined that someone like me, seemingly without a care in the world, had had such a hard time and lived in a world without love. She suddenly thought of her mother, who adored her and would do anything she asked.

Actually, we were both full of mixed emotions. Before I told Wanjun my story, I used to think I was the sorriest child in the world too. My parents did not love me, my cousins ignored me and my aunt and uncle did not give a fig for me. I never had pretty clothes or pocket money. My aunt even begrudged me my school fees and breakfast money.

But that was nothing compared to what she had endured. At least I was a healthy excess-birth girl, people did not think I was peculiar, or point at me or gossip.

12

King of the mountain eagles

I had subdued Lü Meng temporarily and on the surface, he was respectful to me. But behind our backs, he was still up to his tricks. He was a devious so-and-so.

First, a bit of chewing gum turned up on Wanjun's stool. Next, the core disappeared from my bicycle valve so I couldn't pump the tyre up. Then someone stuck a picture of a baby with a huge head on Wanjun's back. The day after that, I found my desk full of rubbish.

You didn't need to be a genius to figure out that that swine Lü Meng was behind all of this. I didn't want to involve Wanjun in more trouble, so I decided to fight back very quietly, on my own.

I was the Chinese class monitor, so I had to give out the workbooks. When I got to Lü Meng, I shouted to him and threw it at him from a distance. The workbook cooperated splendidly. It landed on the concrete floor, right in some mucus spat by a kid who was infamous for hawking and spitting, the 'spit demon', we called him. Lü Meng picked it up and retched with disgust.

I collected dried snot balls from other classmates and wrapped them up in a thick package. Then, in the self-study class, Lü Meng was given his mystery package. He opened it and found the snot balls. He was a bit puzzled and had to peer at them for a while before he figured out what they were. As the class burst out laughing, Lü Meng started to retch again and rushed out of the classroom with his hand over his mouth.

In the music class, Lü Meng sang his little heart out, and did not notice when I quietly got under his desk and tied the laces of his shoes together. When the bell rang for the end of class, and everyone made a beeline for the door, Lü Meng fell flat on his face.

Finally, at the end of the school day, we heard him yelling, 'Hey, damn it, I can't find my bicycle! Has anyone seen my bicycle?'

He sounded desperate. It served him right! I hid under a big tree at a safe distance, and laughed my head off. As he watched the other kids leaving the school yard with their bicycles one by one, Lü Meng's face fell.

Then two girls walked by, laughing, 'That's funny!' said one. 'Who put a bike in the girls' toilet?'

'Is it grey?' Lü Meng asked eagerly, grabbing her arm.

'How did you know? You must be a pervert if you've been in there.' The girl shook him off impatiently.

'What are you talking about? That's my bike! Please! Can you get it for me?' Lü Meng pleaded.

'No way!' The girl was adamant.

By this time, Lü Meng was frantic. He rushed into the girls' toilets. There were shrieks from the girls, and some rowdy boys jeered and pointed at him as he hastily pushed his bicycle outside.

He was red to the gills as he fished his key out of his trouser pocket, shouting, 'Damn it, who was the slimy bastard who put it in there? I'll kill whoever did it!'

I looked up to the sky and laughed. That twerp thought he could get the better of me? No chance!

I gave him such a hard time that eventually Lü Meng got suspicious. How was he going to get back at me? He racked his brains and finally came up with a cunning plan. One Sunday afternoon, he got another boy to agree to go to Xiaoliangzhuang village with him to look me up. His plan was to give my family the idea that I'd been messing with boys and not getting on with my schoolwork.

They knocked at the gate.

'Who is it?!' They heard the Shen Bellow before they saw my aunt, and it scared the hell out of them.

'Is Wu Shanying at home?' asked Lü Meng, making an effort to sound calm.

My aunt opened the gate, saw it was two bratty boys, and shut it in their faces, 'She's gone to see a corpse!'

Lü Meng and his friend were struck dumb. They'd been turned away at the gate before they could even pretend they had a date with me.

'Gone to see a corpse? Did she really say that? Is that the way Shanying's family talk? No wonder that girl's so tough!' The other boy looked frightened.

'Huh!' Lü Meng sounded grumpy. 'Anyway, listen! I can hear people playing the suona, let's go and take a look.'

It was the Yuan family, holding a wake. In the front room of their house, old man Yuan had been laid out, wrapped in a shroud. Anyone could drop in, the Yuans were much too busy to care about intruders. Lü Meng pushed his way through the crowd and the first person he spotted was me, squatting next to the corpse and curiously studying the red gloves the old man was wearing.

'Mother in heaven!' cried Lü Meng when he saw the corpse, and his legs nearly gave way in fright.

By Monday morning, rumours were flying around that, 'Wu Shanying spends her weekends sitting next to dead bodies!' As soon as I appeared at the door of the classroom, Lü Meng stood up and led a chorus from the boys in the back row, banging his desk and shouting, 'Mountain Eagle King! Mighty King!'

All these boys ganging up scared me. What was Lü Meng playing at? I had to tread carefully. I sat down on my stool and my desk buddy leaned over and whispered urgently, 'Wu Shanying, did you really spend Sunday sitting next to a dead body?'

'What?' I frowned, completely confused. What a ridiculous thing to say! And disrespectful too. Yuan Xiaohui's grandfather had died and I'd gone to join in the action. How come the whole class had found out overnight?

'But did you go?' asked my desk buddy. 'Lü Meng got here bright and early today. Is he just trying to spread nasty rumours about you?'

I guffawed. So he was the 'bratty boy' my aunt was going on about. Well, of course. Who else would dare turn up at my aunt's house 'to play with me'. I would have been in deep trouble if it weren't for the fact that the family were used to me playing with boys. I'd always done it.

From then on, the pranks stopped. Lü Meng started to be nice to Wanjun. Not only that, he also started calling me Mountain Eagle any time he saw me. (This was a play on my hukou name, Shanying, which sounded like 'shan-ying' meaning mountain eagle.) Even more marvellous, he actually formed a Mountain Eagle Gang in my honour. I'd always hated the name Wu Shanying, along with my fake hukou ID, ever since I got lumbered with it when I started school. But having my name bandied about by Lü Meng suddenly made me feel like I really was the Mountain Eagle King!

But although he no longer bullied Wanjun or clashed with me, Lü Meng was no saint and carried on bullying other girls from time to time. Once, during a spring outing, Lü Meng chased the girls in the class waving willow fluff he had picked from the trees. As soon as I saw that, I picked a big fat caterpillar from the willow branch and threw it at him. He put on a big show of not being scared, until someone shouted, 'It's moving! It's moving!'

Lü Meng suddenly realized that the thing stuck on his sleeve was a proper genuine caterpillar. He started whimpering in fright.

Wanjun and I laughed so hard that we cried.

'Wu Shanying, do you know the scientific name for this?' asked Ms Liu, who had been watching our antics. She never missed a chance to teach us something new. I shook my head, still laughing myself silly.

'It has a nice name, "catkin",' she said.

'Catkin... catkin...' I repeated after her, and looked at the fluffy stuff she was holding.

Ms Liu went on, 'Hands like catkins, skin like fat, neck like a grub, teeth like gourd pips, forehead like a cicada; eyebrows like the antennae of the silkworm moth, a pretty smile, and expectant eyes,' she quoted from the Tang dynasty poem that describes a beautiful woman. We were deeply impressed that she knew so much.

'How are hands like catkins, Miss?' I asked curiously.

'It's because a beautiful woman's hands are as soft as tender new foliage.'

I took the catkin from Ms Liu. As I studied it carefully, Wanjun joined me.

I heard a voice behind me. 'Don't think you can change your fat carrot fingers into slender catkins just by looking at them!' Lü Meng jeered.

I spun round and jabbed him hard in the forehead. 'You watch it! I'll clobber you!'

There was loud laughter.

Lü Meng did not like being made a fool of in front of Ms Liu and a bunch of girls, and he slunk away with his tail between his legs.

For a while, it was popular to play Slam-the-Beanbag in school. In the ten minutes between classes, the yard was full of playgrounds with kids hurling beanbags at each other. Once, when we girls were having fun, Lü Meng brought a few boys over and insisted on competing with us. We knew we were easily a match for them, so we played.

In the beginning, everything was normal. The boys and girls teams lost and won various rounds. Then the boys realized that Lü Meng was giving away points to me and got annoyed. In the end, they put him and me together and made him join the girls' team.

Their thinking was obviously that if the two of us played together, he wouldn't give away points to me and the game would be fair. But to everyone's surprise, we made an invincible duo, and none of the others even got a look-in.

I grabbed hold of Lü Meng's arm and jumped and bounced around. The boys stood glaring angrily, with no idea what to do. But they had no one but themselves to blame. After all, they had insisted on putting us together. They kept pounding Lü Meng with the bags, until the bags burst and the maize grains they were stuffed with fell on everyone's faces. Scuffling and laughing, we all rushed back to our classroom.

Then there was a craze for a game called 'planes'. We all stood in a single row holding hands. The first one took the hand of the kid next to her and crooked her right leg over their joined hands. When the order was given, the whole line of kids spun clockwise, the first one hopping on her left leg until the line got up enough speed. Then she pulled her leg back and jumped, both legs flying. If she judged it right and they all cooperated, she could fly several circles in the air.

When the boys and girls in our class played it together, Lü Meng would hit the ground when it was his turn to be the plane, apparently because no one was strong enough to hold him up. Lü Meng didn't mind that, but when they laughed at him for being a fatty, he got so angry that he stopped playing. What he did not know was that at a certain point, the Mountain Eagle King (me) would give a wink, and everyone would let go of him and send him crashing ignominiously to the ground.

Once, Wanjun told me, 'Yesterday Lü Meng asked me to join the Mountain Eagle Gang. A tough gang like that, of course I said I'd join!' She was full of admiration for me nowadays. She could see how I messed with Lü Meng behind his back. She was so fearful and lacking in self-esteem that she had spent her life keeping out of people's way. She told me more than once that she really wanted to be like me, playing tough, not afraid of anything.

Actually there was one thing I was afraid of, and that was wearing a skirt. I had grown up scrambling up and down things, and a skirt was a big nuisance when I was doing that. When I had to wear a skirt, I could not sit or stand properly or even be myself.

On School Foundation Day, every class had to put on a show. We were to perform the song 'A Night in the Naval Port', for which the girls all had to wear naval jackets and short skirts. I was really embarrassed. I had never worn a skirt in school. However, that was only the start of the problem.

Early that morning, before the school celebration started, I was standing in the corridor outside the classroom in my skirt, chatting to Wanjun. Suddenly, there was a burst of laughter from behind us. Xiong Jinqiu had crept up behind us, and was holding my skirt up.

I spun around and grabbed her before she could run away, 'You perv! How dare you? You're not getting away with that!' Xiong Jinqiu was an outgoing, cheerful girl, much like me, and normally we got on well. What on earth was she doing playing such a silly joke on me?

I tried to do the same to her, but she was stronger than me. I kept grabbing at her skirt but I couldn't reach it. The most mortifying thing was that Lü Meng and a few other boys were cheering me on, 'Come on, King! Come on, Mighty King! Go for it, Mountain Eagle King!'

By this time, the corridor was packed with onlookers. Xiong Jinqiu and I were still scrapping, neither of us giving an inch. Suddenly, someone shouted a warning, 'Ms Liu's coming!' The other kids headed for the classroom, Xiong Jinqiu stuck her tongue out at me, and followed them.

Furious, I stalked in behind her and gave her a hard whack on the shoulder as I passed. 'See if I don't take care of you after class!' I hissed, and took my seat in the row behind her.

Ms Liu, our class head, walked in. Xiong Jinqiu made a big show of shaking her head from side to side. I was still seething. Ms Liu issued a few reminders about the ceremony and then called Xiong Jinqiu, who was on the class arts committee, onto the podium. She would take us through our song one more time. Xiong Jinqiu stood up with a big smile on her face, and at that very moment, her skirt fell to the floor.

The class erupted.

I looked up, to see her Black Cat Sheriff knickers in full view. Of course I gave a hoot of laughter. Her desk buddy, a boy called Tang

Feng, was speechless. He was normally completely under her thumb. Now he wanted to laugh, but didn't dare to make a sound in case she beat him up later.

I hadn't even taken my revenge and Xiong Jinqiu had messed up, all by herself. I almost wet myself laughing.

It was a terrible humiliation for her. After class, Lü Meng chased her around the yard, singing the Black Cat Sheriff theme tune at the top of his voice.

Xiong Jinqiu was livid. She would happily have minced him up and thrown him into the stew pan. Lü Meng was a blundering idiot who was always shooting his mouth off, but when I heard him sing the Black Cat Sheriff's theme tune, I couldn't help having a good laugh.

Xiong Jinqiu wasn't letting it go. She actually went to Ms Liu and insisted that it was all my fault that she had suffered such embarrassment in front of the whole class. Ms Liu asked me to apologize to her but I refused outright. I never touched her skirt, why should I say sorry to her? Besides, she had lifted my skirt up in the corridor! She was the perp, and she was accusing me. It was ridiculous! I was Ms Liu's trusted helper, and a number of kids sitting in the rows behind us swore I was innocent. So it reached a stalemate.

It turned out that Xiong Jinqiu's skirt had been a size too big, so she had folded the waistband over and pinned it. Normally, it would have been fine, but we had been scuffling in the corridor and the pin came undone. It held while she scooted back into the classroom and sat down on her stool but gave way when she stood to go up to the podium. Her skirt slipped down and her knickers were on show – and I was the luckless suspect.

But I had my defenders: the Mountain Eagle Gang. 'You're not getting away with accusing our King, no chance!'

In the end, she came to me to say sorry, and begged me to call them off. It was weird, I'd somehow ended up as the king of a gang. And I quite liked it.

13

The sunshine boy

'Hello everyone, my name is Lü Yangguang, you can call me Donkey, Sunshine, whatever you like,' the new boy said, when the teacher asked him to go to the podium and introduce himself. We had just started in year six when he transferred to our class from another school. He didn't seem fazed at being in a new school, in fact, he actually joked about his names: Lü (the same surname as Lü Meng) sounded like 'donkey', and Yangguang meant 'sunshine'.

'Dumb donkey!' shouted Lü Meng, who was never stumped for something to say.

The whole class burst into laughter.

'That's a good name!' the new boy gave him a thumbs-up.

'So if he's a dumb donkey, what kind of donkey are you?' I needled Lü Meng, who seemed to have forgotten that he also had a donkey surname.

'I'm whatever kind of a donkey the King says I am!' Lü Meng replied.

'Big-mouth donkey!' said Ms Liu, butting in and taking us all by surprise. Our laughter raised the rafters.

Sunshine was dark-skinned and scrawny. He had a pudding basin haircut and smiling eyes and was kitted out in ill-fitting clothes that looked like hand-me-downs. He was completely open and unaffected, without a trace of deviousness or affectation. As he stepped down from the podium, we could see he was wearing a pair of plain, old-fashioned cloth shoes – rather sweet, we thought.

A week later, Sunshine Lü became the focus of the class. His seat was in the corner of the back row, where he kept his head down, ignoring anything that was going on. But he was a fast mover: during break time he was constantly on the go, in PE he ran faster than anyone else, and when the school bell rang, he shot out of the door. He was not an obvious swot but still managed to come top in the mid-term exams.

'He's superhuman, our Sunshine, he plays all day and still comes first! How does he do it?' I grumbled to Wanjun on our way home from school.

'Don't be taken in,' she said. 'He's a real swot at home! Come and stay at our house tonight. That'll open your eyes.'

Wanjun was being very mysterious and that made me curious, so I stayed over at hers that night.

We had become good friends and by now were almost inseparable. Her mother told me more than once that their door was open for me at any time, because ever since she got to know me, Wanjun seemed to have changed. She had always been moody, shouting at her family at the slightest provocation. But now she was patient and polite, lively and cheerful, and loved to talk and laugh. For twelve years, the love of her family had not managed to save her from the darkness she endured, and yet, in a very short time, our strong friendship had pulled her back from the brink. Wanjun's mother was delighted.

They liked me, and I liked them too. I liked the warmth of their home, I liked the dishes Wanjun's mother cooked, and I liked Wanjun's father, who had a great sense of humour. They embraced my eccentricities, and they made me laugh. Wanjun's mum used to say, half-seriously and half-jokingly, 'Yangyang, when you're grown-up, you can marry into the family and come and live with us!'

'All right,' I'd say. 'But I want a proper wedding sedan to fetch me!'

I was quite used to talking back to my aunt and uncle and I wasn't shy, so I just said the first thing that came into my head.

'Yay! Marry my big brother!' Wanjun was delighted at the idea. We used to laugh our heads off. Even her big brother joined in and sniggered.

When I had lunch at Wanjun's for the first time, I phoned my aunt to tell her. Later, I didn't bother to tell her. I spent the whole day with the Wei family. When I went home in the evening, my aunt scowled and needled me, 'What are you doing back here? Why don't you go and live there from now on?'

I really did stay the night at Wanjun's on many occasions. Every time I called to tell my aunt I wasn't going to be home, she would slam the phone down angrily. I didn't care. I had told her and that was that. What was the point in going home? It wasn't like anyone was expecting me.

That first night, Wanjun and I found a place to hide in a corner upstairs at her house, from where, by craning our necks, we could see what was happening in Sunshine Lü's courtyard. Sunshine certainly kept busy. Washing vegetables, boiling water, cooking rice, washing dishes… He never stopped for a moment.

'So this is what you meant when you said he was a hard worker?' I asked.

'Don't be so impatient. Just watch and you'll see.'

I was puzzled. Wanjun looked mysterious.

As the sky dimmed, the lights went on in the Lü yard. A fat middle-aged woman with her head wrapped in a scarf came to the door. She stood hands on hips in the doorway, swearing like a fishwife at Sunshine Lü and spitting on the ground. She was yelling in some dialect, and Wanjun and I could not understand a word even though we pinned our ears back. The fat woman finally got tired of abusing him. She turned around, spat out another gob of phlegm, and went back indoors. Then we heard a baby crying and grown-ups arguing inside.

The next thing that happened was that Sunshine Lü strolled out with his schoolbag in his left hand and a stool in his right. He sat down on the bench and, with the chopping board where he had been cutting vegetables on his lap, he began to write his homework by the faint light in the porch. When that light suddenly went off, he calmly lit a candle and continued with his homework.

I was appalled. What was this family like? Was the fat fishwife his mother? Why wasn't she looking after the house and cooking?

The next morning, we met Sunshine on our way out of the village to school. He was carrying his schoolbag and munching on half a mantou.

'Oh, you must be the Mountain Eagle King. I'm honoured indeed to meet you!' He saluted me mockingly, putting his palms together in the traditional way.

'Dumb Donkey, don't talk with your mouth full!' I glared at him. Damn it! Even a kid who had just transferred knew my nickname.

'I didn't know you lived near here,' he was still being very polite.

He fell into step beside us.

'We haven't seen you before.'

'That's because I only just moved in,' he said casually as he chewed on his mantou.

'Doesn't your mother cook for you?' I asked, looking at the stale bun.

'My aunt's just had a baby. She's still in the first month.'

'Your aunt?' Wanjun and I chorussed in astonishment. So that wasn't his family and the fat fishwife was not his mother?

'Why are you both looking like that?' Sunshine stuffed the last mouthful of mantou into his mouth, his cheeks bulging like a frog.

'Why aren't you with your mum and dad?'

'They're dead,' he said bluntly. Wanjun and I stood open-mouthed.

Then he laughed. 'You girls are so easy to fool.' At the crossroads, he turned and walked away.

'Damn dumb donkey! He should get a spanking, he doesn't deserve any sympathy!' Wanjun was so annoyed, she stamped her foot.

'Sunshine Lü, are you always as sunny as your name?' I murmured.

As I watched him receding into the distance, I couldn't help remembering how busy he had been the night before, preparing dinner.

Having come first in the exams, Sunshine Lü was not only the teachers' pet, but he also became an idol for the girls. They were always crowding around him asking for help with their maths problems. He was patient as he explained things to them. He used to say, 'When people come and ask me for help, it's showing respect.' He took his role very seriously.

As time went by, some of the boys screwed up their courage and asked him for help when they didn't understand in class and didn't dare to ask the teacher after class. More than once, he was so busy during the break that he didn't even have time to go to the toilet. When the class bell rang and everyone went back to their seats, he shot off to the toilets like an arrow.

Wanjun and I kept a close eye on him on the quiet. We betted that Sunshine was such a live wire that his willingness to help would not last more than a week. Sure enough, a week later, the end-of-class bell had not finished ringing before he had sneaked out the back door of the classroom. On the football field, he was faster than anyone in his tatty cloth shoes, he played harder, and kicked the ball more accurately.

He was all-round popular, and no one in the class ever got at him about his shoes. Until one day, during one of the boys' kick-about football games after PE, his shoe flew off and followed the ball. He scored a goal but his shoe hit the goalie bang in the face.

'Crap! Do people still wear tatty old shoes like this?' The goalie grabbed Sunshine's shoe and flung it in a nearby pile of rubbish.

There was a burst of laughter from the other players, and everyone's eyes were on Sunshine Lü. He flushed angrily, flung himself at the boy and kicked him to the ground with the foot which still had a shoe on. Before the boy could get up, Sunshine pounced on him again, and there was a punch-up on the grass.

'Stop it! Stop fighting!' The other boys closed in and dragged them apart.

'Hey! Sunshine's gone crazy!' exclaimed Wanjun as she jumped off the parallel bars.

'Good for him. If it was me, I'd beat the bastard up too,' I clenched my fists. I really wanted to pile in with Sunshine, and have a go at the mouthy goalkeeper.

'It's only a shoe. He can just pick it out of the rubbish, can't he?' Wanjun thought Sunshine's shoes were a great joke. She used to say to me, 'Doesn't he have any other shoes? Doesn't he feel embarrassed to come to school in a tatty old pair like that?'

'It's nothing to do with his shoes. It is his self-respect,' I told her. Wanjun looked down at her new leather shoes, and then at the worn-out flip-flops I was wearing. She bit her lip and said nothing more. The bell rang for the end of class, and the students walked towards the classroom. Sunshine, still only wearing one shoe, headed towards the rubbish dump, his head down. I followed his lonely figure with my eyes and felt really bad for him. I wanted to say something comforting but could not think what to say. Sunshine did not appear on the field for quite a few days after that.

'The fat woman went crazy last night. She got a broom and gave Sunshine a beating,' said Wanjun one day, not long after his tussle with the goalie.

So Sunshine was getting beaten up at home.

'Why? Is she off her head?'

'It sounded like he was late doing her dinner, as he got back from school late, and she got hungry.'

'The witch! Why can't she cook for herself? She's got hands and feet, hasn't she?' I exclaimed. I hate adults hitting kids, and the first time I set eyes on that fat cow, I knew she was a nasty piece of work.

'Yangyang, there's something I've been wanting to ask you...' Wanjun hesitated. 'Have you got a thing about Sunshine?'

'What on earth makes you think that? Why would I?'

'If you don't, then why are you so bothered by what happens to him?'

'Because we're in the same boat! He's living with relatives and so am I,' I blurted out. 'I'm just curious about him, and I feel sympathetic.'

'I'm sorry, Yangyang, I, I never thought of it like that…' Wanjun scratched her head in embarrassment. 'You being curious about him makes me wonder too. Why don't we just ask him when he comes out into the yard again?'

'Will she let him out tonight if he got a beating last night?'

'We can wait till the old cow's gone to sleep and he's out there with his candle, reading his book.'

'Good idea!' I agreed. That night, we sat on the upstairs balcony where we had a good view of the Lü family's movements but they could not see us. We watched as Sunshine served the old cow her dinner, then did all the washing up and tidied things away. Finally, he emerged with his schoolbag and his stool.

We raced down to their gate and peered through the gap between the gates.

'Psst!' we hissed at him.

Sunshine was engrossed in his homework and didn't hear us.

'Dumb donkey! Dumb donkey!'

He heard his nickname, and looked startled. Then he turned around and looked at the gate.

I raised my voice, 'Hey, Sunshine!'

Lü Yangguang tiptoed over, opened the gate a fraction, and poked his head out, 'What's up?'

Wanjun and I both beckoned him out. Sunshine looked back at the house, where all the lights were out. 'Wait a moment,' he said, and went and blew out the candle on the chopping board.

We went to Wanjun's bedroom, where Lü stood awkwardly, red in the face, fiddling with his hands. He looked so silly that we burst out laughing.

'You want help with your maths?' he asked and glanced at our workbooks spread out on the table.

'Already finished, thanks, we're fine.' Wanjun snapped the books shut.

'Then what's all this about? It's late!' Sunshine scratched his head, looking puzzled.

'Are…are your parents really dead?' Wanjun asked him straight out.

'Wanjun!' I was shocked at her bluntness. Sunshine just laughed, 'So you're checking my hukou, are you?'

'Of course not! We care about you, don't you see?' Wanjun offered him a packet of potato crisps.

'Thanks,' he smiled and took them. 'I was kidding you. They're not dead, but I never see them. I don't know where they are.'

'Why did they abandon you?' I was astonished. I mean, this was a society that favoured males, wasn't it? Why would they have let him go?

'Because they had four boys in a row,' Sunshine was fiddling with the unopened packet of crisps.

'Four boys!' Wanjun and I were open-mouthed with astonishment.

'Yes, I'm the fourth,' Sunshine pointed at himself. 'I don't know what they did with the other three, but I grew up out in the countryside with my grandparents.'

'You didn't live in their village?'

'How could we? The family house got demolished. I was left with my grandparents and my parents got as far away from the family planning officers as they could. I have no idea where they are.' Sunshine burst the crisps packet with a bang.

'That's horrible! They pulled your house down?' I could hardly believe my ears. I had only ever heard of fines from my aunt.

'So many horrible things happened in our village. There was one family where the woman had six baby girls, one after the other. The family planning officers threatened to confiscate the grain stores they had hidden in the cellar, so the family were going to strangle the last baby at birth.' Sunshine told us he was eight when that happened, and he had never forgotten it.

'Having to strangle your own flesh and blood to keep a few bags of grain! It's ridiculous!' Wanjun was so upset that she jumped to her feet.

'Well, she was already born by then and the officers knew the family couldn't pay the fine, and they couldn't pull their house down, so all they could do was confiscate their food supplies. And if they did that, it wouldn't be one baby that died, the whole family would starve.'

Wanjun and I sighed in unison. So there were girls in this world who were much worse off than we were.

'What happened to the little girl?' Wanjun grabbed his arm and gripped it hard.

'When the officers heard what they were planning to do, they unloaded the family's grain again.' Sunshine scratched his head, 'So the little girl survived, but she was taken away.'

'Why?' We both said together.

'It's what they call a transfer. That means when the family can't pay the excess-birth fine, they take the excess-birth baby and give it to someone who can't have children.'

'How do you know so much?'

'Granny told me.'

It's impossible to understand now the absurdity of those policies and how helpless people were against them.

'Why aren't you living with your grandparents then? Why are you here with your uncle and aunt?' I asked, to distract myself from thinking about the baby girl who was nearly strangled and then 'transferred'.

'They got old, and then they died. After that, a bachelor uncle took me in. He found someone to marry, a widow but she didn't want me around, so I was sent to my third uncle.' Sunshine spread his hands wryly and shrugged.

Wanjun and I were truly shocked. For a while, we didn't know what to say.

'Hey, I'd better go. If my aunt finds out, I'll be dead.'

'Wait a minute,' I jumped up. 'Do you hate them?'

'Who? My parents and my uncles and aunt?'

'Everyone, everything.'

'My grandparents were very good to me, so I had a very happy life for my first eight years. My uncle treated me well, and I was happy for the four years I was with him too. He did send me away but I understood why. He'd been a bachelor for so long and he finally managed to get himself a wife. I couldn't expect him to stay single for the rest of his life because of me.'

Suddenly, the skinny kid standing in front of us seemed like a hero. He was only twelve, and yet he sounded so mature and wise.

'What about your uncle and your aunt?' Wanjun stood up too.

'Well, if you've been spying on me from your balcony, you'll know what's been going on.'

'How…how did you know?' Wanjun stammered in confusion.

'So, do you hate your uncle and aunt?' I challenged him, looking him in the eyes.

'They feed me and pay for my classes and give me a place to sleep. I can't hate them.' Sunshine's frankness surprised me. 'My granny used to tell me that as long as someone gave me food, I should be grateful to them. She said there was nothing wrong with a bit of hardship when you're a child. I can live the kind of life I want when I'm grown up and can look after myself,' he said.

His words touched me. At that moment, I felt like an ungrateful little moaning minnie.

14

Brightly coloured days

'But I'm really going to be late, why would I lie to you?'

'I don't believe you'll be late just by washing these pots and pans!'

'I'm not stopping, I'm going to school now!'

'Damn brat, you're so stubborn! I'm coming to the school today to watch what you're doing! Heaven knows what you get up to there. You talk such rubbish!'

I was in year six and we were preparing to graduate from primary and go up to junior high school. We all had to take entrance exams and the school wanted the best possible success rate, so we were all told to be back early before afternoon classes for a self-study period. But my aunt was obsessed with mahjong around then, and for several days in a row, she hadn't even started cooking when I got home for lunch.

That day, it was half past one by the time I had shovelled down my meal and I was going to be late. I grabbed the bike and hurtled towards our gate. However, my aunt blocked my exit and told me I had to wash up a pile of pots and pans first. This led to an almighty row in the yard.

Tears welling up in my eyes and forcing down my resentment, I rode off to school without looking back.

'If you come to the school, you'll see what happens when you're late with lunch and then you force me to stay behind to wash up! You're so unreasonable!' I pedalled as fast as I could through the streets.

My aunt was in hot pursuit on her old bike, 'Damn you, brat! Why are you in such a mad hurry? Slow down! You'll fall off and kill yourself!'

The wind was blowing up a storm and dust filled the air. I could hear her behind me, 'Huh! Now where's that dratted girl gone? She talks such rubbish!'

But as soon as she rode in though the school gate, my aunt lost her swagger.

In the deserted school yard, the poplar leaves rustled in the trees. I put my bicycle away and headed for my classroom. Coming towards me was Ms Liu, our class teacher. I had nowhere to hide.

'What time is this? Why are you late again?' she reprimanded me. Tears of misery filled my eyes, and I looked mutely at the floor.

Just then, we heard a shout, 'Ms Liu, Ms Liu! This girl's so stubborn!' And there was my aunt hurrying towards us.

There were no flies on Ms Liu. She grasped the situation instantly. 'Go on up to your classroom,' she told me. I went. But at the corner of the stairs, I stopped and strained my ears. I heard my aunt protest, 'That dratted girl! Ms Liu, all I was trying to do was get her to wash a few pots. And she flew at me!' I was keen to hear more, but Ms Liu said politely, 'Please calm down, Mrs Shen. Let's go and talk in the office.'

In the classroom, the maths teacher, Ms Qin, was writing maths problems on the blackboard and the others were busy copying them down.

'Miss,' I muttered, my head bent. This was the umpteenth time I had been late.

Ms Qin glanced at me impatiently, 'Come in and sit down.'

Under my classmates' curious stares, I crept to my seat. Tears spattered onto the back of my hand.

'Yangyang, are you okay?' Wanjun scribbled on a scrap of paper and passed it to me.

'It's okay, I just had a row with the old cow,' I wrote back, crumpled my note and threw it at her.

I had never talked about my aunt yelling at me and hitting me because you weren't supposed to wash the family's dirty linen in public. Now, with the washing-up argument, Ms Liu had found out, but I absolutely didn't want all my classmates to know too. I pulled my hanky out of my pocket and wiped my eyes. I just wanted to forget it.

The next day when we went home for lunch, Wanjun came up to me, 'Yangyang, why don't you come and eat with us today? Your aunt might be late again.'

'Thanks, Wanjun, but I can't keep scrounging your food. It's okay, after yesterday's row, she won't forget to cook today.'

Actually, I would have loved to go to Wanjun's, but I felt I was too old now to be begging from other people's tables. They never said anything, but I didn't feel good about it.

That day, my aunt started cooking at half past twelve. I sat down to eat at ten past one. At 1:20, I finished, washed the bowls and chopsticks, and pedalled frantically back to school.

Surely everything would be fine if I got there at 1:30, which was when we were supposed to arrive. I had no idea that my classmates were already in their places as I started my lunch.

During the break, Wanjun cornered me in the corridor and whispered mysteriously, 'Yangyang, I need to tell you something, please don't be angry.'

'What's up? You're scaring me!'

'Before you came today, Ms Liu held a quick class meeting. She said that you had special dispensation to be late, just you. And she said...' Wanjun hesitated.

'What? What did she say?'

'She said the reason you're late is because you have to wash up and do the housework for your aunt.'

Wanjun looked relieved at having got it off her chest, but my head was buzzing, and my eyes had gone blurry. Why had Ms Liu done this? Surely it was enough for her to know? Why did she have to tell the whole class that I was late because I was doing the washing-up? No wonder I had sensed something odd when I walked in today.

'Yangyang, don't take it to heart,' Wanjun urged me. 'I only told you so you wouldn't feel like a fool. Better than being kept in the dark, isn't it? Ms Liu's probably doing it to protect herself too, so if you're late and she doesn't say anything, the rest of them won't think it's favouritism.' Wanjun grabbed my hand and tried to comfort me. Just then, Xiong Jinqiu turned up, 'Hey, look at this, the dishwasher's actually standing in the corridor talking!'

I flew at her and grabbed her hard by the collar. 'Don't you dare say that again! Are you still feeling sorry for yourself because you showed your knickers in class? Well, don't blame me! I already told you what happened, and I don't give a toss if you don't believe me. You don't want to be my friend? Fine. But if you ever call me dishwasher again, I'll beat the hell out of you, even if I get expelled from school for it!'

I don't know where I got the strength from, but she couldn't shake me off, however hard she struggled. She was quite scared at my sudden belligerence, 'It was only a joke. No need to get so worked up about it!'

Well, maybe I had overreacted a bit and got too emotional. I let go of her, and went slowly back to the classroom, my head bent. Behind me, I could hear Wanjun defending me, 'Jinqiu, Yangyang's always been your friend, how could you put her down like that?'

'Hey, it was a joke,' Jinqiu straightened her collar and looked aggrieved.

'A joke? That's your idea of a joke, is it?' Wanjun turned on her heel and stalked back into the classroom, leaving Jinqiu alone in the corridor.

All that afternoon, I couldn't concentrate on the lessons. I could not figure out why Ms Liu had said that. What on earth had she and my aunt talked about? It was all Auntie's fault. If it weren't for her,

Jinqiu would never have called me a dishwasher in front of everyone.

I was desperate that people shouldn't know I was anxious and afraid. But I *was* afraid. I was a really good student, and I didn't want the nickname 'dishwasher' hung around my neck. It was mortifying. I felt everyone's eyes staring at me. I could almost hear their whispers, 'Look at her, she's a dishwasher.'

After school, I stayed on in the classroom by myself and did my homework. The afterglow of the setting sun shining on me was the only warmth I felt that day.

Suddenly, I heard a voice from the back row, 'Got something on your mind?' Sunshine Lü was walking towards me, smiling. I looked around and realized we were the only two left.

'What are you doing here still?' I asked him as I put my things in my schoolbag.

'My uncle took my aunt to stay with her mother. They'll be away for a couple of days.'

I grunted. I wasn't in the mood for chatting.

'I saw what happened in the corridor,' said Sunshine, sitting down at the desk next to mine. My heart skipped a beat. That was the thing I had dreaded, and now it had happened. 'If you're a dishwasher, what am I?' He pulled a funny face at me.

'What do you mean?' I frowned at him.

'If you're a dishwasher, I must be a housework robot.' He roared with laughter.

'If your aunt turned up at the school to complain about your housework, I don't think you'd think it was a joke, do you?' I said sullenly, picked up my schoolbag and turned to go.

'Hey!' He wouldn't let me through the door. 'Don't get angry, I just wanted to say it doesn't matter what other people think of you, you just have to be yourself!'

'I know you're trying to be kind. Thanks, but I really don't need it.' I leaned against one of the desks in the front row.

'Grow a thick skin,' he advised me. 'Otherwise life's exhausting.'

He sat down next to me.

'Don't worry, I'm a lot thicker-skinned than you think.' I really believed there was no one in this world who had a thicker skin than me.

'You know what? Ever since I started in school, I've always been one of the last to bring my fees. Every time the teacher made those of us who hadn't paid up stand up in class, I felt so embarrassed. But I never let it bother me for long. Maybe it's because I'm calm by nature, or just because I was lucky enough up till now to have a very warm family and I met so many good people. For instance, when the other kids had great-looking schoolbags and I didn't, my granny made me one out of a flour sack. It was really cool, and practical. She was good at sewing. And when it was my birthday and we couldn't afford a cake, my grandfather made me a huge eggy laobing in our big iron wok. And when I was in year four, and I couldn't pay for my school uniform, our class teacher bought it for me herself. She never told anyone, so no one in the class knew. Being poor is so embarrassing but I never let it bother me for long, and all my memories are warm ones.'

Sunshine seemed absorbed in his good memories, but his words had touched a raw nerve and made me remember some things I had tried very hard to suppress.

'Not everyone in this world is as lucky as you,' I said.

'What I mean is, Ms Liu was trying to help you but she went about it the wrong way.'

'I don't need sympathy or help!' I grabbed my schoolbag and walked off. I absolutely didn't want him to see me as vulnerable.

'Yangyang!' he shouted after me from the door of the classroom, 'You're the King, we gotta show them what a great king you really are!'

I smiled through my tears, turned and waved at him, 'On your knees with you, this king's going back to the mountain.'

That conversation laid the foundations for a firm friendship between me and Sunshine Lü. From then on, wherever Wanjun and

I were, he was there too. Lots of mornings, we used to kidnap him on the way to school so we could share some hot spicy soup and a fried laobing. We never let him pay. On weekends, we dragged him off with us into the fields to fly a kite or catch grasshoppers. After school, we took him down to the river and played ducks and drakes with flat stones. When we had free activity in our PE class, he taught us to play football.

Whenever he got the chance, Sunshine used to sneak out of the house. Even getting yelled at by his aunt didn't dampen his enjoyment. He used to say that, with us, there was always something to laugh about. The funniest time was when a theatre troupe came to the village. The three of us wriggled our way through the crowd. We got backstage by crawling under the stage, and saw the actors getting their makeup on. When no one was looking, I borrowed a paintbrush and gave Wanjun and Sunshine stripy cat faces. By the time someone in the troupe spotted us, we'd done it and were gone.

In the second half of term, the pressure was on because we had our high school entrance exams at the end of term. Ms Liu not only made us arrive in class early every morning to go over our work, but she also shortened the lunch break to forty minutes. I had a dispensation to arrive late, but I never used it. It would have been humiliating. I preferred to skip breakfast and save my one yuan for lunch at the snack stalls around the school – a bowl of rice noodles, a portion of lamian noodles, a dish of liangpi noodles, a basket of steamed buns, a carton of soy milk or a portion of flatbread kept me going. That way, I didn't need to go home. It was the only way to be in class on time. Auntie was so unreliable, I could only rely on myself, and I cultivated that skill from an early age.

I used the precious early morning time to learn my notes for the day's classes off by heart. That way, I didn't have to worry about doing that on top of the mountain of homework I would have in the evening. That year, I can't remember how many books I memorized. I do remember that just before the exam, the city education authority issued a new policy: 'Primary school graduates will no longer be enrolled in high school based on their test scores. They will be allocated a place according to where their hukou is registered.'

Thank heavens I had the hukou my uncle and aunt had bought for me seven years before. Now, it finally came into its own. There had been horrible times when we had to fill in our personal information on school forms. I used to chew my pen and watch other kids dashing off the names and occupations of their parents, not daring to bring out my hukou in front of them. I was afraid they would see that my document had no father and no mother, and that my birth date was recorded as two years older than my real age. Once, one of my classmates saw my birthdate was recorded as 21st December 1984, and he stared at me and piped up, 'Wow! Were you really born in 1984? What an old woman you are!' And he laughed merrily.

Any time that happened, I would grab their arm and insist, 'You know what? My hukou has the wrong age on it! I was born on 1st January 1986!'

It upset me so much that, when I got home, I would complain to my aunt and uncle, 'I was born in 1986, why have I got the wrong date of birth?'

'Damn brat, you should count your lucky stars you've got a hukou at all! Why are you complaining?' my aunt usually retorted.

'What does it matter anyway? You'll be able to retire from your job two years before anyone else!' added my uncle.

I honestly did not know whether to laugh or cry. Retiring early really was taking the long view. I had not finished elementary school yet, and not even my uncle was retired. Why was he thinking about my retirement? It was ridiculous.

The policy change happened right before we were on the point of going up to high school and suddenly the pressure was off. Some families were happy and some were annoyed, but the kids who used to mock me for my fake hukou were now worried stiff all of a sudden. They mainly had village hukou, and if they had no way of pulling strings with the town high schools, they would end up in a rural high school. They would much rather have had a town hukou like mine. At least then they would have been guaranteed a place in a key high school in town.

'I used to be super annoyed because of the hukou they bought me. Who would have thought it would have come in this useful? Life's a funny thing, isn't it?' I sighed, on my way home from school with Wanjun.

'Hey, you're getting to be such a scholar!' she said. 'You know I've got a phobia about Chinese lessons! Why does Ms Liu make us learn so much stuff off by heart? It makes me want to puke!' Wanjun pretended to gag.

I laughed. 'Don't exaggerate! I don't like all this rote learning either, but I'd rather recite a book than do maths. I only have to look at one problem to get a headache.'

I had hated mathematics ever since Ms Hua had written 'careless' all over my face. And my uncle's rigid teaching methods had only strengthened my deep hatred of the subject.

'That's typical of you, "I'd rather recite a book than do maths",' she said. 'But what a complicated story about your hukou. Say a prayer that we get sent to the same school!'

We were naive enough to imagine that things would definitely turn out the way we wanted them. However, when the announcement in red type was posted outside the school gate a month later, our names appeared on different pages: Wei Wanjun, No. 13 High School; Wu Shanying, No. 12 High School.

'Just when everyone's finally got used to how I look, I have to start again somewhere new. Yangyang, how am I going to manage without you?' Wanjun cried despairingly.

The tears ran down her cheeks, and I put my arm around her shoulders. Any words of comfort felt inadequate. Her big head wasn't growing on my neck. And no matter how uplifting and impassioned I was in encouraging her, it was her that people were going to stare and point at, not me.

'What's up? Has the sky fallen down? Or are you crying for joy because you both got places at good city schools?' We heard a cheery voice and looked up to see Sunshine Lü, beaming in front of us. It suddenly occurred to us to wonder which middle school he was going to. Both Wanjun and I scanned the list.

'Don't bother, this place is too small to hold me,' Sunshine waved his hand in front of my face.

'What do you mean?' I batted his hand away.

'I don't have a hukou, so no school's gonna register me.' He shrugged.

'What?' Wanjun and I cried in unison. We couldn't believe our ears.

'Hush!' he hurriedly pulled us to one side. 'The teachers know but no one else in the class knows.'

I still didn't believe him, 'Haha! Alright, stop making up stories.'

'I'm not lying, really! I told you about my family, didn't I? It's just that I forgot to tell you that I still don't have a hukou, because I was an excess-birth.'

'But your school work is so good, isn't there any school willing to bend the rules and give you a place?' Wanjun frowned. All her own anxieties seemed to have evaporated all of a sudden. After all, Sunshine had no hukou and no school place. It made her own problems look very insignificant.

'This is a world where it's your hukou – not your grades – that counts,' Sunshine said with a mocking smile.

'Can't your uncle and aunt get one for you?' I asked, still incredulous that something this ridiculous could be happening to a friend of mine: the lack of a document was going to deprive him of any more schooling.

'You see, my uncle rents that house, and he has his own wife and kid to support. Even if he had any strings to pull, he wouldn't be able to afford it,' said Sunshine.

Actually, we all knew that his uncle was never going to spend money on a kid who wasn't part of his family.

Wanjun and I were overwhelmed. We didn't know what to say to make him feel better. 'Sunshine!' Just then, Ms Liu, who was nearby, called him over.

They stood by the flower bed next to the teachers' office, and Ms Liu stroked Sunshine's hair and spoke quietly in his ear. Sunshine nodded obediently. The warm sun shone down on them, and the whole scene looked so tender and beautiful.

I began to fantasize that our kind-hearted teacher had decided to adopt him and was going to sort him out a hukou right then and there, so that he could get a place at junior high school, then senior high school, and then get into a prestigious university.

But it was not to be. When we all received our admission letters, Sunshine took the train south to Guangzhou with his uncle and started work. Sunshine was gone. In a farewell letter to Wanjun and me, he wrote, 'My childhood may have been grey, but the days I spent with you two were brightly coloured.' We both burst into floods of tears.

There are starry nights when I find my mind drifting back to that bright boy with the pudding basin haircut and eyes that made slits when he laughed, and the warm words he said to me that sunny afternoon. He came and left in no time at all, staying long enough only to beam a bright light on us and vanish again. Other people may have forgotten him, but I won't. Deep in my heart, I want to believe that Sunshine's life as he grew up was as warm and brilliant as his name.

15

English class monitor

I had imagined that I would be able to go back home to Shandong after I finished elementary school. But all of a sudden, the whole of Dongzha village was demolished. The inhabitants got compensation and moved into rented houses for the time being. My parents said grandly, 'Yangyang, wait until you finish junior high to come back. We'll have a new house by then.' It was such a lame excuse. I didn't care what kind of a house I lived in. All I wanted was to be with my family. Even a straw stook would have felt cosy and warm if we were together.

The long summer holidays were nearly here, and all the kids from the better-off families started cramming English at summer school classes. I knew perfectly well that my aunt and uncle would never give me two hundred yuan to pay for them. I could tell exactly what they would say, 'You'll be learning English in your first year, what'll you do then if you know it all already?'

Rather than be humiliated again, I might as well enjoy my freedom and the lazy summer days. I thought it all through: compared with Sunshine Lü, who had no hukou at all, I was very lucky. Not only could I carry on at school, but I'd been given a place at a key high school in town because I had an urban hukou.

During my wanderings around the village, something on the

second-hand book stall grabbed my attention. It was a fifty-cent Japanese manga comic about a robot cat called Doraemon. As soon as I discovered this big blue lovable cat, my heart was captured. Doraemon was so good-hearted and quick-witted, and so forgiving and caring with Noby. No matter what Noby did, he was always there to look after the boy, to encourage him and support him, and get him out of trouble. Doraemon frequently appeared in my dreams, and he used to get his Anywhere Door out of his pocket and say to me, 'Yangyang, with this, you can go home whenever you want!' Fujiko Fujio's imaginative stories brought me solace that summer. I immersed myself in their world and nothing could bring me back.

My aunt and uncle felt that summer school classes were just another way to squeeze more money out of parents, but the problem was that almost all my classmates attended. When school started, and we were in the first English class, I was dumbfounded to discover that everyone knew the twenty-six letters of the alphabet off by heart. I could not even read them, let alone say them aloud. Worse still, I was left speechless when our English teacher, a plump woman called Ms Gu, covered three lessons from the book in one class. A lot of the kids were not only able to keep up with her, they actually seemed to be enjoying it.

This is crazy! Crazy! Wake up, Ms Gu, not everyone in this class started their English over the summer! I felt like saying as I sat mutely in my corner, praying that she didn't call my name.

Ms Gu, in English, 'How old are you?'

Me, awkwardly standing up to answer, 'I'm fine, thank you.'

The other kids jeered loudly. I was the laughing stock of the class again.

Before the mental fog induced by English had cleared, physics and chemistry made my head spin too. I had hated mathematics, and now I added physics and chemistry to my hated subjects.

I felt completely deflated. I had started with so many hopes for high school.

After a month, we had our first monthly test. These terrifying tests were the weapon used by the class teacher, Ms Zhai Shijie, to sort out the best students from the rest. We were then seated according to our grades. It wasn't forever. If you were determined and bright enough, you could rise to the ranks of the best in the next monthly exam.

There were sixty-six students in the class, eight in a row, eight rows, and two left over. Two wretched students with the worst marks in the test were parked right in each corner in the very back row. I made a mess of my maths, physics, chemistry and English tests but thankfully, I did well in Chinese and that saved me, so I ended up in the third row from the back.

Thank heavens I don't have to sit in the back corner all on my own, I thought. *What kind of a weird way of teaching is this? It's humiliating!* I really could not understand Ms Zhai's 'best-students-at-the-front system'. At the beginning, I tried to work hard, but all the teachers, no matter what subject, only asked questions of kids in the first few rows. Even if those in the rows further back did manage to answer a question, we never got the credit for it. Like Ms Zhai, the other teachers regarded us as trash. They were not real teachers to me; they did not deserve that title. As time went by, the repeated monthly exams almost killed me. I had hardly got around to digesting any new work before the exam came around again. I soon slipped from the third row from the back to the last-but-one row. And back there, while the teacher and her precious pets were immersed in their 'sea of knowledge' at the front of the class, the kids in the back row went to sleep with their heads on the desk, or daydreamed, read comics, or ate snacks, and passed notes back and forth, and did not bother to make a secret of it.

But there were some consolations: I fell in love with San Mao's books and with Watase Yuu's mangas. I was fourteen by then, living in the world they had created, dreaming that one day these lovely people would take me by the hand and we would travel the world together. I basically stopped studying. I became one of Ms Zhai's 'non-studying girls'. And Ms Zhai was so horrible to me that I used to call her the Demoness. It was not only her fierce expression, but there was the fact that she sometimes turned up in morning reading class without makeup, and that was scary. She normally plastered her face in it.

I almost laughed one day when she gave me a telling-off for being late. Her dead-white pointy face and her bloodless lips, coupled with her two pointed canines, made her look just like a witch.

Ms Zhai despised the kids in the back row. The other teachers too, and even the top students in the front rows pulled nasty faces at us all day long. For a whole year, I hardly spoke to my classmates in the front rows and I did not even know the names of many of them. They looked down on me, whereas I regarded them as beneath my notice.

One morning in the first half of our second year, the Demoness suddenly went crazy because there was English homework missing. She got Zou Quan, the English class monitor, to go through every homework book to check who had had the audacity not to finish their work, after she had specifically stated her requirements.

'Oh my god, this is so scary!' I whispered to my desk buddy. 'I'm glad I did my English homework first last night, otherwise she'd kill me!'

But then I heard, 'So it's you three girls! How dare you not do your homework!' The Demoness had a bit of paper in her hand, 'Zhang Li, Cheng Xiaoyan, Wu Shanying! The three of you, come and stand up here, right now!'

'What?' I could hardly believe my ears. I had definitely handed in my homework. I hurried up to the podium, 'Miss, I handed in my homework. Why have you got my name on the list?'

The English monitor, Zou Quan, jumped up. 'You handed in your homework, but you were asked to write each word out ten times, and you only wrote it eight times!'

'Did you hear that? You missed two times for each word. Did you eat them?' the Demoness interrogated me in a loud voice.

I thought my lungs were going to explode. Zou Quan was being so mean. She knew that a whole lot of boys in the back row had done no homework at all. She hadn't told on them. She had landed me in it instead. She had actually counted how many words I had written out. How dare she?!

I so wanted to check that pile of homework books, one by one, and see if the top students had really written every word ten times over.

'Out, all three of you. Go and stand in the corridor and finish your homework!' The Demoness shooed us out impatiently.

I had been shamed in front of the whole class. If it had not been that I didn't want to make a big fuss and involve the kids whom Zou Quan was protecting, I really would have picked up the whole pile of homework books and gone through them one by one.

'Damn it, what a bitch she is!' grumbled Zhang Li when we were outside the door together.

'My desk buddy didn't do his, and she didn't report him!' Cheng Xiaoyan chimed in.

I was even more aggrieved than they were because they hadn't done their homework at all, while I had just missed a tiny bit out. 'She's so prissy, she has her favourite boys, and she's not gonna let the Demoness tell them off. But we're just girls, so she dumps us in it! She's toxic!' I said.

Zou Quan's mother had been showering the Demoness with presents, we knew that, so Zou Quan not only got a place in the front row in the classroom, she was English monitor too, even though her marks were no more than average. We also knew that the Zou family had got rich quick. It seemed like money really was a wonderful thing. Even the Demoness bowed down before it.

There was a reason why Zou Quan had it in for me, and that was because the boy she had a crush on sat behind me. He was a long way away from where the top students sat in the front row. She could only gaze at her heartthrob from a distance, while I sat right in front of him. I was always a bit of a tomboy and got on well with the boys. I liked this one and we often talked and laughed together. Of course, Zou Quan could not fail to notice, and she seethed with resentment towards me.

That Friday, the Demoness made an announcement from the podium, 'At nine o'clock this coming Sunday morning, you will all participate in the Maths Olympiad the city has organized. Let me be clear, I want you all there, I want no absentees!'

I was always desperate to get to the weekend so I could read my comics all night. It was really too bad that I had to get up early and make a show of participating in their stupid maths competition. I was always failing my maths tests, so there wasn't much point in me going along. But the Demoness was adamant, and I wasn't sure if I dared skive off.

That Sunday morning, I bumped into the Demoness at the top of the stairs. 'Wu Shanying, have you been rude to Zou Quan?' she accosted me.

'What? No, I haven't!'

'Then why did her mother come and find me to make a complaint about you?'

'When did she hear me being rude to her? I didn't!'

News travelled fast. I had only a bit of a grumble that Zou Quan landed me in it when I didn't finish my homework. How had it reached her ears? Besides, Zhang Li and Cheng Xiaoyan were the first to start grumbling. Why were all fingers being pointed at me?

'You're so stubborn, girl! There are witnesses and you're still quibbling?!' The Demoness was calling out her witnesses.

'Even if I did, there's no evidence! There's no recording, Zou Quan just picked on anyone, I could just as easily make up a story about her bad-mouthing me!' I said rebelliously.

'Get lost, go home, girl! You're impossible!' Ms Zhai was telling me to get lost? Was this the kind of language a government-funded teacher was supposed to use?

'I don't want to join this stupid dumb Olympiad anyway!' I retorted.

I felt I had been utterly humiliated. I turned around and walked away.

But where could I go? By the time I got to the school gate, I was regretting losing my temper and arguing with the Demoness. It looked like things were going from bad to worse. The thought made me burst into tears.

Then a girl from my class came up to me, 'Wu Shanying, what's the matter? Why are you crying?'

She seemed like my saviour and I spilled out all my grievances.

'Oh, forget it, the old bat just got angry. You come back with me right now. You've got to join the Olympiad.' The girl said briskly, and pulled me back into the school.

'I can't go back!' I protested. 'If I go back and she kicks me out in front of the whole class, it'll be my fault for going in there.'

I felt the blow to my self-esteem keenly, and I really did not want to be humiliated again.

'Right, I'll be honest with you, but don't tell anyone. It was Ms Zhai who asked me to come down and find you. The education authorities have stipulated that every kid has to participate. If you don't go, it'll be a black mark against her. She asked me to come and get you, so you just pretend you don't know anything, go in and sit down and do the test and then you can go home.'

I was really surprised that the Demoness had sent someone for me, and I was a bit dubious as I followed her inside. When I got to the door of the classroom, Ms Zhai glared at me. 'I want your parents here on Monday morning!' she said.

I walked silently to my desk, my head bowed. My parents? She must be joking! Heaven only knows how the Demoness would embellish her story when she told my aunt about my bad behaviour. Besides, knowing Auntie's violent temper, I was willing to bet that she would charge into the classroom and give me a beating. I don't want to die such a wretched death in front of my classmates. I decided that I was not going to get Auntie in, no matter how much the Demoness yelled at me. Monday came, and I sat in my seat, terrified and saying a prayer. I figured that as long as Ms Zhai didn't mention anything during the morning reading session, I would be safe.

All of us in the class sat reading our lesson aloud, and the Demoness paced up and down the podium. Suddenly, she commanded, 'Stop! We're having a class meeting this morning.'

My heart was in my mouth as soon as I heard those words.

'Let me emphasize, and I'm not going to repeat it again, that from now on, English and maths homework, in fact, all the homework your teachers assign you, must be handed in on time! And it's three strikes and you're out! If you fail to complete your work three times, you will leave this school forthwith.'

That scared me rigid. But at least she hadn't made me get my aunt in, I thought, my palms slippery with sweat.

'Now I've got something important to say,' Ms Zhai went on. 'From today, the English class monitor will be Wu Shanying.'

I almost fainted.

There were shouts of, 'Congratulations! Congratulations, Shanying! Make sure you look after us properly! Wow! You got promoted quickly! Congratulations! Shanying, you made it, eh? You better make sure you cover my back!' (This was from one of the back-row boys.)

And after class, more of the back-row kids, Ms Zhai's black sheep, rushed up to congratulate me. It was amazing that one of the ones she regarded as scum of the earth had made it to be class monitor. It was clear they thought that, with me in charge, they could get away without handing in their homework at all!

I secretly decided, then and there, that the Demoness had set me up for this. She had deliberately chosen someone like me, who had failed her English tests, to be class monitor. *I know what you're up to*, I muttered to myself. *You just want me to get into trouble with the other kids every time I collect the homework!* But I wasn't going to fall for that trick. I made up my mind that I would do the job properly and be an exemplary English monitor.

That night, when I got home, I got the tape recorder and listened to my English tape over and over again, until I had memorized quite a long text – for the first time. When the words of English popped easily out of my mouth, one by one, I startled even myself. Before, I used to stumble over even a short piece.

Early the next morning, our heavily pregnant teacher Ms Gu arrived and asked, 'Who's learned the text I taught yesterday? Please come to the podium and recite it.' The top students in the front row buried their heads in their textbooks and went over the words again, but I marched up to the podium, textbook in hand.

Ms Gu looked taken aback when she saw it was me. Looking dubious, she took the textbook from me. It took me two minutes to recite the whole text. I was word-perfect. Ms Gu was astonished.

I took my book back and marched back to my seat, past the rows of the top students. All eyes were on me. I felt like saying, *It was only a text! I memorized tons of stuff when I was Chinese class monitor in primary school! Yeah! The Mountain Eagle King's broken out!*

'Did you really learn all that off by heart, Shanying? Wow, you're awesome!'

'I'm confused, how did you manage that? Did someone put a spell on you? You recited a foreign language!'

'Shanying, you're putting a lot of pressure on us! I can't even recite the first paragraph.'

I threw my textbook down on the table, 'Comrades, no one's gonna oppress me or look down on me, ever again! Sister Shanying's gonna stand tall. I'm in charge from now on!'

When I really made up my mind to do something, nothing could stop me. I gave all my attention to the lesson, and if I didn't understand, I went to the office after class to ask the teacher to explain. When I got home in the evening, I listened to the tape recorder over and over again until I had the text off by heart. In the morning, before I got up, I lay in bed and repeated it to myself. I even rode my bicycle to school holding the handlebar with my left hand and the textbook in my right hand, revising it. I was determined not only to learn the text but to be absolutely word-perfect. My efforts won me hard-earned praise from Ms Gu. But soon she left to have her baby and in her place, we got a young English teacher called Shen Jianping, who just graduated from university.

As soon as he arrived in the classroom the first day, he said in a loud voice, 'Where's my English monitor? Come along, get up so I know who you are!' Everyone's eyes swivelled to the back of the class. I stood up awkwardly. Mr Shen jumped down from the podium and came towards me, 'Comrade Monitor, I need your advice!' He actually bent down to listen to me. I was overwhelmed by all this attention and stood dumbly with a silly smile on my face. The whole class burst out laughing at this comical spectacle.

Right from the start, Mr Shen never played by the rules. He had a very idiosyncratic teaching style. Before class, he would throw the textbook into the desk drawer, and sit with one leg crossed over the other and talk to us, completely off the cuff, about Stephen Chow and films. Then, he would get the textbook out again, and flip through the lesson, pointing out new words and phrases, highlighting the key points, and in fifteen minutes, he was done! The remaining twenty minutes, he would give over to more unscripted chat. He talked about his college life, talked about China's education system, and gossiped about the hottest film celebrities.

Although he only spent fifteen minutes of each class on the textbook lesson, he made us memorise large chunks of text, and learn from it. He gave us his reasons, 'There's no point in me standing up here today talking to you if you don't put your own brains to work. It's too early for you to learn a lot of grammar. Use the tapes and learn the English texts. Read them aloud to improve your feel for the language. The thing is, learning a language means learning to speak it fluently, rather than just answering questions and getting high marks in the exams.'

He was one of a kind, and I liked him very much. He liked me even more. Mr Shen didn't know that I had only just become monitor. What struck him was that his class monitor had crystal clear pronunciation, and learned the texts perfectly. For morning reading sessions, he always made me stand on the podium and recite the text in front of the class. Then, he delegated control to me, and anyone wanting to recite the text came to me. Those were wonderful times. I became a hit in the class.

Mr Shen regularly asked me questions in class, and after class, he often gave me extra time and tutoring. And so I fell madly in love with English. Even in my favourite class, Chinese, I would find myself going through what I had learned in the English class before. I progressed in leaps and bounds. Ms Zhai's glasses almost fell off her nose in astonishment when she saw my results in the mid-term tests. The non-studying girl, as she used to call me, had come first in English! She couldn't quarrel with the marks because the kids sitting around me during the test were either from the back row or were in their first year at high school, that is, a year below me. Even if I had wanted to cheat, there was no one to copy from.

From then on, Ms Zhai used me as an example of what you could achieve if you were determined enough. 'Look at Wu Shanying,' she would say. 'How did she learn English? She had determination and she studied hard! Nothing's impossible in this world if you really want to succeed! You should all learn from Shanying!'

When the Demoness praised me from the podium, I made a big show of gazing devoutly at her, while I muttered quietly, 'Demoness Zhai, you old cow! You never did anything for me, why should I thank you?'

The kids around me could see my expression and hear the weird things I was saying. They had the hardest time controlling their laughter but they were also afraid of Ms Zhai. She might haul them over the coals in front of the whole class. One day, my mocking comments had spectacular results: while Ms Zhai pontificated from the podium, and I looked at her with a fake smile pasted on my face, all those kids in the back rows bent over their desks, their heads bowed. The way their shoulders were twitching, it looked from a distance as if they were sobbing their hearts out, so moved were they by their teacher's sermon. In fact, they were howling with silent laughter.

I had applied myself to English just to prove to the Demoness that I could do it. I never imagined that one day I would be held up as a model to the other students. The thing was, I regularly failed my English tests before that. But anyway, that is what happened. I worked hard and was duly rewarded. Sheer serendipity, really.

If we had not had Mr Shen as a teacher, I might just have plodded through my English classes doggedly the way the others did, instead of falling in love with the language. But from the first moment that he arrived in the class, I liked his youth and energy, his teaching theories, his wit and humour, and the way he treated every student equally. And since he only spent fifteen minutes on the coursework, you had to pay attention to every word and sentence he said.

'I give you complete freedom, and you must give me complete respect,' he used to say, and he was as good as his word. When he had finished teaching us, we could talk amongst ourselves, eat snacks, walk around and go to the toilet at any time without asking him. If English was our last class, we could even knock off early and go home as long as he had finished teaching. I embraced his flexible teaching methods wholeheartedly because he allowed us to control our own learning. But the front-row students relied on learning the teacher's notes by rote, and they did not like it. They got together to write a letter of complaint to the Demoness, demanding a different English teacher. Ms Zhai had always considered Mr Shen's methods odd, and sloppy too. She thought a good teacher should be like her, and force-feed the students' minds with knowledge. She would coach us in all the key questions that were going to come up in the exam. Her message was, *Make sure you remember every single bit of this! A forty-five minute class is not enough for me, so how could fifteen minutes be enough when Shen Jianping teaches.*

A vigorous campaign to get rid of Mr Shen began. The Demoness appealed to the head to condemn him for neglect of his duties and not taking the students' futures seriously. Parents of the top students came and doorstepped the head in his office, demanding that their child should get a new English teacher. 'Otherwise, I'll transfer my child to another school tomorrow!' they threatened.

There were cries of, 'Why does my precious girl have to suffer such a useless teacher?' And, 'How can a teacher let the children run wild like that?'

A week after these protests, my favourite teacher Mr Shen resigned and was gone forever. Before leaving, he said to me with a smile, 'I'm leaving, but don't get upset or sad. If I hadn't been pushed out today, I would have left sooner or later anyway. I have my dream, and now I'm off to be the real me! You're my star student. Remember, you're in charge of your own learning. And you should learn because you love it, and work hard of your own volition, not because the teacher or your parents make you, or because you've got exams! Give it your best efforts, girl, and the day will come when you make a name for yourself and, as long as you remember your old teacher, I'll be happy!'

Mr Shen patted me on the shoulder, turned and got on his motorbike (we always thought that was so cool!), grabbed the helmet from the handlebar, and buckled it on. Then he revved the accelerator, and roared off towards the school gate. I watched him go but I didn't cry. Mr Shen was gone because he had fulfilled his mission. I had learned that no one in this world is always there to watch over you and lead you by the hand. My mentor had taken me to the door, but the next steps depended on me.

I had become English monitor and a top student by accident. My road to studying English was going to be a very long one, and even I had no clear idea just how long.

16

The volcano erupts

'Damn brat! Phone!'
Auntie bellowed into the yard from the front room.

'Coming!'

I hurriedly finished hanging out my clothes on the clothesline strung across the middle of the yard.

'You'll wear out your clothes if you keep on washing them,' my aunt grumbled and scowled at me.

'I'm not asking you to wash my clothes, why are you so bothered?' I shot back resentfully.

'But water and washing powder cost money!!'

She was on about money again.

It didn't matter that I had hardly any decent clothes when I was in primary school, but now I was in high school and my aunt was still insisting, 'We shouldn't spoil the brat with new clothes.' But every teenage girl wants to dress up, doesn't she? Even if I couldn't, at least I wanted clean, tidy clothes. That was why I had to keep washing the few garments I had. At a time when I should have been at my prettiest, I did not look pretty at all.

When I talked back, she would get angry, and when she got angry, she shouted at me. I ignored her, went straight indoors and picked up the phone.

'Yangyang, are you arguing with your aunt again?'

'It's nothing, just her usual grouses. Ignore her.'

'Okay, hey, I've got good news. My uncle's Shar Pei has had a litter of puppies. They're super cute. Are you busy? Why don't we go and see them?'

'Okay, I'm coming.'

I hung up and went out into the yard, where my aunt was still muttering to herself. I grabbed the bicycle from where it was propped in the corner and was about to whizz out of the gate, when I heard, 'Where are you off to, damn brat! Not going to see your Big Head friend again?'

'Her name's not Big Head, and she's my good friend!'

'It makes me feel sick just to look at her, and you spend all day around her. Come back right now, you damn brat!' my aunt yelled, but the pedals under my feet had suddenly acquired wings and I sped away. She knew perfectly well that Wanjun's big head was down to having had hydrocephalus as a baby, but she was utterly unsympathetic. She constantly made fun of her and tried to stop me from playing with her. The fact that Wanjun was a close friend was something she never understood and never would.

I was dog-tired by the time we got to her uncle's house, but there were no puppies to be seen. In fact, her uncle said, 'Wanjun, the bitch has been very protective of her puppies these days. She even growls at us when we feed her. She'll settle down in a little bit, why don't you come back then and see them?'

Wanjun went inside to say hello to the family, leaving me to get my breath back in the yard. I was just playing with a parrot in a hanging cage, when suddenly the Shar Pei bitch shot out of her kennel in the corner, charged towards me and sank her teeth into my calf. My yells brought Wanjun's uncle outside and he gave the dog a kick that sent her flying. She picked herself up and slunk back to her kennel.

I was still yelling in pain, 'Ow! Ow!'

I carefully pulled up my trouser leg. The dog had taken a lump out of my right calf and blood was pouring down my leg.

'Be brave now. I'll put some iodine on it. It'll be fine in a minute,' Uncle Wei said, and gently dabbed at the wound with a cotton swab.

'Ah-ah-ah-ah-' I shrieked.

Poor Wanjun, who was squatting beside me, looked very upset. 'I'm so sorry, Yangyang, if I hadn't left you by yourself, she wouldn't have bitten you.'

'Don't worry about it, if I hadn't been teasing the parrot, the dog wouldn't have come for me,' I said between gritted teeth.

'Your friend got bitten before I'd even finished speaking,' said Wanjun's aunt. 'But now you've got the iodine on, it'll be fine in a couple of days.' And she patted me comfortingly on the shoulder.

It was a shame. We'd been so looking forward to seeing the puppies and now look at what had happened. On the way back, Wanjun was so apologetic that I had to keep comforting her. It hurt like hell though. When I arrived home and limped into the yard, pushing my bicycle, the only thing I wanted was to go to my room and have a good rest. But my uncle, who was tending his grapes, spotted something was up.

'What's wrong with your leg? It was fine when you went out,' he said.

'I got bitten by a stray dog when I was playing.' I dared not tell him the truth.

'What?' He glared at me. 'You got bitten, huh? You go to the clinic and get a rabies jab, right now! If you get rabies, it's no joke!'

I turned around and limped out of the gate without a word.

'Who told you that just wiping it with iodine to disinfect it would make it better?' the doctor in the clinic said sternly. 'This rabies has an incubation period. If you don't get an injection immediately and treat the wound properly, you might be in real trouble.'

The tears ran down my cheeks.

The clinic was just across the street from our house, but my legs felt like they had lead weights tied to them. I didn't want to go back home, but there was nowhere else to go.

As soon as I stepped through the gate, my uncle began to interrogate me, 'You tell me the truth now, whose dog bit you?'

I bowed my head and said nothing. 'Whose dog was it?' he repeated, and banged the table with his fist.

'The Shar Pei from Wanjun's uncle's house,' I said, trembling with fright.

'Damn brat, you lied to me! You said it was a stray. How many rabid strays are there roaming around? You tell more and more lies nowadays!'

It's because I was afraid you'd be angry and not let me play with Wanjun, that's why I lied! I thought to myself. After all, it wasn't as if I wanted to be bitten. I was suffering from a nasty dog bite, and he was completely unsympathetic.

'And you can take the clinic bill to her uncle's house straightaway. How dare they be so irresponsible when it was their dog that bit you?! Why should I pay up? Go on, off you go!'

All he was focused on was getting his money back from the dog owner. I crumpled the receipts in my hand and seethed with hatred for my uncle.

Wanjun and I were like sisters, so I was really embarrassed to have to go and ask her uncle for money. As the sun glared down on me, I just wished I could evaporate. I stood at Wanjun's gate. I had been here so often, but now I felt overwhelmed. I couldn't open my mouth, let alone face Wanjun.

Suddenly there she was, standing in front of me, 'Yangyang, why are you here? Weren't you going home to have a rest?'

'I... I...,' I still couldn't speak.

'What's wrong? Are you sick?' Wanjun came up to me and put a supportive arm around me, her face full of concern.

'Wanjun, can you take me to your uncle's house again?'

'What on earth's the matter? Spit it out!'

'My uncle's insisting I have to give this to your uncle,' I mustered my courage and showed her the clinic receipts.

Wanjun still looked puzzled.

'My uncle said I had to have a rabies jab in case. And...and he wants your uncle to pay him back.'

I could not look her in the eye.

'You wait for me here, I'll be right back,' she said. She glanced at the receipts, then without further ado, pushed her bicycle out of the yard and was gone.

Fifteen minutes later, Wanjun handed me two hundred yuan from her uncle.

'Off you go, and give the money to your uncle,' she said. 'He was right – it was down to them to pay the clinic bills. Yangyang, you really need to rest when you get home. I'm so sorry.'

I could think of nothing to say.

As I pedalled home gripping the money in my hand, the road seemed endless. I was mortified. If it had been someone else's dog, I would have gone and argued with the owner without a second thought. But this was my best friend's uncle. I had no idea what was going through Wanjun's head, or what she had said to Uncle Wei. All I knew was that at the moment I took the money from her, something changed between us. Our friendship was no longer as warm and untroubled as before.

Before my injury had healed, more troubles came to bite me at school. Once the first monthly test was over, we 'bottom-of-the-class' students were separated from the top students in the front rows. They were to be given lessons in the computer room by a top teacher. After all, they represented the future of the school, and of the country too.

My marks for English and Chinese were among the best, but my maths, physics and chemistry pulled me right down. I tried so hard, but I just did not have the brains for science and I could not get the lessons into my head. I was a one-sided student: my marks in English and Chinese were excellent but they were not going to make up for my failures in science. The school decided it was a waste of time for me to take the senior high school exam because my overall marks would not be good enough. So there were no computer-room lessons for me.

Our class teacher, the Demoness, had made no bones about focusing her teaching on the top students but now, these inequalities were blatantly institutionalised. Our school divided the class into winners and losers. So in year three, the Demoness became the undisputed ruler of the school.

With the class split in two, the 'losers' became more and more rebellious. They had this label hung around their necks, and they acted up to it. In the meantime, the school put its hope in the top students, the ones who were being taught in the computer room. The bottom set were left kicking their heels. But although Mr Shen was gone, my enthusiasm for learning English was undimmed. 'You should learn because you love it, and work hard of your own volition, not because the teacher or your parents make you.' I would never forget what my teacher had taught me.

The days passed, and I kept wishing I could disappear. I did not exchange a word with my uncle for a long time after I was bitten by the dog. He looked grim-faced and aggrieved. I kept out of his way. So long as I avoided lighting the fuse that might cause him to explode, he and I could coexist.

One evening, I was cycling home from school. As usual, I was starving by this time. I got home and was just about to go to the kitchen to find something to eat, when I heard my uncle's voice from the sitting room.

'What's up?' I stood listlessly in the doorway.

'Your cousin and his wife went to get a wardrobe this afternoon and they haven't come back. Go and see if they need any help. Follow the path at the east end of the village, and you should be able to see them,' Uncle said severely. 'You can give them a hand pushing the cart. You're a big girl now, it's time you learned to pitch in and help the family out, brat!'

I had no problem with working, but just then, I was ravenous. He hadn't even asked me if I'd had anything to eat, or said, 'Get yourself a bite before you go to keep you going.'

In this family, my needs were always ignored.

My stomach rumbled as I walked along in the darkness. I had avoided the path to the east of the village ever since the police found a woman's body in a stinking ditch alongside it a year ago.

I tried to keep my spirits up. Suddenly, a bicycle shot past. I cried out in fright, and the rider turned around and yelled back, 'What are you shouting for? You scared the hell out of me!'

'Damn you! You're the one who scared me!' I muttered angrily at his retreating back.

I carried on walking another few hundred metres, peering into the distance whenever the light in a yard made it possible for me to see anything. I could not see anyone, and began to think maybe my cousin and his wife had taken another way home. I scampered home as quickly as I could.

'Damn brat, how come you're back so soon?' my uncle demanded roughly as soon as I walked in.

'I didn't find them. I thought they must have come back another way.'

'You didn't find them? You didn't even try looking for them, did you? How dare you lie to me? Go back and look for them! I don't believe you couldn't find them!'

Back out into the darkness again, I burst into floods of tears. By now, I was not afraid of ghosts. I was much too angry with my uncle and his unpredictable temper. I hated him for glaring at me and flaring up all the time. The concept of keeping cool did not exist for him.

When he was happy, any and everything was plain sailing. When he was upset, everyone had to suffer with him. He saw me as a poor wretch, a punchbag whom he could beat black and blue whenever he chose.

I stumbled through the darkness, weeping and cursing him. I was not afraid anymore, because right now, my anger was protecting me.

Then I heard a voice, 'Yangyang, what are you doing here?'

Not far away, my cousin and his wife were pushing the cart towards me, and she had seen my small figure in the darkness.

'Uncle told me to come,' I said, wiping away tears with my sleeve.

'It was only a wardrobe, we didn't need your help. I don't know what your uncle was thinking, making you come all this way.' My cousin's wife often defended me. She said she could never understand the way my aunt's family treated me.

'Come on, it's late, let's get back. Have you had anything to eat yet?'

I shook my head, and she sighed, 'You go on back and eat. We'll manage on our own.'

But I bent my head, leaned down and silently helped her with pushing the cart.

'Your father! I can't stand this anymore. All your family does is bully Yangyang all day long!' she complained as we walked along. My cousin knew that he was in the wrong, so he didn't say a word. He had bullied me ever since I arrived as a small kid.

Back home, I locked myself in my room. It was night, I had had nothing to eat and I was so angry. At first, I lay in bed crying. Then all kinds of strange ideas began to pop into my head. *Tomorrow I'll pack my bag and go to the Shaolin Temple on Mount Song. I'll live as a monk, learn kungfu, eat vegetarian food and become a Buddhist! But what if they don't want me? I'll kneel down and beg them to take me in! If that doesn't work, I'll go to a nunnery. I'll spend the rest of my life hiding out in the mountains and never come back!*

Eventually, I fell asleep. Early the next morning, I picked up my schoolbag and went to school as usual. I put my strange fancies of the night before to the back of my mind. I was only sixteen and still at school. Where could I go? I had no place that was mine, either at home or at school. I had no idea what the future held, if I would ever have a home or where it would be. When we broke for lunch, I hovered outside the phone booth near the school. When I finally plucked up the courage to go in, I picked up the phone, then put it down again. Finally, after tussling with myself, I dialed Shen Wenming's number.

In my mind, I was very clear that even if he was violent, I would rather be with my parents than stay another day with my unpredictable, volatile uncle.

I told him, 'We're about to take the senior high school exams, when are you coming to get me?'

'I'll be there as soon as you've done your exams, okay?'

'You promise? Please come and get me as soon as you can, I don't want to stay here a moment longer.'

'What's wrong? Has someone been beating you?'

'No, I just can't stand looking at Uncle's angry face all day long.'

'Well, don't keep talking back to him then, no wonder he's angry if you've been pissing him off!'

'I haven't been pissing him off! Anyway, now you know. But please don't phone them. If he knows I asked you to take me back to Shandong, he'll do his nut.'

I put the phone down and heaved a sigh of relief. Soon, I could leave this vale of woe behind me. I had a few fond memories, of course, but I had to go. They had done me the kindness of rearing me, but I did not know how much longer I could put up with living in a family where emotional bombs went off all day long.

On the way home, the sun shone brightly and there was a pleasant breeze. I thought of leaving here for good and felt a surge of elation. I was smiling as I pushed my bike into the yard. But my joy evaporated when I caught sight of my uncle glowering at me from the front doorstep. My instinct told me something really bad must have happened. Sure enough, no sooner had I put the bike away than he bellowed at me, 'Stand right where you are!'

I stood motionless in the middle of the yard.

'Did you call your dad?'

I looked down and said nothing.

'Damn brat, you went behind my back and accused me, didn't you? Shen Wenming called to tell me to leave you alone! Huh, who's he to talk?!'

The tears swam in my eyes.

'You ungrateful brat! I don't know why I bothered with you!'

Uncle was trembling with anger. My aunt stood at the door of the kitchen, sighing. She had brought her niece here, and now look what had happened. What else could she do except sigh?

Eleven years of accumulated resentment burst out of me. 'Why did you take me in?' I shouted. 'Did I have a choice? I didn't ask you to. It was your choice to foster me!'

There was a loud crack as my aunt whacked me across the face.

'All you ever do is hit me, isn't it? It's all your fault. If you hadn't meddled in what didn't concern you, I wouldn't have landed up here, living this miserable existence,' I said, forcing the tears back. My right cheek burned painfully from her slap.

'If it hadn't been for your aunt, you would have starved to death!' My uncle was so angry that his voice cracked.

'Well, I'd rather be dead. It would have saved me from this misery,' I said coldly, and turned and went to my room. I opened the cupboard and took out the big zipped laundry bag I had been keeping there, and began packing my books and other things in it.

'The exams are more than two weeks away, why are you packing already?'

I had not noticed my aunt in the doorway. She looked at my bulging bag, and suddenly choked up.

I turned my back on her, and my own tears pattered down. Ungrateful or not, I couldn't wait to be gone. The atmosphere, both in the room and in the yard, was so oppressive that I felt like I was suffocating.

I was constantly being told off in this family. They got a kick out of shouting at me, pouring cold water over me, telling me off in public, getting hysterical over the tiniest things, and putting me down at every turn. Whether it was the way I sat at the dinner table or the way I held my bowl or my chopsticks, I couldn't do anything right. I was a pig when I ate too much, and picky when I ate too little. It got so bad that I was sure other people were eyeballing me and mocking me in public too. Subsequently, I kept telling myself that no one was watching me or mocking me, and no one was suddenly going to let fly at me, everyone else was much too busy with their own food. It took a long time before I could eat with my classmates, and longer still before I overcame my fears.

I had grown up knowing that if I got into trouble, I had to hide it from the family. There was no point in going home to tell them, I would just get another telling off and a beating. To them, I was an object of ridicule and antipathy. If there was something I did not know how to do or did wrong, there was no one to guide me or tell me how to do it right. I simply got a tongue-lashing. So I learned to keep quiet and put up with it.

From when I started primary school, I could cook, wash and clean on my own. I was not in the habit of asking anyone else – I did not want to bother them. I hardly ever got sick and when I did, I just rested until it got better. One winter, a whole lot of purplish blood clots started coming out of my nose. When I told my aunt, she said, 'Damn brat, it's because you're greedy. You ate too much dry food and it's given you internal heat. No more than you deserve!' So I just had to put up with it. One hanky after another got covered in blood stains. I thought I was going to die. After a while, however, the good Lord took pity on me. He must have known no one loved me, so he took special care of me. The bleeding stopped on its own.

I was never given milk or calcium tablets as a child, and in the second year of junior high school, I began to suffer from calcium deficiency. I suddenly lost a bit of one of my front teeth. That black hole in my tooth every time I opened my mouth looked really nasty. When I got home that day, I asked my aunt if she would take me to the dentist. She bared her full set of false teeth and spat at me, 'What do you need a filling for, damn brat? Does it put you in a panic if you don't spend money for a day?' She had spent a lot of money on her own teeth but she put me down for wanting one small filling. Fine, if she wouldn't take me, I'd save up and take myself. A week later, I took the breakfast money I had saved and about fifteen yuan I had borrowed from my classmates and went to a small dental clinic nearby. The dentist was a quack. He did not even wash his hands before telling me to lie in the chair and open my mouth. Then, without a word of warning, he began to drill where my tooth had broken. I screamed, and cried from the pain. The dentist stopped his work, charged me ten yuan for the visit and sent me home. That night, the left-hand side of my face and my nose swelled up. The family ignored me, when they were not giving my swollen face disgusted looks. They certainly did not offer me any comfort or anti-inflammatories.

I never experienced affection from the family. In fact, the atmosphere in which I grew up was utterly bleak. Gradually, I became over-sensitive. I used to search people's faces, in case I did something wrong and offended them. If anyone was kind or a friend gave me a present, I would find myself crying, unable to stop. I spent eleven years in a home where the only words spoken to me were cold and unpleasant. I got used to the abuse. However, human endurance has its limits, and one day all volcanoes will erupt.

17

Where is my home?

I left without a shadow of regret. I had few memories of laughter in that family. There was more sadness than joy. The moment the train left the station, I felt as if a weight had fallen from my shoulders. After eleven years, I could tentatively begin to make my own way in life.

I had dreamed so often of my family – my father, mother and sisters – but when I woke from my dreams, my family was always so far away and fuzzy. I wanted a home, nothing fancy, or even very big, but a place where there was love and laughter.

After eleven long years, the snot-nosed girl wailing for her Nana was finally going home. I remembered the summer holiday I had spent there, playing with my sisters in the alley, and our shouts and laughter and chatter echoed in my ears. It seemed like yesterday.

'Yangyang, you're back!' My mother met me at the gate with a smile on her face. I had dreamed this scene countless times. But when the dream became reality, I could not bring myself to shout, 'Mum!'

'Dinner's ready! Go and wash your hands,' she said, taking my bag from me.

Then I heard Star, 'Yangyang! Come and see! Mum's made lots of nice food today!'

She grabbed me by the hand and pulled me towards the kitchen.

At dinner, as we helped ourselves to rice, there was a yelp from my third sister, Serene, 'Hey! Why are you scooping the rice from the middle? What a mess you've made!' She was looking at the hole I had made in the middle of the pot of rice. She snatched the ladle from me and carefully smoothed the rice back into the hole from the edge.

'Idiot!' I said impatiently, picked up my rice bowl and headed for the sitting room. 'It's just a rotten old bowl of rice! Why does it matter which part of the pot it came from? What a lot of stupid rules you have!' My good mood had evaporated.

'Yangyang, calm down, that's just the way she is, you better get used to it. I don't pay any attention,' said Star in my ear.

Shen Wenming spoke, 'You two were always whispering when you were kids. Are you going to carry on the same way now you're grown up? Be careful you don't bite each other's ears off!' He was right. During that summer holiday five years ago, Star and I always ganged up on Serene. When we found something fun to do, we kept it a secret from Serene and never invited her to join in. And when we went to our shared bed at night, Star always insisted on sleeping next to me.

Serene was quick-tempered, and nosy too, and was constantly fighting with Star. Sometimes their arguments ended in a fight and the result was often that both of them got a beating from Shen Wenming, who was even more hot-tempered. In his narrow view of the world, it was not a question of who was right or wrong. A disobedient child got a beating. That was the best way to educate children.

When they were little, Star and Serene had shared a bed and a quilt. If ever Star turned over in the night and accidentally touched Serene, Serene would reach out and dig her nails into Star. Poor Star was covered in scratches and bruises and if she cried, Shen Wenming beat both of them then and there. So that summer when I visited, I became a natural ally for Star: we had similar temperaments, I saw myself as a protector of the weak, and I had plenty of tricks up my sleeve. We quickly became a thorn in Serene's side. So much so that for years after, she used to say that she must have been a changeling, or why would her sisters have been so mean to her? It was ironic when you think about it. I, the kid who was farmed out, never doubted who my real parents were, whereas Serene didn't see herself as one of the family just because her spiky temper alienated them.

As for Moon, she was the adored eldest daughter. She was also four years older than me, five years older than Serene, and six years older than Star, so she spent her time with young people of her own age. She could not be bothered to take Serene and Star along, and they did not bother with her. When I came back, the four of us were finally together again, but she was off at university. So she was largely absent as we three grew up. Meanwhile, I had landed in the family, an interloper, a prickly teenager. In just a few months, I had a terrible fight with Serene, quarreled with my mother, and was slapped across the face by Shen Wenming.

Serene was stubborn and hot-tempered. She was always meddling and she used to flip about the most trivial things, often upsetting the rest of the family too. I could fly off the handle too, but in general I was very easy-going, and just so long as you didn't cross the line with me, I could laugh at just about anything. When I did lose my temper, there was no stopping me. I used to get so annoyed with Serene that we often came to blows, verbally or physically, and neither of us would give in. After these rows, we used not to speak for days on end.

Star was an introverted child who minded her own business. She liked nothing more than to bury her nose in her textbooks, ignoring what was going on around her. When I stood up to Serene, Star never put her oar in. To put it more politely, all she was concerned about was her schoolwork. She made a big deal about being neutral but really, she was intent on protecting herself. After all, as the smallest, she had often been bullied, and she had perfected the art of turning a blind eye.

One day, Star was in the bathroom having a shower and Serene needed the toilet. She knocked urgently on the door until finally, Star shouted through the door, 'I'm getting dressed!'

Serene shouted back, 'I'm going to pee myself while you're getting dressed! I won't be looking at you, so what are you getting all shy about?' And she battered and pounded on the door again. I was sprawled on the sofa in the sitting room, watching events unfold but content to let them get on with it. They were both amazingly stubborn: one trying to kick the door in, the other determined to keep her out.

The banging was deafening, but there was no sound of movement in the bathroom.

Serene shrieked with frustration and darted into the kitchen. She came back with a big kitchen knife and started hacking at the door handle, 'Open this door! Open this door right now!' Still no sound came from the bathroom.

Holy shit! This is awesome! I couldn't help thinking. I was genuinely interested to see how determined Serene was. Was she actually going to break through the bathroom door with a kitchen knife? If she did that, she would cop it from Shen Wenming when he came home. He would beat her half to death. The more I thought about it, the more I felt the laughter bubbling up inside me. But if I didn't hold it in, she might lunge at me with the knife. Just as Serene was chopping madly at the door, it banged open. Star walked calmly out, her head wrapped in a towel and carrying her washbasin. She didn't even look at Serene and just headed straight for the balcony.

I clicked my tongue in astonishment. I looked at Star standing with her back to us, completely undaunted. I could hardly believe her composure. If it were me, I would probably have jabbed the toilet plunger at Serene and got into a fight with her. On the other hand, if it were really me in the bathroom, I might have let Serene in when she first knocked on the door. I couldn't see what was so funny about hogging the bathroom when someone else really needed a shit. I couldn't help admiring Star's inner strength, however. If I could be as calm as her, I won't be constantly at loggerheads with Serene, sometimes even keeping up hostilities for days at a time.

One day, our mother went shopping and could not cook our lunch. Serene saw the note she left behind and started to mutter, 'She's so annoying! Why's she gone shopping? Why hasn't she made our lunch? Doesn't she know how precious my time is? I don't have a second to spare!'

Meantime, Star and I had eaten a steamed mantou with a bit of pickles and were engrossed in our schoolwork. Serene had no right to complain about her time being precious. What's more, our mother was not our slave. She could cook if she wanted to and she had every right not to if she didn't want to. Serene was fifteen years old by then. She had two arms and two legs. She could cook for herself.

Star and I carried on with what we were doing, and eventually Serene stopped her grumbling. The only sounds to be heard in the house were the rustling of pages. Half an hour later, our mother came hurrying in, laden down with shopping bags. As soon as she got through the door, Serene rushed into the living room. ready to berate her. When she saw our mother taking a shoe box out of one of the bags, she exploded. Mum hadn't been at home like she should have been, cooking our lunch, and all because she wanted to buy a new pair of shoes, blah, blah, blah. 'Spend, spend, spend, is that all you can do? Do you know what time it is? I've got my exams, my time's precious, and you're out buying shoes? And you're always going on at me to study hard!' she yelled.

Star and I were sitting on the sofa admiring Mum's new shoes. She and Mum pretended they hadn't heard, and ignored her. But I just couldn't do that. Her constant carping was really winding me up.

'Are you ever going to stop? That's enough!' I shot back. 'Why shouldn't our Mum buy a pair of shoes? Is no one entitled to any time for themselves? Do they have to dance attendance on you twenty-four seven?'

'It's nothing to do with you, I wasn't talking to you! Just butt out of it, sicko!' said Serene, exasperated. She was never going to accept any criticism.

I did not say a word. I got up, grabbed one of the new shoes on the table and I whacked her across the face with it.

She shrieked.

Then, not to be outdone, she hit me back with the other shoe.

'You little bitch!'

Now I was really riled. I made a fist and threw a punch at her.

'Stop fighting! Stop fighting this minute!' shouted Mum, and she and Star pulled us apart and made us calm down.

Serene was constantly criticizing Mum. This was just one small incident among many. I really hated the way our mother and Star put up with it. Maybe they were used to her abuse, but I wasn't prepared to put up with it. For me, there was only one way to deal with someone like this: hit her. That was the only way to vent my anger. If our mother would not keep her under control, then I would teach her how to behave.

For a long time after that, Serene and I limited ourselves to glaring at each other. Since we were living under one roof, that made for a strained atmosphere. While I fought our mother's corner, however, both Serene and Mum talked and laughed as if nothing had happened. I was upset that not only did Mum not thank me, but not long afterwards, she said something that hurt me deeply.

One breezy autumn day, the afternoon was bright and sunny, so Mum got us all together to sort out the clothes cupboards. The weather was getting colder. It was time to put away our summer stuff and give our autumn clothes an airing. That day, as I watched them bring out lovely, brightly coloured jumpers one after another, I felt very upset. The thing was, when I was a child, I had so longed for a jumper with a cartoon design of my very own. But my aunt was too lazy to knit one for me, and there was no way my cousins would. In the end, all I got was an ugly, plain pink one that Mingmei had originally knitted for herself until it shrank in the wash.

'You knitted these sweaters for my sisters?' I asked Mum, casually picking up one of them.

'Yup, I knitted them all. When they were little, I used to look at fashion books and knit them jumpers.'

She seemed oblivious to my distress as she pulled one out and showed it off proudly.

'Didn't it ever occur to you to knit one for me?' I looked her straight in the eye as my hands gripped it.

'Well, I thought you were being well looked-after by your auntie. I mean it looked like that from the photos she sent. You were nicely dressed.'

'That's because she put on new clothes on me every time she took a picture. You didn't look beneath the surface! Besides, even if I'd had thousands of jumpers, none of them would have been knitted by you! When you were knitting for your first, third and fourth daughters, didn't it occur to you that you had a second daughter thousands of miles away? Did you ever wonder, even once, how I was doing? About whether I had a nice cosy new sweater? No! You never thought of me, not once!'

As I got these words off my chest, my hands trembled.

'Oh, for heaven's sake, why do you let it bother you so much?' Mum said.

She didn't realize she had said the wrong thing until she met my eyes.

Was I letting it bother me too much? No way! There was no one in this world who was less bothered than me. If I was that bothered, I would not have set foot in this house! They had cast me off for eleven years, and had I ever complained or criticized? No! Never! I never told them what I had been through. They just saw me as a bad-mannered, wild child who had suddenly arrived from the back of beyond.

I still remembered how when I came back for my grandfather's funeral, Serene and Star at first wanted to spend every second with me, and suddenly, they vanished. When I found them hiding behind the carved cabinet in my granny's house, they were stuffing their faces with a box of butter cakes.

'Why didn't you get some for me?' I asked.

'Mum only gave us two yuan,' they said straight out, without batting an eyelid. It was clear that no matter how much they argued, Serene and Star would always be sisters and our mother's beloved daughters. While I was an outsider, not worthy of even spending a yuan on for cakes.

Five years later, when I mentioned this to Mum, she insisted that she would never have left me out like that and I must have misremembered it. Ridiculous. How could I misremember something like that?

Trivial incidents – jumpers and cupcakes – but it was in these seemingly insignificant events that my mother showed her partiality. Maybe she never realized the special place she held in my heart. I didn't say and she didn't ask. We lived under the same roof but we might as well have been thousands of miles apart.

Whenever we talked about her one visit to me in Nanyang, she just burbled away, saying the first thing that came into her head, with no regard for my feelings.

'The time I went to Nanyang to see you, God it was cold, and there was no heating. I caught a cold the next day.'

'That bed was so hard. I just couldn't sleep. I got up in the middle of the night, wrapped myself in a quilt and spent the night on the sofa.'

'I was only there a few days and your aunt spent all her time gossiping with your father, and your uncle had a big frown on his face and said nothing all day long. It was such a dead atmosphere, I'd have fallen into depression if I'd stayed any longer.'

And so on and so forth.

No heating, hard beds, depressing atmosphere, and she could not stand it after just a few days? But her daughter, her own flesh and blood, had to stick it out for eleven years! No doubt she meant no harm, but her words wounded me. Still, I was silent. I refused to argue.

What was the point of endless fighting? We were a stubborn bunch in this family, every one of us. They insisted they did not owe me anything, while I insisted the opposite. The long years of separation had created an invisible rift between us. On the surface, I was lively and carefree, but inwardly I seethed with resentment. Still I kept it all inside – my pain, my grievances, my disappointment and my despair. I made no noise, I was always the child whom people paid no heed to as if I was transparent. I acted as if I had accepted reality. In fact, I made myself forget my longing for my mother's love because that was the only way not to suffer.

If my mother blabbed, Shen Wenming blabbed even more than she did. He was not your classic, loving father-figure. He talked endlessly, and most of what he said was nonsense. When it was funny, you thought, hey, this old man is very humorous. When he was being pigheaded, he was just incredibly annoying and unreasonable.

He was a self-confessed male chauvinist and more or less ignored his wife, although she bore the brunt of all the housework and care of us girls without complaint. In the meantime, he told the whole wide world what a hard life he had, earning money to keep his family. He made himself out to be some kind of benevolent ruler over his little domain (his family), within which everything belonged to him. On days when there were no arguments going on, he would deliberately pick on something to complain about: the food was bad or the house was a mess, or anything else. Nothing was too small or trivial for him to criticise. Sometimes, he went on so much that he drove our mother mad and then there would be a serious row.

Once, he wound her up so much that she ended up in hospital, and while she was away, we took him to task and gave him a serious talking-to.

'You're like a bear with a sore head with our mother. Why? She's so good to you, but you're always losing your temper with her! What kind of a man are you? Any man with a bit of nous goes out and makes big money and gets things done! It's only men with no brains and ability that take it out on their women! You never do anything at home, you sit around like the Empress Dowager all day long while our mother works her fingers to the bone for us all. You're always complaining about one thing or the other. How can you be the master of the house and still have such a foul mouth on you?'

The three of us had a good go at him. He was furious. 'Get out! Get out of my sight!' he roared, clenching his fists and trembling with rage.

We girls were pretty much grown up by now, so it was natural we would protect our mother.

The days when Shen Wenming ruled the world were gone forever. Maybe it's because he didn't even try to act like a proper father, so I didn't treat him as one. He shot his mouth off, but I gave as good as I got. If he annoyed me, I was going to get the better of him come what may. Many times, Shen Wenming was driven almost apoplectic with rage by his gabby second daughter. Then he would resort to brute force. After all, that was what he was good at, beating children.

On my first Spring Festival back in Shandong, Moon came home for the holiday from her university in Beijing. Before she arrived, Shen Wenming bought a huge quantity of anthracite. He stored it on the balcony and spent the days messing with the stove to get it burning really well, so that his precious eldest daughter would not freeze. (The rest of us didn't matter.)

'You're only lighting it because she's coming back,' I confronted him at the dinner table. 'If it wasn't for her, we'd be living in an icehouse.'

'You better watch it, or I'll whack you across the face!' Shen Wenming shot back and threw his chopsticks down, making Star cower in fright.

'What's the problem? It's obvious she's your pet. Are we not allowed to say so? She always has been. If she wasn't coming back, would you even bother?'

'Get lost!' he roared, his face contorted with fury. There was an awkward silence around the table.

Okay, I'd get lost. I wasn't scared. I threw down my bowl and chopsticks, and went to the shoe cupboard. Mum hadn't said a word but now she spoke up, 'It's cold, where are you going?'

'To my aunt's house.' As soon as I said that, I regretted it. Star had explained to me that we could not go there during the Chinese New

Year because if any of us went to our aunt's house, she would give us a present of money; and then when our cousins came to our house, my mother would have to reciprocate and give them a red envelope each. It was just a way for the parents to swap money, really. And our family was poor, so Mum never took us to pay a New Year's visit to her relatives.

'What are you going to do at your auntie's? Everyone is busy at New Year,' she said.

'What's wrong with dropping in on her? Especially as I'm not welcome here.'

'Because if you go at New Year, you're just asking for money!'

'Who said I was asking for money? Even if she gave it to me, I wouldn't take it!' I was really upset at that. Why did she think I was only interested in scrounging? I remembered how affectionate my aunt had been to me that summer holiday. I remembered her goodness and kindness. I just wanted to meet her, talk to her, nothing more.

'If I say you're not going, then you're not going! Stop answering back!' Shen Wenming grabbed one tatty slipper off his foot and threw it at me, and hit me right on my shoulder. I grabbed it and hurled it back. With a crash, it landed in his bowl. 'I'll teach you to answer back! You think I can't keep you under control?' Shen Wenming jumped to his feet, marched up to me and slapped my face.

'Harder, hit harder, why don't you?' I tried to hold the tears back, but they leaked out anyway.

'Get out! Get out of here and don't come back! If I'd known you were going to be so unruly, I'd have strangled you as soon as you were born!'

'You'd have been doing me a favour. That way, I wouldn't have had such a hard time, or had anything to do with people like you! Where were you all when I was a kid and needed looking after? Why are you both so keen on controlling me now that I'm grown up? It's too late now. I never asked to be born! You insisted on having one daughter after another just because you wanted a son!'

Pow! Shen Wenming, in paroxysms of rage, slapped me again. He and his sister, Auntie Wenjie, really were two of a kind. Slapping people was all they were programmed to do.

I flung the door open and rushed out. No one came after me. Perhaps they were just used to Shen Wenming's violence, or maybe they didn't like my rebellious nature. This was supposed to be my home, but I was just an intruder. They were a family who had lived under one roof and loved each other for all those years. The proof was in our family hukou document hidden at the bottom of the drawer, which did not have my name in it.

I walked through the ice and snow, the bitter cold wind on my burning face. I seethed with suppressed resentment and grievances, and couldn't stop the tears dripping down. Since everyone thought I didn't exist, maybe I really shouldn't be here. I was overwhelmed with feelings of loneliness and helplessness. The world was such a big place, where was my home in it?

18

Spilling the beans

One bright moonlit night, my sister Moon and I had our first heart-to-heart.

'When I was in Beijing, the other two told me that Shen Wenming slapped you across the face.'

'And they told me that when you were in high school, he slapped you too, for flunking your school work.'

'Hah! No one in this family can escape Shen Wenming's clutches, can they?'

'Do you know why I get back to college as quickly as I can, every time I come back on holiday?'

'I bet it's to see your boyfriend! What other reason could it be?'

'Only half-right! There's another reason: I hate coming home, it's so depressing.'

I frowned and stared at her, nonplussed. She was the favourite daughter. Why didn't she like it here?

'Don't look at me like that. You know what? It was because I was the first that they wrapped me in cotton wool. I had no life of my own for twenty years. I felt stifled. So getting a college place and leaving home was a release. Even if I spent all day in that tiny six-bunk room and did nothing else, I'd prefer it to being here. I refused to stay here for one more day!'

'What do you mean depressing? They treat you so well, I can see that. They adore you.'

'Yes, I admit they haven't treated me badly in the material sense. What I mean is, mentally and emotionally, do you understand what I mean?'

'Mentally and emotionally? That's because you never had it tough when you were a kid. You should experience a bit more hardship. That'll make your emotional tension seem like nothing.'

'You're not getting it, are you? Never mind, forget it, forget I ever said it.'

'Hey, why are you being so serious? Can't you take a joke?'

'Okay, well anyway, because I was the eldest daughter, they were super strict with me. They controlled every tiny thing I did, all day long. And if I didn't do it well enough, one would be responsible for giving me a lecture, while the other took on giving me a beating. Not that the beatings were too bad, so long as I didn't put up a fight. Starting with my very earliest memories, there was never a time when anyone was interested in what I was thinking or what I wanted to do. I was really envious of the good relationship that other kids had with their parents. They could play with their Mum and Dad like kids do, and when there was something serious to deal with, there would be a discussion, and they all settled things harmoniously. Maybe it's because they were too repressive when I was a teenager but now, whenever they talk to me, I just want out. When they ask how I am and how my studies are going, I want to throw the phone at the wall. Every time I hang up, I go and hide on the rooftop and have a cry. I know I'm at a safe distance in Beijing, but I still try and avoid talking to them. I'm afraid that I'm going to blow up like a volcano. I've trodden so carefully all these years, and I'm tired of it.'

I thought to myself, *They've controlled you since you were a kid? I wanted someone to control me but no one did.* The more people don't have something, the more they desperately want it. A kid with no parents does not even get this kind of warped love, while one with parents is not grateful for it and wants something better. I wanted to be angry with her, but then I had second thoughts. It would only make things worse for me, and upset her. Some things are better left unsaid.

Moon went on, 'When I was young, money was really tight because they had to pay off the family planning fines debt. They were always quarreling over money. Shen Wenming has always been difficult about money. If you ever ask for any, he'll find every way to avoid giving you any. Even if it's to pay tuition fees, he'll put it off as long as he can.'

'Shen Wenming and Shen Wenjie are two of a kind,' I said. 'That's exactly how our aunt used to behave. When I was little, if I ever asked for money, she'd make it as difficult as possible for me – she felt bad if she didn't. From my one yuan for breakfast to sixty yuan or so for my school uniform, she never once gave it willingly. Of course, she had to give it to me in the end but she just wanted to upset me first.'

'I'm not surprised they begrudged us money,' said Moon. 'That was their money and they had to earn it. Of course they weren't going to splash it around!'

'You're absolutely right. So we need to get financially independent as soon as we can! I really have had enough of begging and scrounging.'

'Mum's had to do it for nearly twenty years,' My sister said with a sigh. 'I'll never forget one winter's night when they had a row about money and he beat her and slammed out of the house. He left her alone in the pitch dark sobbing her heart out. I was ten and all I could do was hide by the gate, as far away as I could get, and watch helplessly. I was scared, I didn't dare go and comfort her, let alone go back to my bed alone.'

Just thinking back at that childhood nightmare made the tears trickle down my sister's face. She choked on her words and fell silent.

I reached out and gripped her hand. I did not know how to comfort her. Or perhaps, in all honesty, I did not want to comfort her. Okay, she was scared and scarred psychologically, but they didn't beat or swear at her. I had suffered verbal and physical abuse, and when I cried at night, there was no one to comfort me. When I was slapped and punched, I was too weak to fight back and, worse still, I had nowhere to run to. That was real terror.

What I said was, 'All the same, no matter how much she cried or how helpless she was, when the sun rose the next day, she was still your mother, the person you could rely on. I've only ever had myself. What's more, she was an adult, she had choices, she could fight back or run away. But I just had to accept my fate.'

'Yes, you're quite right. I can't feel too sorry for our mother. All these years, she always said that if it weren't for us, she'd have divorced him a long time ago. But the fact is, she just got used to the way Shen Wenming behaved towards her. When he came back at the end of the day after work, she felt sorry for him. He used to come in and lie down on the sofa, and she would bring his dinner to him. He stuffed his belly and went straight to sleep, leaving a shambles on the table for her to clean up. She takes care of everything for him: washing, cooking, cleaning. He has no idea how much he has to be grateful for. He takes everything she does for granted. In his eyes, he's head of the family and he's the only one who works his fingers to the bone to put food on the table.'

I said nothing, but I was not surprised by her words, even though she was the favoured eldest daughter. It had taken me only one year, since my return to Shandong, to see the brutality that everyone hated so much. Six years ago, he had given me a kick hard enough to send me flying and destroy his relationship with me. He had wounded my already fragile self-esteem, and when he told my favourite aunt that I was a thief, that had scarred me.

Shen Wenming frequently said, 'This is my house. If you don't like it, you can go!' And he always suited the action to the words. The first thing he did when he woke up every morning was turn on the TV. Whether it was four o'clock in the morning or eleven at night, the TV had to be available for him twenty-four seven. He did not care how much he was disturbing the rest of us. The TV was his life, he couldn't live without it.

We all asked him to keep it down, but he justified himself by saying things like, 'Just get used to it. If every little noise wakes you up, then don't sleep! You've just got into bad habits!' In his view, there was nothing wrong with him, everyone else was at fault.

In the depths of winter, we kept the doors and windows closed and he used to chain-smoke in the living room while he was watching TV. The whole house was wreathed in stinking smoke. If you asked him politely to smoke on the balcony, he refused pointblank. If you opened the living room window to get a bit of air in, he slammed it shut and yelled, 'Get out! Out! I'm freezing to death in here!' You might be poisoned by his smoke, but he wasn't going to die in a cold draught.

We had an air-conditioning unit in the living room and at the height of the summer heat, it came into its own. We liked to keep the doors of our three bedrooms open at night so we could sleep comfortably. Surely nothing wrong with that, was there? Well, for Shen Wenming, there was. Turn on the air conditioner overnight? Are you kidding me? What a waste of electricity! So, at the dead of night, when everyone was asleep, he would get up and press the 'Off' switch. Within half an hour, we would all be awake and lathered in sweat.

He kept the TV on constantly and that wasn't wasting electricity, but he thought it was a waste of electricity to turn on the air conditioner at night for the whole family. He was the head of the family, he did what he wanted. He was the ultimate selfish man.

He constantly complained about being hard up. 'Do you know how much it costs to keep the air conditioner running overnight? Not a single one of you brings in a cent! All you do is spend all my hard-earned money!'

But while he pleaded poverty, he let opportunities to make money slip through his hands. He had a second-hand Dongfeng van that he wanted to sell but he reckoned the buyer's offer was too low, so he refused it. So that blue van sat for five years in the Dongzha village office's compound. Eventually, he sold it for scrap for 2,000 yuan instead of the 20,000 yuan the buyer had offered him.

'It's my van and I'll sell it cheaply if I want, but no one's gonna take advantage of me!' he proclaimed.

Once he had made a loss on it, no one else was allowed to express their opinions. He made stupidity into quite an art.

When the house had been demolished and the family was relocated, we were lucky enough to get a place with a shop front on a busy street. My mother wanted to open a tailoring shop so that when she had a bit of spare time, she could make and mend clothes or furniture covers and earn a bit of money to put towards the housekeeping. The most important thing was that she could earn her own money instead of constantly badgering Shen Wenming for the housekeeping. But he put his foot down. He was adamant no matter how hard she tried to persuade him. Instead, he hoarded all sorts of tat and filled the front room with it. Discarded furniture and scrap metal he had found by the roadside was all treasure in his eyes. One day it would be a broken toilet, another, an old pressure cooker, or a pile of bowls and chopsticks thrown out by a restaurant. The room was full of rubbish.

That front room could have brought in quite a lot of money in rent. Instead, he turned it into a rubbish tip from which he didn't make a cent. But it did not matter how often you told him, he was not convinced. According to him, this was his treasure, it made him feel wealthy, and we just didn't understand. 'Someone might want it,' he used to say.

Time passed and Shen Wenming went into partnership with someone else and opened a solar water heater shop. Before the business got going properly, he had to set himself up in style as the big boss. He bought himself an executive desk and chair – fine. But why a 1.8-metre sprung-mattress bed? Was he planning to take siestas in it when the business tired him out? Worse still, as soon as he opened the shop, he started drinking and did not stop. He drank with one customer after another all day long, and when he staggered back into the house roaring drunk after work, we would get no peace. He was like a bed bug pickled in alcohol. His eyes were always bloodshot, and his whole body reeked of alcohol. He never even had time to sober up. After three months, his solar water heater shop (no after-sales service provided) closed its doors for good.

For a long time after that, he drank obsessively. If you tried to stop him, he yelled at you. If you let him drink, he would stumble into a drainage ditch and sleep there all night. He broke his nose and his arm, and his face swelled up, but still he drank. One of his alcoholic friends got liver cancer and died before he was fifty. The rest of us tried to use this as a warning to make him stop, but he just said, 'Well, he couldn't take his drink like I can! He was no good!'

We kept trying. 'Right, so, he couldn't take it and he went to meet his maker. So who's left to compare yourself to now?' But it was no good.

After Shen Wenming quit his job and started his doomed solar heating business, Mum had been very worried about him. He had earned a good salary for the past few years. But now the IOUs piled up, one of his biggest debtors being a bastard from the Family Planning Office. From the very beginning, Mum had warned him not to give the man goods on credit. Everyone in Dongzha village knew the man was a rogue who borrowed money and never paid it back. Worse still, he had spent years levying fines on the villagers for breaking the family planning laws. Some of those fines had put families on the breadline for years. But Shen Wenming would not listen. He insisted on lending money to him, and bragging to anyone who would listen, 'Huh! Don't you believe it, he wouldn't dare mess with me!'

One day, he boosted his courage with some drinks and went to collect the debt. Only, he got into a big argument with the man's cronies and got beaten up badly for his pains. Shen Wenming had studied kung fu for ten years when he was young, and he used to swagger around Dongzha village as if he was untouchable. As a youth, he could easily beat up a worthy opponent and reduce him to abject terror. But now he was in his fifties, and no matter how strong he was, there was no way he could get the better of a thirty-something.

When I got there, he was lying on the ground with a brick in his hand, threatening to kill the man. There was a huge crowd of onlookers, but no one was willing to help him up. Not surprising when you looked at his bloody face. Who was going to help a brute like that? What did he think he was doing, getting into a punch-up at his age? I was furious with him, but it was my father lying there after all and I had a smidgen of sympathy. However, just as I reached out to pull him up so I could get him to the clinic, he flung me off. He gave me such a hefty shove that I sat down in the muddy ditch. What little sympathy I had had vanished like the mud splashes I made as I fell.

The beating was reported to the police and the miscreant was apprehended. He did not have any money, so he offered to let out the front room of his own house and any rental earnings could go to repay the debt.

But Shen Wenming was adamant. 'No! I want cash!' he declared. A promise of rental from some bullshit shop front wasn't worth the paper it was written on, in his view.

Fine, so the debtor withdrew his offer. A few years passed, and the shop front became more and more valuable, while none of the cash he was owed went into his pocket. The debtor was serving a prison sentence for the assault and Shen Wenming was no better off. As he watched the shoppers streaming in and out of the premises, he felt very sorry for himself. So what did he do? He gave our mother a beating because she had wanted him to do the deal with his attacker. He yelled at her for being a stupid bitch who knew nothing about anything. He was as short-sighted and opinionated a man as ever walked this earth. Some people are born losers and can never make big money. Shen Wenming was so obstinate and selfish that I'm sure the God of Wealth took one look at him and turned his back on him in disgust.

Shen Wenming's complaints always went something like, 'If it hadn't been for me, you would all have starved to death! You think it was easy for me to support my family? You're all a bunch of ungrateful wretches who do nothing but eat and drink and never thank me!'

I felt like saying, *We can all see that you've had a hard life. But you're always claiming credit for yourself, over and over again, and we're sick of it. The more you boast, the more it puts us off. Bringing up a child should be a selfless, loving act, but you've made it fee-paying and loveless.*

Many times, it was not that we didn't want to get close to him, but that he never, ever acted like a husband and a father. Everything he said and did showed how selfish, self-seeking and ignorant he was. That was why he didn't get any respect.

On their wedding night, he apparently instructed our mother to bring him hot water so he could wash his feet, and then ordered her to wash them for him. Mum ignored him, and he kicked over the big wash bowl, flooding the bedroom. The next day he was still annoyed, so he went out and drank the whole day. When he was drunk, he roamed around the village, arguing with the gossiping women or sleeping it off in a smelly gutter.

When he was ill, Mum bought herbal medicine and prepared it for him, and did her best to take care of him. But when she was sick, he abandoned her for the whole day, and fed himself from street stalls. When he saw her about to take her medicine, he jeered at her, 'What are you taking that for? You're going to die anyway.' He was really foul-mouthed.

As a young couple, they once went on a boat trip from Yantai to Dalian. It was an overnight trip and they bought themselves seat tickets. Strangely, Mum did not see hide nor hair of Shen Wenming all night. He swaggered up to her early the next morning when she was standing on deck watching the sunrise, complaining, 'Ai-ya! The couchettes on this ship are so uncomfortable, I'm aching all over!' He had actually upgraded himself to a couchette where he slept soundly, and abandoned his wife as she spent the whole night in a seat in economy class.

When family planning controls were at their most stringent, the local officials were constantly urging him to have a vasectomy or Mum to have her tubes tied. Mum was unhappy, because she had had four children and was not in good health. If she had the operation, when would she get time to recover her strength? Besides, a vasectomy was a minor operation for a man. But he was adamant. In the end, our mother had the operation, and she never did recover her health fully.

When they moved house, Mum quietly threw away some of the stuff he had been hoarding: the scrap metal and a grease-stained sleeping mat. When he found out, he was furious. He accused her of wasting money, and then gave her a beating, just as if they had never shared more than two decades of married life. The rubbish he hoarded was precious, and no one was allowed to throw it out even if he didn't use it. Throwing it away was more than disrespectful to him, it was a hostile act.

There was a long period when my paternal grandfather was seriously ill and in such pain that he often called for help by knocking on the wall with his walking stick at night. The rest of the family were very patient when they went to tend to the old man. Not Shen Wenming. Once, he was sound asleep in the bunk bed beside him, and the old man, unable to wake him, started knocking on the wall again. Without further ado, Shen Wenming grabbed his father's walking stick and threw it into the yard. The old man was not having that. He hammered on the wall with his bare hands. Shen Wenming, deprived of his night's sleep, flared up. Grabbing the old man's hand, he slammed it hard against the wall, 'That'll teach you to knock!'

The next morning, when he got home, he said smugly to Mum, 'I sorted him out. See how he behaved himself last night?' Mum was silent, her back turned to him. You could almost hear her say, *This is your own father and he's dying! Can't you make more of an effort to care for him? How can you be so heartless?*

But you could not wash the family's dirty linen in public. Who could we tell? And who would understand? People would just make fun of us, or make nasty comments behind our backs. Besides, outside the home, Shen Wenming was always smiling and cheerful. Everyone said he was such a good-tempered man and that there weren't many as decent as he was. If any of us had tried to say what he was really like, who would believe us? His line was, 'I'm your father and I'm bigger than you! If you're not going to obey me, then beat it!'

We might as well not have had a father.

19

Breaking free

On 1st January 2004, I was eighteen years old and I celebrated my birthday for the first time in my life.

When I was little, my aunt and uncle always said, 'Why do you want to have a birthday? You've got food to eat. Every day's a birthday for you!'

To be fair, they were of a generation who counted themselves lucky not to be hungry or suffering other hardships. They had never had a birthday themselves, so they were not going to celebrate mine. Birthdays were a luxury.

That morning, I found 'Happy Birthday, Yangyang' written in coloured chalk on the classroom blackboard. I hurriedly wiped the blackboard clean but secretly I was delighted. I walked to my desk with everyone's eyes on me, and there I found a blue birthday card with a cartoon design on it: snowflakes swirled in the sky, and a little girl holding a present stood on tiptoe and kissed a little boy on his rosy cheek.

I opened the card carefully. Inside, there was '生', 'birth', hand-written in the centre of the card, and underneath, a line of smaller writing, 'see page 11 of your politics textbook'. I quickly pulled the book out of the pile on my desk and found an identical card tucked into page 11, with the character '日', 'day', written in it. And so on, until I had assembled cards with all four characters writ large: '生日 快乐' Happy Birthday.

I thought that would be the end of the surprises, but there was more to come. When I reached into my desk for my pencil case, I found a heart-shaped blue box. Inside it, a rhinestone bracelet made of little blue stars glittered and winked at me. The card read, 'Happy birthday, Yangyang. This is just a little gift, I hope you like it, please don't turn me down in front of everyone. Signed, DP.'

What a sweet boy. In fact, I had turned him down before, and I was surprised he was so determined. I smiled to myself as I took out the bracelet and put it on my left wrist. He was sitting not far from me, and out of the corner of my eye I could see that he was pleased. It gave me a nice warm feeling to know that I had an admirer.

Yucai Senior High School was only about fifteen minutes away from where I lived, and I walked there on my own every day. I was busy now. Life consisted of home – school, school – home. During my three years of junior high school, I had given myself too much freedom. It took money and connections to get into this key high school. I told myself that it was time to buckle down and focus on my studies.

I was an enthusiastic student, especially in Chinese, history and English classes. My teachers and my classmates all thought I was one of the best. So when the first mid-term exam results came out, everyone expected to see my name in the top ten.

I took my time as I calmly scanned the list from top to bottom. Finally, there I was, ranked among the last twenty. I know very well that marks in arts and science subjects were averaged out, so I had no chance of getting into the top ten. It had been the same in Nanyang, where we were put into the top classes or the bottom classes depending on the overall marks we got. And now, in Jining, we were divided into three tiers based on our overall marks. It was not just those two schools, but the same system was used throughout China's education system. We have a saying, 'The leaders hand down policies, their subordinates have to put them into practice.' The state only rates overall exam scores, so all schools have to follow suit.

Many years have passed, and I have no idea what happened to my old teacher Shen Jianping. He taught me how to learn and how to think about learning in the right way. He had his feet on the ground; for him, substance, not form, was everything. If all teachers were like him, they could bring about earth-shaking changes in China's education system: China would have to stop teaching to the test; teachers would aim to develop students' all-round abilities, in ethics, knowledge, and physical prowess. But they weren't. It was like the whole country was having a 'Down with Shen Jianping' campaign.

The second half of the term, in that first year of senior high school, we were divided into science or arts classes, and my arts class had a total of sixty students. There were only twelve boys, and the rest were all girls. I had a few good friends in the class, but most of the girls were either swats or messed around all day. I was not a swat; I did my reading thoroughly but I liked our relaxation time too.

As time went by, I had less and less to do with the girls in my class. Some of them were nuts – they used to play a game which involved grabbing each other's tits in public. This was worse than the skirt-lifters of my primary school. I preferred to be alone.

In my second year of senior high school, I fell in love with authors like Wang Zengqi, Liang Shiqiu, Lu Yao, Shen Congwen, Lin Haiyin, Yu Hua, Wang Xiaobo, Natsume Soseki, George Orwell and W. Somerset Maugham. As I immersed myself in their worlds, they made an indelible impression on me.

My childhood traumas continued to cast a shadow over my teenage years. For a long time, I could not break free. I was not close to either of my parents, and I certainly did not miss my aunt and uncle and cousins. I was lively and cheerful on the surface but sensitive and vulnerable on the inside. I yearned for love, but I was prickly too. Being alone in my room did not make me feel lonely. Quite the opposite, I felt free. I was so good at keeping my distance that I was unable to get close to anyone. The noise and bustle of family life just made me feel empty. I did not feel part of it, even though I put on a good front.

Luckily, I had access to a vast array of books that worked on me like a tonic. They not only healed my emotional wounds but also taught me how to empathize, how to let go of the past and how to save myself. They told me that there is always light at the end of the tunnel. My emergence into the light came through the worlds described in books. I learned self-restraint and maturity. Through books, I gained the confidence to deal with loneliness. I had been abandoned, unloved and neglected, but I had an instinctive hunger for knowledge and I could learn on my own. I wanted to grow up as quickly as possible so that I could steer my own path through life.

At the end of senior high school, we took our university entrance examinations. After that, I got on the train and took a solo trip back to Nanyang. Three years had gone by but I had not forgotten the land that once nurtured me. As dawn broke, I emerged from the train station, and hopped into a blue, three-wheeler 'beng beng' van. They were open-sided and the morning breeze blew in my face as we passed along the familiar city streets that I had been away from for so long.

Nothing seemed to have changed. Baihe Bridge teemed with morning joggers, people practising opera or Tai Chi, and fishermen. The sun shone on the river, the breeze ruffled the weeping willows on the bank and the fisherman cast their nets.

As the van turned into Zaolin Street, I found myself looking around for something. The moment my eyes alighted on the black fascia board with the gilded lettering that read 'Tonglezhai', I felt a surge of happiness. I had spent many a cicada-loud afternoon in this small bookstore. It had become my refuge, a place where I could wander through forests of manga books and immerse myself in the world created by Fujiko Fujio.

At a small shop selling breakfast on the street, early risers sat at square wooden tables eating fried laomo, drinking hot spicy soup, munching crispy fried youtiao sticks, and spooning in soft tofu. The steam rose from the cooking pot at the shop door as the woman owner stirred the contents deftly with a long wooden spoon. My long-numbed nose twitched at the pungent smell of Chinese herbal medicine mixed with the spicy aroma of beef broth.

As we headed towards Xiaoliangzhuang village, I saw two ponytailed little girls walking along hand in hand, talking and laughing. I twisted around and stared back at them. Wanjun and I had once been like that too, the best of friends and without a care in the world, hadn't we? The van stopped by the sturdy poplar tree in front of my aunt's house. I paid the fare and thanked the driver. Then I stood there with my big backpack and looked around. After three years, I was back.

Children ran back and forth in the alley, engrossed in their games. I could hear the crackle and pop of stir-frying vegetables, their aroma filling the air. There were the yard walls, the carved eaves, the flowers growing under small trees in the corner of the yards, the cool mint planted in old wooden tubs, and the morning glory that crawled up and over the walls and through cracks, their green leaves contrasting vividly with the blue of the sky.

The gate was ajar and I walked in. The yard was lush with fragrant plants, and there was my uncle engrossed in watering the hydrangeas. I stood at the entrance quietly watching him.

I heard a bellow from the front room, 'Buy, buy, buy! You little beggar, you never stop asking for money so you can stuff your face! You don't want to eat the food I put on the table, all you want is rubbish from street stalls!'

It was my aunt telling off her five-year-old granddaughter, Li Menglin.

'I'm not a beggar! I just want to buy something!' Menglin hurled the tea cup she was holding to the ground.

'Ai-ya, this'll teach you!' My aunt slapped her face.

Menglin burst into a wail, 'Wah! My granny hit me, Grandad!'

And she ran out to the yard, her hands over her face.

'She wouldn't hit you if you didn't make her angry,' said my uncle, carrying on with his watering and not looking up.

Just then, Menglin spotted me standing at the gate. I cocked my head and smiled and waved to her. She put her finger in her mouth and crept behind Uncle, tugging on his white sweatshirt.

Finally, my uncle raised his head and looked towards the gate. Our eyes met, and I saw a tremor in the hand holding the watering can.

'Hello, Uncle.' I smiled and walked into the yard.

'Yangyang's back!'

My uncle's deep voice quavered.

My aunt came out holding the teacup fragments in her hand, and stopped in astonishment when she saw me.

'Hello, Auntie,' I greeted her with a smile.

'Damn brat! You damn brat!' She bellowed as she threw the broken bits into the rubbish bin. 'Why didn't you tell me you were coming?'

'So I could give you a nice surprise,' I said, letting her slap me on the shoulder.

Uncle's nose had suddenly gone red and his eyes were swimming, so that he had to turn away and give them a quick wipe. I had been away for three years. For a whole three years, I had allowed my resentments to simmer and had stubbornly refused to contact them. No doubt they thought that I wanted nothing more to do with them and would never come back.

'What is it, Granny?' Menglin went to her and tugged at her jacket.

My aunt grabbed my hand in excitement. 'Come along now, say hello to your auntie, this is Auntie Yangyang!'

'Auntie Yangyang? Are you really Auntie Yangyang?' Menglin wiped her tears on her sleeve and smiled at me. 'My granny tells me stories about you every night!' She looked up at me and said earnestly, 'I like the ones about when you were little best!'

I took Menglin's chubby little hand. I looked at my aunt and uncle – their hair had gone quite grey in my absence – and felt quite choked up.

'Did you travel overnight? You must be exhausted. Go and have a lie-down.' My aunt steered me indoors and my uncle put down the watering can, got his walking stick which had been hanging on the vine trellis, and followed.

'I brought some presents from Shandong for you and uncle, Auntie,' I said. 'The Misandao honey cakes you like and Uncle's favourite Yutang pickles, oh, and two bottles of Confucius wine.' I took the gifts out of my backpack.

'Oh, you're such a good girl! You haven't forgotten your aunt and uncle! All the Shen girls are so good-mannered. Our nieces on your Uncle Li's side, we've given them so much help and they're doing really well for themselves, but do they ever give a thought to us stuck out here in the countryside? But look how well we did with our Shen girl!' my aunt said in a loud voice, though my uncle was no longer in the yard. I knew she was making the point that his agreeing to bring up her niece had all been worthwhile.

'Yangyang, Yangyang!' Uncle shouted, coming back into the yard.

'Yes!' I went to see what was up.

'Are you hungry? I've bought you some of your favourite xiaolong dumplings.'

'Thanks, Uncle.'

I was a little uncomfortable at this unaccustomed attentiveness. Then Menglin yelled from the doorway, where she stood chewing her nails, 'Grandad, I want dumplings!'

'Damn brat! You're into everything! These are for your Auntie Yangyang!' My aunt pulled Menglin indoors. 'Come along and eat your dough balls!'

'No, don't want them!' Menglin yelled. She broke free and scurried to hide behind me.

'Damn brat! So stubborn. Just you wait! I'll give you what-for!' My aunt gave Menglin's forehead a fierce jab.

Shades of my past came rushing back. That Shen Bellow! It was as if I was a little kid again. I suddenly realized that my aunt didn't have it in for me personally. She was just born with a vile temper. She was treating her own granddaughter exactly the same way.

I put down my xiaolong dumplings and took her hand, 'Come on, Menglin, let's go and wash our hands, and then we can eat them together, okay?'

I led her over to the sink in the yard.

'Auntie Yangyang, will you stay here?' she asked sweetly. I smiled and stroked her head.

I had not forgotten how much I too used to long for a guardian angel at my side.

'Meow!' A kitten lay along one of the vine branches, and I looked up and examined them for the first time. They had grown up with me, those vines. Now, after nearly twenty years, they were beginning to look their age. The luxuriant growth they used to put on was a thing of the past. All that was left were four or five sparse clusters of grapes, a dismal sight. I still vividly remembered happy times spent under the trellises as a child. Now, the beauty of the eighteen vines existed only in my dreams.

After breakfast, I took a shower and then a nap. It had been a tiring overnight journey, and I slept through till the afternoon. I got up and headed to the front room, where I could hear the ceiling fan whirring, rubbing the sleep from my eyes. The sound of the TV was turned right down, and my uncle was hunched over it, squinting at the screen.

'Oh, you're up. Are you hungry? Look, your aunt's made you some jiaozi for lunch.'

Uncle lifted the lid of the pot and brought out a large bowl of dumplings.

'Wow, jiaozi!' I grabbed a stool, sat down and began to stuff them into my mouth.

'There are plenty more in the pot,' Uncle said.

'Thanks, these are enough.'

'Where's Auntie gone?' I asked as I ate.

'Gone to play mahjong. She's addicted to it, she has to play every day.'

Uncle cleared his throat, got slowly to his feet, went to the doorway, hawked, and spat a large gob of phlegm onto the concrete outside. I winced and frowned. He had not changed.

As the cicadas chirred, the fan creaked, and the TV muttered to itself, we chatted idly. Somehow or another, the conversation turned to the time I was bitten by a dog when I was a kid.

'You lied to me, you said it was a stray from somewhere!'

'Well, you should think about why I did that. It was because you never liked my friend Wanjun and you wouldn't let me play with her. If I told you that her uncle's dog had bitten me, you'd have made sure I never played with her again.'

'Don't talk nonsense. Damn brat, you always did talk nonsense!'

'All the same, there's always a reason why a child tells lies. And you didn't even take me to the clinic, even when I had a bad bite like that...'

I had hardly finished speaking before my uncle exploded with wrath, 'Why should I take you to the clinic?'

'Why? Because you were the adult and you were looking after me! That dog bite hurt, and it traumatised me too. But you weren't bothered. All you did was give me a terrible telling-off and make me go and ask her family for money!'

It was all so long in the past but my emotions still felt raw. I burst into tears and ran into the bedroom.

Suddenly, Uncle seemed to realize how rough and rude he had been. He frowned and started pacing around the yard, his hands behind his back. Then he spoke, 'We're out of mung beans, here's some money, why don't you take the bike and go and buy two pounds in the market?'

I was sitting on the bed in floods of tears and he was asking me to buy mung beans?

'I'm not a kid anymore and you've really upset me. I'll pack my bag and leave now,' I muttered.

'Go on, buy us two pounds of soybeans too, and you can keep the change,' he said, holding out a hundred-yuan note, as if I'd never spoken.

'I'm not going!' I turned and looked out the window.

'Go on.'

'Nope.'

'Go on.'

There was silence. Stalemate. Finally, since he obviously wasn't going to leave the room, I got off the bed, grabbed the money and disappeared into the yard. The stubborn old man had never apologized to anyone in his entire life, nor had he ever spoken any words of comfort. Sending me shopping and telling me to keep the change was a big concession.

I didn't know why I had lost control like that, but whenever any memories of my childhood came up, a heap of suppressed grievances and resentments came up too. I thought I had come to terms with my past, but the truth was that, at heart, I was still a hurt little girl.

I bought the mung beans and soybeans. Once I was back, I washed my face and went back into the bedroom again.

'Yangyang!' I heard my uncle shout from the yard.

Ugh! He was annoying! Why couldn't he leave me alone? I scrunched the pillow between my hands. 'Yangyang!' He shouted again.

'What's wrong?' I went to the door of the front room and said irritably.

'Go upstairs to the storage room and bring down the floor fan, will you?'

'If it's not one thing, it's another, with you!' I pulled a face and obeyed reluctantly.

I put the fan down in the middle of the yard and disappeared back indoors.

Meanwhile, under the blazing sun, my uncle stood at the sink, carefully wiping each fan blade with a wet rag. Beads of sweat rolled down, and after a while, his white sweatshirt was so drenched with sweat, it was almost see-through.

Eventually, I could not help myself. I went out into the yard and said to him, 'It's too hot, what are you doing wiping it now?'

'I'm giving it a wash and a wipe while it's sunny, then it'll dry off and when you go to bed, you can have it on and keep cool.'

I felt quite emotional. This uncle of mine had done everything to make me hate him, and yet he still loved me. He couldn't express it in words, but he showed it with his actions and I was moved.

'You go in and take a rest,' I said. 'I'll finish it.'

I took the dirty rag off him and handed him a clean wet towel. He wiped his face, exclaiming, 'What a good girl you are, so grown-up!'

A good girl? That was funny. If only he had called me that before. I had always been good and grown-up, but he had only just realised. If only he had been just a little less ready to fly off the handle when I was a kid, and watched what was happening around him, and cared about us children, been gentler with us, more affectionate to my aunt, and more patient with me, how different things might have been.

The night before I went back to Shandong, at the dinner table, my uncle frowned and cleared his throat several times, but somehow he could not get any words out.

'Spit it out, Uncle!' I said with an encouraging smile, and put down my bowl and chopsticks.

After living under one roof for so long, I had noticed a pattern in the way my aunt and uncle reacted. In my uncle's case, he typically frowned and cleared his throat several times over, then stared off into the distance for a few seconds before he finally spoke. After this prelude had played out, he would launch into a long spiel.

'You'll be going to university soon and, as your uncle, I want to say a few things to you before you go. You came to us when you were quite small, and as you grew up, you got told off and beaten pretty often. If I'm truthful, I'd have to say that all of us were nasty to you. But it was only because you were so disobedient that we all took it out on you. Even if you don't say anything, we know you still hold it against us.'

Uncle stopped speaking and put down his chopsticks.

'Uncle, please don't say anymore,' I said. 'Everything you've said shows how little you understand me. If I still hated you, I wouldn't be sitting here now. I might have been cheeky but I've never held grudges. Now I want to say something to you, Uncle, and don't be angry. You're a well-read man, but you live in the past, you still live in the shadow of the Cultural Revolution. In the shadows you created. Then you went and married a woman you didn't love, and you two have spent most of your lives having terrible rows. And that's shaped your personality and the path your life has taken as well. You're an old stick-in-the-mud who's never going to change!'

I completely ignored my aunt as I blurted all this out, although she was sitting at the table too.

'Ai-ya! That's the most sensible thing I've heard in decades!' Not only was my aunt not angry, she actually laughed out loud.

'Hey, it's too late to say anything now. I can't change my bad temper. It'll be like this till I die. If it hadn't been for your aunt agreeing to be my wife, I'm pretty sure I'd still be an old bachelor!' said my uncle. He had been keeping his feelings in for thirty years, and now it all came out. He said he had always felt that he had married beneath him with Auntie. He had imagined marrying an educated woman but ended up with someone who was ignorant, rough and rude. He had always been full of complaints about God's injustice to him, and the tricks fate had played on him, and ignored what was right in front of his eyes. Finally, he was beginning to see what he did have: a wife to see him through to the end of his life.

Auntie jumped in at this point. 'You don't need to tell me what I am, I know perfectly well that I'm rough and ready,' she retorted. 'All the years we've been together, you've been angry with me. But even though you look down on me, I respect myself for what I am. You're more educated than me, but I'm more capable than you are. You're such a good-for-nothing, if I left you, you'd never find another wife like me no matter how hard you tried!' She was making the point that as a Shen family girl, she was every bit as good as he and his Li family were.

'That's enough of that! The Lis are a family of scholars! If we hadn't had all these government campaigns, I might have been a university professor by now.'

'Huh! Pull the other one! With a face like yours? Why don't you go and look in the mirror? The Shens were a fine family too. If we hadn't had all these government campaigns, I'd have been a proper Miss Shen!'

Miss Shen? For my aunt, with her broad shoulders and stocky build, to describe herself as a proper miss was hilarious and my uncle and I burst out laughing. The joyous sounds carried through the window and filled their little yard. Just then, a gust of wind blew in, stirring the air, and suddenly it was as if everything was finally resolved.

20

The way they were then

Professor Li and Miss Shen. If the clock could be turned back, if there had been no class struggle or Cultural Revolution, fate would never have brought together Li Yige from his family of scholars and Shen Wenjie from a rich landlord family. They were poles apart.

When she was young, Shen Wenjie was as good as any man. Mixing cement to build a house, hefting bricks to build a yard wall, hoeing the ground by hand, transporting goods to wherever they were needed with a barrow, driving a tractor and ploughing, she could turn her hand to anything.

She quickly earned high praise from the commune work team, 'Wives from other parts know about hard graft. That girl from Shandong beats the lot of us.'

In those days, work points were earned instead of wages, and my aunt's physical strength and energy and outspoken character meant that she quickly fitted in and became known as a 'good girl'.

When the good girl gave birth and became a mother, she mistakenly thought that her husband would take good care of her, but in fact he did nothing at all to help. When the baby was hungry, cried or peed, it was down to Shen Wenjie to deal with it by herself. Without the help of a mother-in-law, and with her own mother far away in Shandong, my aunt had to put up and shut up.

Both the farm work and the baby needed to be taken care of, and Shen Wenjie could not count on her husband, who was always out and about. So instead of the traditional yuezi, the one-month confinement to recover from the birth, she had to swaddle the baby, put it in a bamboo basket and take it down to the fields. She would feed the baby and lay it under the tree, while she gritted her teeth and got on with the work.

After a day of hard labour, there was no rest when she got home. There was washing and cooking and the baby to look after. Shen Wenjie had no time either for the yuezi or for postnatal depression. There was so much to do, inside the house and out, that she had to be a superwoman to keep her head above water.

Another daughter was born, then a son, and things went on like this for many years. She brought up the three children all on her own. When things were at their most difficult and she was weighed down with responsibilities, she got into the habit of making snap decisions and taking shortcuts to get things done.

She would steam a big pot of mantou buns to last the family for a week; pickle a big pot of vegetables, enough for a month; turn dirty clothes inside out and wear them again; splash a bit of water on any vegetables she had just dug up and fry them in the wok; keep the dirty bowls and chopsticks for the next time; and deal with any kid who made a fuss by giving them a slap.

She managed to get by and, in time, my three cousins finished school and got steady factory jobs. But neither the nitty-gritty of family life nor the passing of the years smoothed her rough edges. In fact, she seemed to get more abrasive as she had more spare time. The family said it was the menopause but whatever it was, I erupted at age five into their seemingly calm world. Throw together a menopausal woman seething with resentments and complaints, a cynical, embittered victim of the Cultural Revolution with frustrated ambitions, and an excess-birth girl traumatized at being abandoned by her parents; and the results were never going to be anything other than dramatic.

Auntie Wenjie's explosive temper first showed itself on the train when she threatened me, 'If you don't stop crying, I'll throw you out of the window.' She had offered to help out her younger brother and his wife with the best of intentions, but she was a very impatient caregiver. When she was a young woman, after the birth of her eldest daughter Li Ruomei, she used to take her to the fields in a bamboo basket every day, and lay the baby under the tree after she'd fed her, so that she could keep her eye on her and get on with the farm work. When winter came, she tied Ruomei tightly to the bed and left her behind. The days and months passed and the toddler spent all day every day in a filthy nappy looking helplessly out of the window.

Wenjie and Yige came to blows about every little tiny thing to do with bringing up their baby. After one of the worst rows, Wenjie threw herself into the lake. Yige plunged in, dragged her ashore and gave her a violent slap across the face. The onlookers all felt very sorry for her.

Wenjie often said that if she had known that marriage would be such torment, she would never have married him. But such was the hand fate dealt her.

Wenjie's landlord family were traditional and believed that, 'A virtuous woman has no special talent.' So Wenjie, as the eldest daughter, was given the absolute minimum of schooling and could only read a few characters. She was also nothing special to look at. But she was known for her fiery temper, plus she had three younger brothers trained in martial arts, so no one messed with her.

Just when she got to an age when they should be looking for a husband for her, Land Reform got underway and all of her family, including her, were condemned as landlords. Overnight, their fortunes plummeted: their land was confiscated, the house was divided up. But the younger brothers were still in school, and the parents were old and frail, so the task of earning work points and food for all of them fell on her shoulders.

She was out in the fields, day after day, year after year, in all weather, getting up in the dark and working till late. It would have been a hard life for a strong young man, let alone a girl in her early twenties.

Wenjie yearned to escape these hardships by moving far away, marrying a good man and living a good life.

Into these pleasant daydreams walked Li Yige.

He was from Jinxiang County, Shandong Province, and had been born into a well-known family of scholars. During the Anti-Rightist movement of the 1950s, they were also condemned as landlords because they had a scrap more land than their neighbours. Yige's father, Li Fengsheng, had been born in the nineteenth century, graduated from Yenching University in Beijing and worked as an administrator in the county government. His wife, a gentle, well-educated woman, gave him three daughters and two sons, but died soon after the youngest son was born.

During the War of Liberation, Li Fengsheng fought for the Nationalists. He had every intention of going home and missed his five children, and when the war ended in 1949, he made a last-minute decision not to follow the Nationalist Army to Taiwan. Instead, he took refuge in a coal mine in Huainan where he got a job. It was not until his eldest son Li Yiheng volunteered during the Korean War, that the father felt able to return to his hometown in Jinxiang, Shandong, where he could count on some status as the dependent of his heroic son.

Yige's eldest sister had brought Yige up, and the father who suddenly landed on them after so many years was a stranger. Father and son, both of them uncommunicative by nature, did not get on. Li Fengsheng bought an ox so he could pose as a good peasant. But he was effete and over-educated and had no clue about farming. Neither the ox nor his own body would obey him.

The village leaders took pity on him and gave him a job teaching at the village school. The trouble was that Li Fengsheng had been brought up in the old traditions and was not going to change them now. He was in the habit of hitting children on the palm of their hands with a ruler. There was one particular naughty kid in the class whom he hit so hard that his hand swelled up. The parents angrily reported to the county government that he was a counter-revolutionary intent on getting his own back on the poor and lower-middle peasants by inflicting corporal punishment on their children.

It was such a ridiculous time, politically, that Li Fengsheng was sentenced to five years in a laogai prison camp, and his younger son Li Yige was forced to leave school because he had a 'bad background'. His father eventually came out of prison but still had to undergo 'reform by the masses'. Father and son moved into an old, abandoned pigsty, where they slept on piles of sorghum stalks at night and did collective labour assigned by the production team by day.

So as he grew up, Yige was always short of food and clothing. With no hope of getting back into education, he had no future to look forward to. He began to take out his suppressed resentment on his father, and the pair were constantly at loggerheads.

After the Korean War, Li Yige's eldest brother Yiheng was allocated a job in the Nanyang County Commercial Bureau in Henan. By this time, he was married and settled, and was anxious to do something to help his father and younger brother in Shandong. He asked friends with connections to get his brother a job in Nanyang in the army or a factory or a school. But nothing worked out because of Yige's 'bad political background'. Yige was sensitive and began to feel like he had the plague: no one dared touch him and anyone who did, caught it.

Li Yige suffered from a complicated mixture of feelings: he felt inferior, and was depressed, indecisive and irritable. However, when the government encouraged people to move to the Dongbei provinces in the far North-East, Shandongers went in their droves and Yige was tempted. He took with him some money his siblings had put together for him, but he arrived in those vast open spaces alone and friendless. In the winter ice and snow, he could find nothing to do. He was too scrawny to cut wood or carry coal. His savings were almost gone and eventually one day he lay down in a snowdrift in despair. Why had he not left school earlier and learned to farm, like his sister? What use were schoolbooks anyway? What you needed to survive was physical strength.

However, there was light at the end of the tunnel. Yige's eldest brother happened to have been posted as a cadre to the Liying brigade of Nanyang Angao Commune, where he met a brigade cadre called Yang Hetang in the commune canteen and they became close friends. After the commune canteens were dissolved, Yang Hetang would still visit Li Yiheng at the Nanyang County Commercial Bureau every time he went to town.

Once, Yiheng happened to mention the fact that his younger brother had come back from the North-East but was not getting on well. Yang Hetang immediately said generously, 'Send him to me! He'll be fine if I'm here!'

And that was how Li Yige ended up in Angao, Nanyang, Henan province. It was a landscape of hills riven with sheer valleys, quite unlike the vast plains of Shandong where you could see for miles. The fertile land for farming was in the valley bottoms, while the soil on the hilltops was poor and unproductive.

The locals did not travel much and mostly stayed put, even in times of famine elsewhere. The varied topography meant that the valley bottoms produced crops during droughts and the hillsides were fertile when the valleys flooded. They were also prudent. They prepared for times of scarcity by wrapping bundles of dried vegetables in lotus leaves and hanging them on the house beams: dried sweet potato leaves, mooli shoots, cabbage leaves, dried slices of sweet potato and pumpkin, and dried red radishes.

The air was clean, the people warm and honest, and Li Yige, who had suffered so much in Shandong, finally began to feel at home.

Now that Yige had finally settled down, his father and siblings began to worry about getting him married. It was not that he had never thought about romance himself. But his background, as the son of a Nationalist father and a scholar family, had left him with an abiding sense of inferiority. If he found a wife and they had children, might they not suffer discrimination too?

He made up his mind to stay a bachelor for the rest of his life. And yet... he was a healthy man and he could not quite let go of the idea of looking for a woman. As he got older and approached thirty, the longings grew.

In families from a bad political background, the so-called Five Black Categories, the women could find husbands from 'good' backgrounds so long as they were willing to cut themselves off from their own families. It was different for the men: it was pie in the sky to think of finding a woman with a good background. Yige knew that the local girls would never give him a second glance. His only chance was to go back to Shandong and blag his way into a marriage by concealing his past.

In the meantime, his eldest sister, who was still in Jining, wrote and asked him to go home: a matchmaker had found him a decent girl and wanted to introduce them. Before he left, his big brother and his wife dressed him up in his brother's cadre suit, complete with his green army cap and watch. They even gave him a Serve the People lapel badge to pin on.

When he arrived, however, his smart cadre's outfit could not hide his gauche manners and the rictus of a grin plastered all over his face. Unsurprisingly, his intended, a woman called Lin Xiuzhen, hurried away with her family without even stopping to eat a meal. They thought he was thick, even mentally retarded. Yige had always been introverted, and now he became even more taciturn. His sister was at her wits end to find him a match. Another go-between was called on, and she had a silver tongue.

She described Shen Wenjie to him, 'This girl is good-looking, hardworking and capable, whoever takes her home will be blessed! Besides, her grandfather Shen Liuye was well-known as a good man in Jining back then. This is a fine family. Any girl from that family will be fine too!'

To the Shens, she said of Li Yige, 'This young man is talented, educated, and the scion of a scholar family. His elder brother served with honour in the Korean War and has a job as an important official in Henan. If you marry him, you can go and enjoy life in Henan!'

Full of hopes and longings, Shen Wenjie met Li Yige with her mother. The man in front of her seemed cultured, if a little shy. She was tempted, especially by the thought of living a leisurely life in a house full of books. She was thrilled that the days of hard labour might finally have come to an end.

Finally, he had found a woman, but Yige was hesitant. Wenjie, who was solidly built and swarthy, was a far cry from the original girl, Xiuzhen, who was graceful and delicate. Was this the best he could do? That night, he talked to his sister.

She was blunt. 'Lin Xiuzhen didn't want you, forget her. What's wrong with Wenjie, eh? You go out and take a look at any girl in the street. Are there any better-looking than her? Don't be so picky! You're like a pig that won't eat pumpkin!'

Yige sat on a stool, head bent and wringing his hands. His sister finally took pity on him. She softened her voice and said, 'Besides, you know quite well what things are like for our family. You should be happy to have found anyone willing to marry you. You're a poor specimen, how can you hope to find a gorgeous girl and get her to go into your battered old cage? The whole family has pulled out all the stops to help you find a wife, and you're not satisfied! If you're so fussy, they won't try again.'

His sister's words touched a raw nerve. It was true what she said. Without the family's help, he would not even get to touch this woman's toes, let alone hold her in his arms.

On 2nd October 1968, Li Yige and Shen Wenjie were married in Jining, Shandong.

When they arrived in Henan, Wenjie was dumbfounded. It was all fictitious, the big house with two rooms, the plot of farmland, and the secure job. Instead, there was a dilapidated thatched hut, a bed built of mud bricks, and borrowed pots and pans. She had imagined a happy life for herself, far away from home and family, but the reality was worse than her home in Shandong.

Wenjie had gone to primary school but could scarcely read and write, while Yige had been in high school and read poetry. Two people with absolutely nothing in common had been thrown together by fate and circumstance. They were fettered to their marriage by politics. It was a union typical of those times. The young couple quarreled constantly over the slightest thing, got furious, and even came to blows, but neither would give way to the other. For Li Yige, marriage became the way in which he vented his emotions.

All his young life, he had had lofty ambitions that were doomed to be unfulfilled, and he had ended up disillusioned with learning. No matter how much you studied, nothing beat having a strong physique. So he made his daughters and son get factory jobs after they finished high school.

Although Wenjie spent all her time complaining, she was a good housekeeper. While Yige was away working, she took care of everything, building the house, bringing up the children, washing and cooking. Fate is a wonderful thing. If Li Yige had really married the gentle, delicate Lin Xiuzhen, their lives would not have been half as satisfactory. It was thanks to strong, capable Wenjie that these two strangers were able to put down roots in Nanyang, and the family could blossom and bear fruit.

21

Sungrass

In September 2006, when I first walked through the gate of my university, I knew that from then on, I was responsible for my own life. I did not want to look back. It had taken me twenty years of hard work to finally get control over my destiny. It was around then that I received a letter from my uncle.

My dear Yangyang,

It has been months since you left. I hope you are well.

Your aunt and I were delighted to hear that things went well for you in Xi'an. In the photo you sent of you standing in front of the university, you have such a big smile on your face. Every time your aunt picks it up, she makes a point of saying that you are the pride and joy of the Shen family. I can hear how happy she is. I was not destined to get into university myself, but I am pleased and overjoyed to have such a clever niece.

Since you left, I have had a lot to think about. I realise that when we fostered you, we let you down in so many ways, and never gave you the care and affection that you deserved. When you were with us, we didn't think you were so important but now you have gone, not even the eighteen vines can fill the gap you left. The yard is empty, and so are our hearts.

In 1991, your aunt brought this small person to live with us in Nanyang. Eleven years later, that girl could not wait to leave. You were filled with rage against us. We did not care about you when you are here but now we miss you deeply. It is only when you lose something that you realise how much it meant to you.

Yangyang, please forgive the mistakes we made. Our generation finds it hard to talk about everything we suffered. The misfortunes of our family, the lack of affection, the hardships, and our resentment of the injustices of those times deprived us of love and we never learnt how to express it. This was true for our children, and the same is true for you.

When you get to my age, you see things clearly. As you said, one's personality determines one's fate, and my timidity and weakness made me passive, so that I ended up in this small village. And your aunt, the woman I rejected in my innermost being from the word go, has stayed with me all these years, brought up my children and helped me keep the family going. If it were not for her, I would have stayed a bachelor, I am sure of that.

Yangyang, you always were a kind-hearted, generous, strong, independent girl, always full of life. Fate brought you to us, but it is your character that has determined your destiny. If you had been a docile, obedient little thing, your Nana would never have asked your aunt to take you away. Your grandparents adored you, you know, and they indulged you in everything, but when you became as naughty as the Monkey King, they could not control you and had to send you away.

This little monkey suffered all kinds of trials and tribulations growing up, but finally she found the true way, and now she is flying free. We are thrilled at how hard she has worked. She had a bumpy ride in childhood but she did not let that become an excuse for sitting back and complaining; she made it a reason for fighting back and growing stronger. Remember the song 'Little Weed' you used to sing when you were small?

Whenever I think of the expression on your face as you sang it, I feel quite emotional. Remember, little weed, you are indomitable and no matter where you go, our thoughts and good wishes will go with you. There will always be a home for you in Xiaoliangzhuang.

The vines in the yard are getting feebler by the year. They are nowhere near as good as before. It is the same with people, when they reach that point in their lives. So you take care of yourself. 'Good health is an asset of the revolution', as they say!

We are both doing well, please don't worry about us.

The soft afternoon sunlight shone through the windowpane onto my face, and onto this heartfelt letter from my uncle. I had never felt so loved.

Fifteen years ago, when I was uprooted from my grandparents' hothouse, I realized that I had to work hard and adapt to survive. Even a small, puny weed like me could grow strong in any environment and anywhere. I could weather any storms and survive any amount of damage, and come up smiling at the sunrise, growing stronger, bit by bit.

I had always known that I was lucky compared to other excess-birth children, those who were abandoned or died at birth. I had the love of Nana and Grandad for the first five years of my life, and with them I lived happy and carefree. Thanks to their love, I had a sunny personality as a little girl. I was incredibly fortunate to be able to live with them. If it had not been for those early years with them, if I had gone straight to my uncle and aunt, I would have been a very different person.

It was only much later that I learned that my uncle had lost his mother at the age of three, and had had a loveless childhood too. He was forced to drop out of school because of his family's bad political background. He was a depressed and frustrated man when he married my aunt, a near-illiterate woman with a vile temper.

There was a time when I hated them so much, hated them for

taking me in and making me suffer, hated them for ruining my happy childhood. I used to long to go home and leave this loveless family. As I grew up, I began to understand how they had suffered and I came to terms with the past. The government's family planning policy left an indelible mark on the lives of that generation.

Although the one-child-per-family era has ended, the wounds it inflicted over three decades have not healed. People lost their jobs and families were fined, women were injured and baby girls were abandoned. Time only heals surface scratches, and there are still women with their hearts full of pain.

For a long time after I went home to Shandong, I was overwhelmed with sadness. I blamed my parents for giving me up, resented my aunt for not looking after me, and I felt worthless. I felt I had been abandoned by the whole world. I wanted to die, but lacked the courage. I did not understand why my parents brought me into this world but let me go, then took me back but did not love me. I was finally home with my Mum and Dad, but I was lonely and depressed. I was no longer the happy little girl with a smile on my face.

I was never any good at acting girly and I never tried it with my parents. I often did not even call them Mum and Dad. It used to annoy my father, and sometimes other family members used to wind him up by asking why I was like this with him. I hated the way they made sarcastic comments about me and joked about my birth.

'If your big sister had been a boy, your Mum and Dad wouldn't have had you.'

'You have your sister to thank for your existence.'

'If it weren't for me stopping him, your father would have left you out in the fields to die!'

'Why didn't you have a little willy? You should have been a boy!'

I was often near to tears at their comments. Why on earth did they keep going on about me being an excess-birth child who should not have been born and nearly got left out to die? It was their fault, not mine, I was innocent. I did not choose to be born breaking the family planning rules. I hated them. My self-esteem deserted me and I became over-sensitive, suspicious and anxious. I stopped talking and turned cynical and embittered. I became very prickly, put up the barriers and shut myself off. I was not alone in that. I realised later, having read the accounts of other excess-birth children on the Internet, and read a lot of psychology books, that these were normal emotions. But I needed to focus on finding a way out so that I could leave this sadness and resentment behind.

Some things were unforgivable, so I would not forgive them. But I wanted to accept myself, with all my resentments, accept the fact that I had grown up unloved, neglected, and with bad parents. Bleeding and injured though I was, I needed to move on by myself.

To this day, I dislike going home. I still do not have a good father-daughter relationship with Shen Wenming. I still like spending long periods alone. I'm used to taking care of myself. I still want hugs, but I am wary – there is a black hole in my life that can never be filled.

As I drew closer to my mother, I listened to her stories of the past, understood her better, and her limitations. I tried to imagine her childhood, her teenage years, her marriage, her suffering and her tears. If she had not come from a bad family background, she could have gone to university and her studies could have given her a completely different life. However, she was timid by nature and let her parents arrange everything for her. They made her drop out of school and marry a man she did not love. She was trapped and unfulfilled during the best years of her life.

If it had not been for the Cultural Revolution, my parents would never have married. If it had not been for the family planning policy, my life would have been perfectly ordinary. If my aunt had not bought me a hukou and made me go to school and get an education, my life would have been dire. The reason why school was so important to me was that it taught me to see how constraining my birth family was, to make changes there, and then give something back to them.

I might have stayed with, 'If they had not hurt me then…' Because it is always easier to blame others than to take responsibility for one's own growth. Blaming everyone except myself meant that I did not have to face my own shortcomings. I could believe that my problems were all other people's, and there was nothing wrong with me. But what would have been the point?

History cannot be rewritten. What's done is done. No matter how much I hated those who hurt me, the hurt could not be erased. The only result would be to trap me in pain which would only get worse. It was unrealistic to imagine that harm could be undone, nor was there much point in resenting my parents and society in general. What did help me was to cut myself off from that harm and not to let those feelings control my life.

In due course, I met a man who became my boyfriend and was very good to me. An only child, he had had a happy childhood and was kind and gentle. He understood me, he sympathized, he cared about me and for me. He gave me everything I wanted: to be loved. However, as we got to know each other, I often found myself hurting him and abusing him verbally. Finally, he burst out, 'I don't blame you, it's not your fault, it's their fault, your aunt, your uncle.' And I suddenly realized that I had become a copy of my aunt and uncle. All those years of cold, cruel words had left scars that could not be erased.

I had not realized until that point, nor did I want to admit, how important a role my childhood still played in my adult life. I stubbornly persisted in believing that I was who I was because that was what I wanted to be. I was such a prickly hedgehog that I was hurting other people and myself. I could not see who I was until I pulled out each spine one by one. It is a long and painful process to see oneself clearly, as is the process of returning to one's childhood. Time after time, I sat alone at home with the tears streaming down my face. I could not control my feelings or my tears. I went back to being the pain-in-the-neck crybaby I had been as a kid.

'She's got older but she hasn't grown up. Growing up requires love. She's never been loved, so how can she grow up? I want to give her a lot of love so she won't be hurt again, and she can grow up healthy and happy.'

The words of someone who values and loves me the way I have never been loved since I was taken away from my Nana and Grandad. I am so grateful for the way he cherishes me. With him, I feel warm, safe and happy. He has given me unconditional love and made me understand that every girl is worthy of love, that it is worth learning to love oneself.

In the process of growing up, all excess-birth children have faced unendurable disappointments. These have torn us apart and inflicted wounds that will never heal, and which still cause us pain. This is unfortunate, but it has also allowed us to develop extraordinary abilities – in our powers of observation, our memory, our ability to heal ourselves. Suffering has enriched us.

To this day, there is a paucity of literature about excess-birth children. If this continues, when we depart this life in the natural course of things, my generation will disappear without a trace. The passage of history smoothes over people's resentment and anger. Ten, twenty, a hundred years hence, who will remember us?

> Not as fragrant as flowers, not as tall as trees,
> I am a weed that nobody knows.
> I am not lonely, I am not worried,
> I have friends all over the world.
> Spring breeze, oh, spring breeze, blow me green,
> Sunshine, oh, sunshine, shine me bright.
> Rivers and mountains, nurture me,
> Earth and mother hug me tight.

The song so familiar from my childhood echoes in my ears as I get up and go to my desk, my heart suddenly filled with energy. Sunshine Lü, Wei Wanjun and me, as well as millions of others who were born as excess-birth children and lived their lives hidden away, we were all sungrass blooming brilliantly in the darkness. None of us has been beaten down by suffering. Amid the darkness, we have chosen to be grateful, we have chosen to make changes, both within ourselves, and within our birth families. We have walked out of the shadows towards the light.

It is a wonderful thing to survive. I want to write down everything I have heard and seen and experienced. I want the world to hear our voices. We have survived and we will survive!

1 When Grandad was young

2 Mum and her brother
when they were young

3-4 Dearest Nana

5-6 Dearest Grandad

7 Mum and Dad's wedding photograph

8 The big Shen family

9 Mum and Dad with Moon, when she was three months old

10 One year old Yangyang

11-13 Nana and two year old Yangyang

14 With Moon and chubby third sister Serene

15-16 Grandad and fourth sister Star

17 Star and I in Sunzha village

18-19 Moon with Mum and Dad in Beijing

20 From right to left: Mum, her elder sister (my favorite aunt), and their sister-in-law at Nana's

21 Four of us sisters with Nana, Grandad, and our cousins, who are the children of my favourite aunt

22 From left to right: Star, Moon, Yangyang and Serene

23 The whole family on a day out in a city near Sunzha

24 Mum with the four of us

25-28 Rare happy moments with my sisters shortly
before I was taken away to Nanyang

29-31 A day out in Qufu with Moon and Dad

32 When Auntie Wenjie
was young

33 Auntie Wenjie
in her late forties

34 Auntie Wenjie's family in Nanyang
Seated (left to right): Auntie Wenjie, Mingze and Uncle Yige
Standing (left to right): Mingmei and Ruomei

35 Uncle and Auntie Wenjie

36 Uncle in front of Yellow Crane Tower in Wuhan

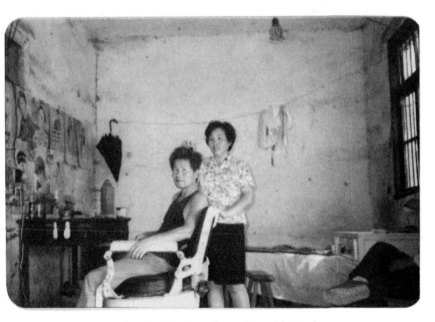

37 Auntie Wenjie at her salon with Uncle

38 Unhappy me with Mingmei some time after my arrival to Nanyang

39 Before putting on make up
for a 'professional' photoshoot

40 After putting on the typical
'90s make-up for kids

41 The little toy gun Auntie Wenjie used to entice me to leave with her

42 Auntie Wenjie's family with Uncle's niece, Wu Shanying (bottom left), whose Hukou was sold to us

43 The woman on the chair is Uncle's sister-in-law and also my aunt "by law" as stated in my Hukou

44 Mingze photobombed by me in the living room

45 Smiling like a fool despite my wounded thumb from playing
at the concrete factory near home

46 With Mingze at
a park near home

47 Mingze under the
grape vines in our yard

48 With Uncle, in front of the grape vines we planted together

49 With Auntie Wenjie's big family

50 When I was forced to wear a
dress for the sake of a picture

51 With Mingmei

52 With the neighbour's daughters in their cute hand-knitted sweaters

53 With my classmates, who all had uniforms

54 Happy sisters all together in Jining

55 The lucky Star who finally went back home

56-57 Sisters and their Mum in Jining

58 Four of us with our little cousin (Mum's nephew) on
a cold rainy day after Grandpa's funeral in Jining

59 Nana and Grandad in front of their newly renovated home

60 Auntie Wenjie and Uncle
with Grandpa, who passed
away in Jining at 66 years old

61 Grandma and Grandpa

ABOUT THE AUTHOR

Born in Shandong, SHEN YANG came to the world as an excess child and does not legally exist. As one of the millions of China's 'invisible children', she was forced to live in the shadows of the Chinese society. Amidst a troubled childhood, Shen Yang found solace in literature and graduated in Applied English. She has since completed a scriptwriting course in Beijing Film Academy and now lives in Shanghai, where she crafts her latest works.

ABOUT THE TRANSLATOR

Photo by Alex Hofford

NICKY HARMAN lives in the UK and is a full-time translator of Chinese literary works. She has won several awards, including the 2020 Special Book Award, China, the 2015 Mao Tai Cup People's Literature Chinese-English translation prize, and the 2013 China International Translation Contest, Chinese-to-English section. When not translating, she promotes contemporary Chinese fiction through teaching, blogs, talks and her work on Paper-Republic.org.